THE WAY OF ST JAMES

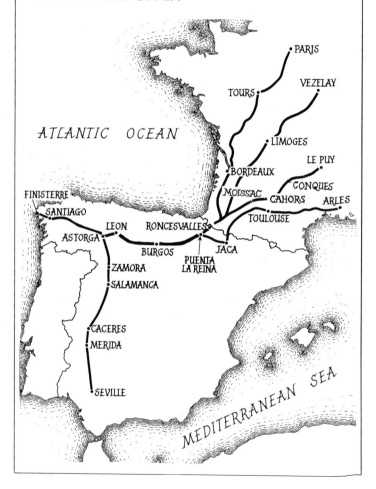

THE MAJOR PILGRIM ROUTES THROUGH FRANCE AND SPAIN

ATLANTIC OCEAN

PARIS

VEZELAY

TOURS

LIMOGES

LE PUY

BORDEAUX

CONQUES

MOISSAC

CAHORS

ARLES

FINISTERRE

TOULOUSE

SANTIAGO

LEON

RONCESVALLES

ASTORGA

JACA

BURGOS

PUENTE LA REINA

ZAMORA

SALAMANCA

CACERES

MERIDA

SEVILLE

MEDITERRANEAN SEA

THE WAY OF ST JAMES
LE PUY TO SANTIAGO
A Walker's Guide

by
Alison Raju

CICERONE PRESS
MILNTHORPE, CUMBRIA

© A. Raju 1999
ISBN 1 85284 271 7

First Edition 1999
Reprinted 2000, 2002

In memory of
Dr. Patrick Hurley
who took the colour photographs for
the Spanish section of this book.

Son tres días,	There are three days,
Hoy,	Today,
Mañana,	Tomorrow,
y tuve ayer.	and I had yesterday.
Son tres días,	There are three days,
Hoy,	Today,
Mañana,	Tomorrow,
y tengo hoy.	and I have today.
Son tres tiempos,	There are three times,
Ayer,	Yesterday,
Hoy,	Today,
y con Dios, tendré mañana.	and with God, I shall have tomorrow.

Patrick Hurley 6 vi 94

Photographs for the French section by Maurice and Marigold Fox

Front cover: Cahors. The Pont Valentré and the River Lot

CONTENTS

INTRODUCTION 7

   History 10

   Topography, economy and language 17

   Before you go 23

   Planning your schedule 24

   Equipment 24

   There and Back 26

   Being there 27

   Using this guide 35

THE ROUTE 43

APPENDIXES

   A   .GR651: Variant along the Vallée du Célé 225

   B.   *Camino aragonés* 226

   C.   Santiago to Finisterre 227

   D.   Outline Guide to the Camino Mozárabe

         Vía de la Plata 238

   E.   *Refugios* in Spain 242

   F.   Suggestions for further reading 244

   G.   Glossary 247

   H.   Index of principal placenames 251

Advice to Readers

Readers are advised that whilst every effort is taken by the author to ensure the accuracy of this guidebook, changes can occur which may affect the contents. It is advisable to check locally on transport, accommodation, shops etc but even rights-of-way can be altered.

The publisher would welcome notes of any such changes

Le Puy. Statue of St James in Cathedral

INTRODUCTION

The Way of St. James as described in this book is a long-distance footpath with a difference. People have been walking it - as a pilgrimage route - for over a thousand years and in 1987 the section from the Spanish monastery at Roncesvalles in the foothills of the Pyrenees to Santiago de Compostela became the first European Cultural Itinerary. Its almost 1500 kilometres from Le Puy-en-Velay in the Haute Loire to the City of the Apostle in the western reaches of Galicia have changed little in all that time. For although parts of it have now become modern tarred roads and many of its "hospitals" and other accommodation set up by religious orders along the way to minister to the needs of pilgrims have long since disappeared, the route through France and the *camino* as it is known in Spain still pass through the same villages, climb the same hills, cross the same rivers and visit the same chapels, churches, cathedrals and other monuments as did the path taken by our predecessors in centuries gone by.

The Way of St. James is also a long-distance footpath with a difference in that many of those who walk the route through France and the vast majority of those who start on the Spanish side of the Pyrenees are not experienced walkers at all. Many have never done any serious walking in their lives and many will never do any again, for here, as in the past, walking is a means of transport, a means to an end, rather than an activity for its own sake. Most long-distance footpaths also avoid not only large towns but even quite small villages as well; the Way of St. James, on the other hand, because of its historic origins and the need for shelter, deliberately seeks them out. Several thousand people walk the Way every year, whether from points on the *camino* in Spain, from the Pyrenees, from different parts of France or from even further afield: it is not uncommon, even nowadays, to meet Swiss, German, Belgian or Dutch pilgrims, for example, who have set out from home to make the entire journey on foot. However, one of the differences between the modern pilgrim and his historical counterpart, whether he or she walks, goes by bicycle or on horseback, is that very few return home by the same means of transport. The modern pilgrim route has thus become a "one-way street" and it is unusual, today, to encounter anyone with either enough time or the inclination to return to his or her point of departure by the same means as he or she set out.

People make the journey to Santiago for a variety of reasons - historical, cultural, religious, as a significant action or event in their lives - and it is something that many Spaniards in particular think of doing at least once in their lifetime, even if they do not actually manage to. Twentieth-century pilgrims are people of all ages and walks of life, the majority from Spain, but with a great many each year from France, Switzerland, Belgium, Holland and Germany and others from much further away. (In contrast there are relatively few from Britain at present.) Many travel alone, many in twos and threes, many in quite large groups, particularly those on foot. Many complete the entire journey in one stretch; others, with more limited time, walk only from León or Astorga, or cover a section at a time over several years. Most who walk the Way of St. James, and especially those who have been able to do the whole route in one go, would probably agree afterwards, however, that it has changed their lives in some way, even though they may never have set out with this intention at all.

This book replaces the two previous volumes published by Cicerone Press: Hal Bishop's guide to the French section from Le Puy to the Pyrenees, *The Way of St. James: GR65* (1989) and the present author's *The Way of St. James: Spain* (1994). Both guides were in need of revision due to the many changes made to the route after their publication, alterations caused by redistribution of agricultural land and road building programmes in France and by the diversion of the *camino* in parts of Spain away from the main roads which formed its historic route onto safer and more pleasant alternative tracks, a move promoted by the massive influx of pilgrims during the 1993 *Año Santo* (Holy Year). The publisher has now decided to combine the two sections (of one and the same route, in effect) into a single volume. The Way described here thus begins in Le Puy-en-Velay, following the GR65 of the French long-distance footpath network, and continues through southern and south-western France to Saint-Jean-Pied-de-Port. From there it crosses the Pyrenees into Spain and wends its way through Navarra, Castilla y León and Galicia to Santiago de Compostela. However, those who wish to walk only the Spanish section will find it more convenient to do so from Saint-Jean-Pied-de-Port than Roncesvalles, despite having a stiff climb on their first day: it is easier to reach the former by public transport (Paris - Bayonne - Saint-Jean) than by going to Madrid, Bilbao or Irun and then backtracking to the latter. On the other hand, those who prefer to walk the French section one year and the Spanish the next would do well to consider continuing to Pamplona and making the break there: not only is this city easy to reach by bus or train but the crossing of the Pyrenees would then come at the end of the first half of the journey when the pilgrim is likely to be fitter than at the start of the second. For those who feel that their pilgrimage would be incomplete unless they continued to Finisterre a description of this route is given in the Appendixes at the end of the volume. This is followed by outline guides to the *Vía de la Plata*, to the 54km variant (the GR651) along the Vallée du Célé from Béduer to Bouziès in the French section between Conques and Cahors, to the *camino aragonés* from the Spanish border to Puenta la Reina and by a glossary of geographical and other frequently encountered terms. A list of suggestions for further reading is given in the bibliography.

The walk from Le Puy to Santiago can be completed in nine to ten weeks by anyone who is fairly fit and also likes to visit places of interest along the way. It can be undertaken in sections, too, by those who lack the time to do it all in one go or who would just like to cover certain sections, and indications are given in the text as to how to reach (or leave) the main towns along the Way. Anyone in Britain who is thinking of walking, cycling or riding any part of the route should certainly consider contacting the Confraternity of St. James for advice and membership - their annually updated guides to accommodation and facilities on both the French and Spanish parts of the route are extremely useful (see last page of this book for the address). Cyclists will find it *extremely difficult* to follow the walker's route through France, even on mountain bikes and in the sections in which they are not prohibited anyway, and it is not recommended that they attempt it; stretches that *are* suitable, however, are indicated in the text. On the other hand, most parts of the *camino* in Spain are accessible to mountain though *not* to touring bikes. (See *The Way of St James - a Cyclist's Guide* by John Higginson, Cicerone Press. This is a complete cycling guide from Le Puy to Santiago, using touring bikes.

HISTORY

Pilgrims have been travelling to Santiago de Compostela on foot or on horseback (and more recently by bicycle) for over a thousand years. (Godescalc, Bishop of Le Puy, who went there in AD 951, was one of the first.) At the height of its popularity in the eleventh and twelfth centuries over half a million people are said to have made the pilgrimage from different parts of Europe each year, the majority of them from France.

Pilgrimages had been popular amongst Christians ever since Constantine the Great had the Church of the Holy Sepulchre built over the site of Christ's burial in Jerusalem, in AD 326, and the discovery, shortly afterwards, of the Holy Cross itself. Those journeying to this shrine were known as *palmeros* (palmers) whilst *romeros* went to Rome, the burial place of Saint Peter, the other great centre of Christian pilgrimage in the Middle Ages, along with Santiago de Compostela after the finding of the remains of Saint James the Great (son of Zebedee, brother of John and Christ's cousin). The high point of this third pilgrimage occurred between the years 1000 and 1500 but although numbers dwindled after that, due to the Reformation and other, political, factors, the stream of pilgrims making the trudge westwards from different parts of Europe to the far reaches of Galicia in north-west Spain never completely dried up and in the late twentieth century is making something of a comeback. The Cathedral authorities in Santiago maintain a register of pilgrims and in 1991 recorded a total of 7274 travelling on foot, bicycle or horseback (compared with 5760 in 1989, the year of the Pope's August visit there, and 4918 in 1990). In the 1993 Holy Year (a year in which St. James' day, July 25th, falls on a Sunday, and in which special dispensations are available - see below) a record 99,436 pilgrims received their *compostelas* (certificate of pilgrimage) though not all, by any means, began in Roncesvalles, let alone further afield. The numbers fell, predictably, in 1994 (15,863), though they began to rise again in 1995 (19,821) and 1996 (23,218) and will no doubt continue to do so, with another "avalanche" expected in the next Holy Year (1999).

Legend

After the death of Christ the disciples dispersed to different parts of the then known world, to spread the Gospel as they had been bidden. St. James went to Spain, we are told, where he spent a couple of years evangelising, though apparently without a great deal of success. He then returned to Jerusalem but was beheaded by Herod shortly afterwards, in AD 44. Immediately following his martyrdom, however, his followers are said to have taken his body to Jaffa, on the coast, where a ship was miraculously waiting for them and they set off back to Spain. They landed in Iria Flavia on the coast of Galicia, present-day Padrón, some 20km from what is now Santiago de Compostela, after a journey (and in a *stone* boat!) which is purported to have taken only a week, thereby providing proof of angelic assistance. The body was then buried in a tomb on a hillside, along with, later on, two of his followers, and then forgotten for the next 750 years. The story is, in fact, considerably more complicated than this but these are the bare bones.

Early in the ninth century Pelagius, a hermit living in that part of Spain, had a vision (which he subsequently reported to Theodomir, bishop of Iria Flavia) in which he saw a very large bright star, surrounded by a ring of smaller ones, shining over a deserted spot in the hills. The matter was investigated and a tomb found there containing three bodies. They were immediately identified as those of St. James and two of his followers and when Alfonso II, King of the Asturias (791-824) went there he declared St. James the patron saint of Spain. He built a church and a small monastery over the tomb in the saint's honour, around which a town grew up. It was known as *campus de la stella* or *campus stellae*, later shortened to *compostela*. This is one explanation of the origin of the name. Another is that it derives from the Latin *componere* (to bury), as a Roman cemetery or early Christian necropolis is known to have existed under the site of the present-day cathedral in Santiago - and where the remains of St. James are still believed to be housed today.

The pilgrimage

News of the discovery soon spread. It was encouraged to do so, moreover, both by Archbishop Gelmírez and the cathedral authorities, who were anxious to promote the town as a pilgrimage centre, thus attracting money to the area, and by the monks of Cluny, who saw in it the opportunity to assist the Spanish church in their long struggle against the Moors. Both factions were also helped by the fact that the Turks had seized the Holy Sepulchre in 1078, thus putting a stop to pilgrimages to Jerusalem. However, Santiago was attractive as a potential pilgrim "venue" in other respects too, as it fulfilled the various criteria necessary to make a pilgrimage there worthy of merit. It was far away (from most parts of France, for example) and difficult to reach, thus requiring a good deal of hardship and endurance to get there (and back again too, of course). It was dangerous (wolves, bandits, fever, rivers that were difficult to cross, unscrupulous ferrymen) as well as being in Spain, then locked tight in struggle with the Moors, and for this reason many pilgrims travelled in quite large groups. (A considerable corpus of pilgrim songs from previous centuries still exists, sung as they walked along.)

The road itself, both through France and in Spain, was also well supplied with shrines, relics and other sights worth seeing. As traffic increased roads, bridges and hospices were built and the pilgrimage churches, characterised by their ambulatories round the inside of the building in order to facilitate viewing of the relics exposed behind the high altar, were endowed with a growing number of such items, thus ensuring that pilgrims would pass that way to see them. Many churches were dedicated to St. James and many more contain his statue, whether as a pilgrim (*Santiago peregrino*) or (in Spain) as the Moor-slayer (*Santiago matamoros*). He is the subject of paintings and stained glass too, with a halo as St. James the Apostle, without which he is portrayed as a pilgrim. A considerable number of very tiny chapels or *ermitas* dedicated to St. Roch (San Roque in Spanish), the pilgrim saint from Montpellier, were also built along the way though many of those on the Le Puy route through France were originally dedicated to St. James. After a pilgrimage to Rome St. Roch devoted his life to caring for plague victims but withdrew to live in a forest when he contracted a disease which left him with an unsightly sore on his left thigh. For this reason he is depicted in art with the front flap of his coat turned back, to warn people to keep away from him, and is accompanied by the faithful dog, often with a loaf of bread in his mouth, who brought the saint his daily rations. Legend has confused him with *Santiago peregrino* at times, though, and he not infrequently appears in a "pilgrim version" as well, with added hat, staff and cockle shells on his clothing. Many churches and chapels of St. James changed their dedication in the sixteenth and seventeenth centuries, however, in recognition of St. Roch's role in curing plague victims, which explains the apparent scarcity of churches and chapels of St. James along the route from Le Puy to the Pyrenees today, in contrast to the pilgrim road through Spain.

Why did people go on pilgrimages anyway? For a variety of reasons. As a profession of faith, as a form of punishment (a system of fixed penalties for certain crimes/sins was in operation during the Middle Ages), as a means of atonement, as a way of acquiring merit (and thus, for example, reducing or, in certain cases, cutting in half the amount of time spent in Purgatory) and as an opportunity to venerate the relics of the many saints available along the principal routes to Santiago. (Indulgences were available to those who visited shrines.) No doubt, too, there were some who were just glad of the opportunity to escape their surroundings and later there were professional pilgrims who would (for a fee) undertake to do the pilgrimage on behalf of someone else who could afford the money but not the time to do it him or herself. Those with the means to do so went on horseback and some wealthy people made the pilgrimage along with a considerable retinue. The majority of pilgrims went on foot, however, and even amongst the rich there were some who preferred to walk, rather than ride, because of the greater "merit" they would attain afterwards.

The pilgrim in former times was not at all sure that he would eventually reach his destination, let alone return home in one piece, so before setting out he took leave of his family and employer, made his will and generally put his affairs in order. He (or she) obtained his credentials (pilgrim passport) from his bishop or church, which he could then present in order to obtain food and lodging in the many pilgrim "hospitals" and other establishments along the way. This was both a precaution against the growing number of *coquillards* or pseudo-pilgrims and as a means of providing proof of his journey: he had his papers stamped at different stages along the way so that once he arrived in Santiago he could obtain his

Compostela or certificate of pilgrimage from the Cathedral authorities there. This in turn entitled him to stay in the pilgrim shelters on his return journey as well as furnishing evidence, if needed, that he had actually made the pilgrimage successfully.

The pilgrim had his staff and scrip blessed in church before setting out and travelled light, carrying little else but a gourd for water and his scallop shell. This singled him out as a pilgrim, rather than as any other type of traveller, and is the symbol embedded above doorways and in other places on the many and varied buildings that accommodated them along the different pilgrim roads. Pilgrims with funds could obviously stay in inns and other publicly available lodgings but probably the vast majority stayed in the different hospices and other facilities specially provided for them. Some of these were in towns, whether in the centre or outside the walls to cater both for latecomers and possibly contagious pilgrims, whilst others were in the middle of the countryside, often by bridges or at the crossing of important pilgrim feeder roads: examples are the former hospital by the Pont d'Artigues near Saint-Antoine, run by the Order of the Knights of Santiago, and the Chapelle d'Abrin, shortly before La Romieu, the surviving part of the Commandery of St. John of Jerusalem at the junction of the routes from Le Puy and the road from Moissac to Aire-sur-l'Adour via Agen. Much of the pilgrim accommodation was provided by religious orders such as these, the Benedictines and the Antonins, by churches and civic authorities, as well as by benevolent individuals. The facilities offered varied considerably from one establishment to another and records survive from many of them indicating exactly what was provided for the pilgrim.

There are different explanations as to the origins of the *coquille Saint Jacques* but one is that when the followers of St. James arrived in the port of Iria Flavia with the apostle's body they saw a man riding along the beach (a bridegroom in some versions) whose horse took fright and then plunged into the sea. When they reemerged both horse and rider were covered from head to foot in scallop shells (and even today the beaches in this part of Galicia are strewn with them). It was customary to set out in the springtime in order to reach Santiago for the feast of St. James on July 25th and return home for the winter. This was especially true in Holy Years, those in which

July 25th falls on a Sunday (the next ones are in 1999 and 2004), the only time the *Puerta Santa* or Holy Door of the Cathedral of Santiago is open. This is sealed up at the end of each such year and then symbolically broken down again by the Archbishop in a special ceremony in the evening of December 31st preceding the new Holy Year, a year during which special concessions and indulgences were, and still are, available to pilgrims. On returning home many joined confraternities of former pilgrims in their own countries, the forerunners of the modern-day associations of "Friends of St. James" that now exist in several countries to support, promote and encourage the different routes to Santiago.

Many pilgrims wrote accounts of their experiences but as early as the twelfth century the first real "travel guide" was produced, probably between 1140-50. Its author was for a long time believed to be one Aimery Picaud, a cleric from Parthenay-le-Vieux in the Poitou region of France, and it formed part of a Latin manuscript known as the *Codex Calixtinus*. However, instead of relating the journey of one particular individual this was intended as a guide for the use of prospective (especially French) pilgrims. It describes the four roads through France (see below) and divides the route from the Pyrenees to Santiago into thirteen (somewhat unequal) stages. It lists, with comments, the places through which the *camino francés* passes, indicates some of the hazards pilgrims may encounter and contains advice on the good and bad rivers along the way, indicating which are safe to drink and which should be avoided. The author also describes in some detail the inhabitants of the different regions through which the prospective pilgrim will pass, their language (including one of the earliest lists of Basque words), customs and characteristics, none of which compares at all favourably, in his opinion, with those of the people of his native Poitou. He includes a list of shrines to be visited along the different roads through France, a description of the city of Santiago and its churches and a detailed account of the cathedral's history, architecture and canons. It is now thought that this guide was not, in fact, written by one person but was a compilation, designed, under the influence of the energetic bishop Diego Gelmírez, to promote Santiago de Compostela as a pilgrimage centre. Regardless of its authorship, however, this guide once attributed to Aimery Picaud was certainly instrumental in popularising the itineraries of the four main pilgrim roads through France and the *camino francés* in Spain. It has recently been translated into English: see bibliography.

Routes to Santiago
The route described in this book is not, in fact, the one and only "Way of St. James". In former times, when pilgrims set out from their own front doors and made their way to Santiago from many different places, several well-established routes grew up (see map). In France, for example, there were four main departure points, each with several "feeder roads" (such as the one from Rocamadour to Moissac) joining them at different points along the way. The route from Paris, the *Via Turonensis*, passed through Orléans, Tours, Poitiers, Bordeaux and Dax. From Vézelay pilgrims took the *Via Lemovicensis* through Limoges, Périgeux, Bazas and Mont-de-Marsan while those from Le Puy took the *Via Podensis* and passed through Conques, Cahors, Moissac, Aire-sur-l'Adour and Navarrenx. All three routes joined up near Ostabat on the French side of the Pyrenees, to continue over the mountains to Roncesvalles and on across the north of Spain as the *camino francés* or "French road". The fourth way, from Arles, and known as the *Via Tolosana*, visited Saint-Gilles du Gard, Toulouse, Auch and Oloron but crossed the Pyrenees further east at the Col de Somport, from where it is known as the *camino aragonés*, before merging with the other three at Puenta la Reina.

Although the name *camino de Santiago* has become synonymous with the *camino francés* in Spain other important routes included the northern one along the Costa Cantabrica, passing through Hernani, Zumaya, Guernica, Bilbao, Lareda and Castenada before turning inland to reach Santiago via Oviedo and Lugo. This was the path taken by many English pilgrims, who went by ship as far as Bordeaux and then continued on foot, whilst others sailed to La Coruña and then walked the rest of the way along one of the *Rutas del Mar*, one of which was known as the *camino inglés*. The *Vía de la Plata* or *camino mozárabe*, on the other hand, was the way taken by pilgrims from the south of Spain and others joining it by sea in Seville, passing through Mérida, Cáceres, Salamanca and Zamora before joining the *camino francés* at Astorga. (An outline guide to this route - fully waymarked today - is given in Appendix D.) There were also routes from the east coast of Spain as well as two *caminos*, south to north, through Portugal, one inland, the other along the coast. The "Way of St. James" described here therefore corresponds to the ones known, respectively, as the *Via Podensis* and the *camino francés*, no doubt the most widely used and best documented of the many pilgrim roads to Santiago. It begins in Le Puy-en-Velay and passes through Conques, Figeac, Cahors, Moissac, Aire-sur-l'Adour, Saint-Jean-Pied-de-Port, Roncesvalles, Pamplona, Estella, Logroño, Burgos, Sahagún, León, Astorga, Ponferrada, Villafranca del Bierzo and Sarria. It is also known that many pilgrims in former times continued their journey beyond Santiago to what was then the end of the known world in Finisterre, a walkers' route described in Appendix C.

TOPOGRAPHY, ECONOMY AND LANGUAGE

The *Vía Podensis*, the French part of the Way of St. James described in this book, begins in Le Puy-en-Velay in the *département* of the Haute-Loire and on the south-eastern edge of the Auvergne, a town famous for its bobbin-lace industry, its brown lentils and a pilgrimage centre in its own right. The Velay is a volcanic region, its often barren landscape punctuated by innumerable *puys* (tall conical hills, derived from the Latin *podium*) and latticed with ancient tracks and lanes frequently marked with old wayside crosses. From here the route makes its way across the Margeride plateau and through the Gévaudan, an area best known for the mysterious wild beast (*la bête du Gévaudan*) who claimed so many lives there towards the end of the eighteenth century. After that, continuing to climb, it eases its way up onto the even higher open plateau land of the Aubrac, with its *drailles* (wide drove roads), its *burons* (shepherds' bothies) and its lush green meadows rising to nearly 4,000 feet. Here flocks were driven up from the valleys below every year to spend the summer months grazing there, an activity known as *transhumance* in which pastors and their several hundred animals each would make their way up there on foot, a journey often lasting several days in each direction. Today this task is normally carried out in vehicles though an attempt at reviving the tradition has taken place; the tall wooden statue of a pastor in the village of Aubrac was placed there to mark the first such expedition in 1990.

After the Aubrac the landscape changes dramatically and the route continues down through the deep wooded gorges of the Lot valley and along the river itself to Estaing, before climbing up again and then plunging down into Conques (the name itself means "small valley"), deep in the recesses of the hills. By this time the GR65 has reached the old region of the Rouergue. After emerging from here the countryside begins to open out again somewhat, before continuing through the chalky wooded area of the Quercy with its traditonal dovecotes (*pigeonniers*), its half-timbered houses, its *caselles* and *gaviotes* (small round hut-like buildings of drystone wall construction) and its not infrequent dolmens. After that the *Vía Podensis* makes its way to Cahors through the *causse*, a term denoting an undulating limestone plateau covered with scrubby vegetation, little water and few distinguishing features.

By now the observant pilgrim will have noted the many Occitan terms used in placenames - *mas, borie, couderc*, for example (see glossary for others) - a language (not a dialect) of Latin origin. Historically France was divided, linguistically, into two main sections, the northern half with its *langue d'oïl*, the south with its *langue d'oc*, each quite separate languages and so named because of their respective terms for the word "yes". Occitan (often referred to as "Provençal" as well) has an extensive literature from the Middle Ages and later and was the only language spoken throughout the whole of the south of what we now know as France. Because the northern *langue d'oïl* was the one used in the Royal court and because administrative power was increasingly centred in Paris, this became the official "French" language spoken today. Occitan is still used by older people in country districts but there are probably few speakers left in the late twentieth century for whom it is their mother-tongue. In recent decades there has been a revival of interest in the language and as well as the emergence of modern authors writing in Occitan it can now be taught in schools and taken as a subsidiary subject both in the *baccalauréat* and at university level, as can Basque and Breton in other areas of France. Occitan also has several dialects, Béarnais and Gascon being those the pilgrim will encounter in placenames along the Way of St. James (*luy, gave*, for example).

After Cahors the countryside gradually flattens out, beginning with the rolling landscapes of the Tarn et Garonne and then, after crossing the Garonne itself near Moissac, on through the Gers (the least wooded *département* in France), with its rural bullrings, its castles and *bastides* (fortified market towns) perched on hilltops, punctuating the vast undulating fields of corn, sunflowers and other crops. This is the old Armagnac region, famous for the drink of that name, after which the pilgrim goes on into the *département* of the Landes near Aire-sur-l'Adour. Here the landscape is almost completely flat arable land, its scenery not very interesting and with few distinguishing features. Its large-scale agriculture is the consequence of the *remembrement* of recent decades, the regrouping of small, uneconomic portions of land into larger, more viable units and resulting in huge geometrically laid-out fields with irrigation channels and few hedge boundaries. Then, slowly, the terrain becomes hillier again as the pilgrim passes through the Béarn, once a separate kingdom, before the route makes its way towards the foothills of the Pyrenees and the Basque country.

The Basque country as a geographical entity (as opposed to the present-day Spanish autonomous *región* of the *País vasco*) flanks both sides of the Pyrenees, three of its provinces in France (Laborde, Bassa-Navarre and Soule), the other four in Spain (Álava, Guipúzcoa, Navarre and Viscaya). As you approach Saint-Jean-le-Vieux and Saint-Jean-Pied-de-Port you will begin to notice features that you will also encounter well into Spain - placenames in both languages (Basque and French or Castilian), for example, and a changing local architecture. In both countries the large Basque houses with their overhanging eaves, often ornately decorated, outside staircases and balconies running the whole length of one or more sides of the building are common, as is also the *frontón* or pelota court, to be found in almost every village of any size. The Basque language (*Euskerra* in Basque, *Vascuence* in Castilian) is unrelated to any of the Romance languages and its origins are still the subject of scholarly debate. It is an official language in the four Basque provinces in Spain, alongside Castilian, and is much in evidence in Navarre, whether in ordinary conversation, on television (in bars, for example), on signs, notices and placename boards.

After the high mountains and deep valleys of the Pyrenees, where sheep are a common sight, the landscape changes, flattening out to become more undulating as the *camino* makes its way down to Pamplona, a fortress town set up on a hill in the middle of a wide, fertile plain. It also gets hotter and dustier in summer, when it rarely rains, and the older vernacular houses are brown, built in adobe with red pantile roofs. This area has much in common with the landscape of Castille-León, though you remain in Navarre until the outskirts of Logroño.

La Rioja, like Navarre, is both a province and an autonomous *región* (Spain is divided into seventeen of the latter, each containing one or several *provincias*) and is well known for its excellent wines. It is also characterised by a deep red clay soil, contrasting sharply with the golden corn in summer, the bright blue of the sky and the dark green of many of the trees, particularly in the early morning and evening light, and you will come across a number of potteries or *alfarerías*, especially in the section between Logroño and Nájera. From here to Burgos, before it climbs up into the woods in the Montes de Oca, the *camino* continues its way through undulating countryside where you will encounter, in common with many other parts of Spain, large flocks of sheep and goats, often on the move with their shepherds and goatherds, in search of new grazing on cornfields that have just been harvested.

As you continue into Castille-León, one of the largest of the autonomous regions (with nine provinces), you will meet the first of a special type of local inhabitant: the *cigüeña*. The ubiquitous stork has a nest (and sometimes as many as three or four) on the tower of nearly every church and is a characteristic sight in this part of Spain, as are also the seemingly endless cornfields. After Burgos the *camino* wends its way up onto the *meseta*, the high plateau or tableland where the walker often has the feeling of being on the "roof of the world", after which it descends through the rolling countryside of the province of Palencia into the flat plains of León where several places include the suffix *del Páramo* (bleak plateau/plain) in their names. (Other places along the Way of St. James in Spain end in *del Camino*, evidence of the route the pilgrims took in former times.)

After Astorga the *camino* enters the Montes de León, slowly, at first, through the area known as the Maragatería. There are different theories as to the origins of the people in this area, who have their own distinctive customs, traditions and music, one of which is that, because of their isolated situation, they are the descendants of a very ancient race who escaped the effects of successive invasions. There are many abandoned or semi-abandoned villages in this section, although some are now coming to life again, due, in part, to the revival of interest in the *camino de Santiago*. An example of a typical *maragato* village, now a National Monument and worth a short detour, is Castrillo de los Polvares, just off the route beyond Astorga. After the Cruz de Fierro the *camino* enters the mountainous area of El Bierzo, sometimes thought of as Galicia's fifth province, with its fertile valleys and excellent wines, though the latter are not yet as internationally well known as those of La Rioja.

After Vega de Valcarce, still, in fact, in the province of León but totally different from the landscape where the *camino* enters it 7km before Sahagún, the pilgrim road climbs up and up, through chestnut woods and then out into open country up to El Cebreiro at 1300m, shortly before which it enters Galicia. From here the route changes dramatically in character.

Galicia is the autonomous *región* comprising the provinces of Lugo, Orense, Pontevedra and La Coruña. It has its own language (not a dialect), related to Portuguese, and which, together with *castellano* (ie. "Spanish") is used as an official language in the region. As a result you will find that not only will people reply to you in *gallego* but that all road signs, official notices etc. appear in both languages. The spelling of placenames often varies between the two languages and as at present the *castellano* forms have not yet been officially standardised the names you see on maps and notices may differ from what you see on signposts and on entry to villages big enough to have placename boards. Some of the more common variants are the interchange of "b" and "v" (as in Valos/Balos, for example), "o" and "ou" and "e" and "ei".

Galicia is a very green, lush area for the most part, with the highest rainfall in Spain. Unlike the south of Spain with its enormous *latifundios* (very large properties) the land in Galicia is divided (and subdivided) into tiny, often uneconomic individual holdings (*minifundios*), the result of centuries of sharing out land between its owner's descendants. As a result you will frequently see people working in the fields (many of whom are women) doing tasks by hand that would elsewhere be done more economically by machine. Unlike parts of Navarre and Castille-León, too, where villages are often very far apart but whose buildings are tightly concentrated together, those in Galicia are often tiny, not far from each other and much more spread out so that you are not usually very far from a building of some kind. The region is also criss-crossed with a veritable maze of old green lanes, which wend their way through fields separated from each other by stone boundaries made of large slabs set on end like rows of giant teeth, so that without some kind of waymarking systen the *camino* would be almost impossible to follow. Another characteristic feature of the Galician countryside is the *hórreo*: a long rectangular granary, of stone or, sometimes, brick, raised up on pillars and used for storing potatoes and corncobs. They have slightly pitched roofs with a cross at one end, a decorative knob at the other. *Hórreos* vary greatly in length, from those that are only 3-4m long to enormous structures with two or three compartments and that stretch for 20-30m.

Due to its location Galicia remained isolated from the influence of much of what was happening to the rest of Spain in former centuries and as a result still retains evidence of its Celtic origins. The *palloza*, a round stone dwelling with a thatched roof, dates from these times and several are to be found in the vilage of El Cebreiro, while traditional Galician music uses the *gaita* (bagpipe). (Those interested in the architecture, working life and customs of Galicia should visit the Museo do Pobo Galego when they reach Santiago.)

Galicia is also a very heavily wooded area, many of the trees centuries old, and as a result is very pleasant to walk in, even in the height of summer. Unfortunately, however, in recent years, large areas of its forests have been devastated by an epidemic of huge fires, suspected to have been started deliberately but quite why or by whom no one really seems to know. Those who continue on to Finisterre will also see something of the Galician coastline, with its *rías*, the fjord-like inlets along the Atlantic from the border of Portugal to the province of Asturias on the Costa Verde.

BEFORE YOU GO

a) Read up as much as you can about the Way, its history, art, architecture and geography, as well as other people's accounts of their journeys. A short bibliography is given in Appendix F.

b) If you are one of the many people walking the Way who are not already used to walking or to carrying a rucksack day-in day-out, get in plenty of practice before you go. Consider joining your local rambling club at least six months in advance and go out with them as often as you possibly can. Most clubs have walks of different lengths and speeds so you can start with a shorter, slower one if you need to and gradually build up your speed and stamina. The advantages of this are that you can walk with other people (usually friendly), walk in the countryside, have someone to lead who knows the way and suitable places to walk (which you may not) and you can also practise walking in hilly places (which you will need). Then, start increasing the amount of weight and gear you take out with you until you can carry what you need. After that, go out walking on at least two days in a row on several occasions, in hilly places, carrying all your proposed gear with you: it's a very different matter walking 30 kilometres on a "one-off" basis from getting up again the following morning, probably stiff and possibly footsore, and starting out all over again. In this way you should have an enjoyable journey, with troublefree feet and back.

c) Don't expect *anybody* - anybody at all - to speak English! Assume you will have to speak either French or Spanish all the time, according to where you are, for everything you need, however complicated. So, if you are not already fairly fluent, consider a year's evening classes or home study with tapes in your preparations: you will find yourself extremely isolated if you are unable not merely to carry out practical transactions but also to converse with the (very many) French and Spanish pilgrims and other people you will meet along the Way.

d) Decide what type of footwear you will be taking - walking shoes, lightweight boots, heavy (thick-soled) trainers, etc., and break them in *before* you go.

PLANNING YOUR SCHEDULE

As already indicated, Le Puy to Santiago can be walked comfortably in nine or ten weeks by anyone who is fairly fit, leaving plenty of time to visit places of interest along the Way. Allow plenty of time when planning your itinerary, though, especially if you are not an experienced walker. Start with fairly short stages and always stop *before* you are tired. You can increase the distances as you get fitter and into the swing of things.

Try not to plan too tight a schedule but allow plenty of time and flexibility to account for unforeseen circumstances (pleasant or otherwise). Where and how many rest days you take is up to you (though Conques, Cahors, Moissac, Burgos and León are "musts"), as is also whether you include several short days' walking in your programme, arriving at your destination during the late morning so as to have the remainder of the day completely free. If you are extremely tired, though, or having trouble with your feet, a complete day off works wonders (particularly in a small place with no "sights" to be visited) and is well worth the seeming disruption to your schedule that it might initially seem to be. Allow at least three days to visit Santiago at the end - there is plenty to see and you will also meet up with many of the other walkers you have met along the Way.

EQUIPMENT

1. **Rucksack**. At least 50 litres if carrying a sleeping bag.
2. **Footwear** - both to walk in and a spare pair of lightweight trainers/espadrilles/sandals etc.
3. **Waterproofs**. Even in summer it may rain, especially in Galicia. A "poncho" (ie. cape with a hood and space inside for a rucksack) is far more useful (and far less hot) than a cagoule or anorak.
4. **Pullover**. Much of the route is high up and it can get cold at night, even in summer.
5. **First aid kit** (including a needle for draining blisters). The type of elastoplast sold by the metre is more useful than individual dressings. Scissors. High-factor sunscreen if you burn easily.
6. **Torch**.

7.   **Large water bottle**. At least two litres if walking in July and August.

8.   **Sleeping bag**. Essential if staying in *refugios* in Spain. However, if you are only doing the French section and are staying in *gîtes d'étape* a sheet sleeping bag will be sufficient as blankets are provided.

9.   **Sleeping mat**. Useful if staying in *refugios*, where you may have to sleep on the floor and also for siestas in the open air.

10. **Stick**. Useful for fending off/frightening dogs and testing boggy terrain.

11. **Guidebook**.

12. **Maps**.

13. **Compass**.

14. **Whistle**.

15. **Sun hat** (preferably with wide brim).

16. **Small dictionary**.

17. **Mug, spoon and knife**.

18. If you are addicted to tea/coffee or can't get going in the morning without a hot drink a "camping gaz" type **stove** is a great advantage, even though it will add extra weight to your luggage. This is especially useful in summer when you will probably set out very early - 5.30 or 6am - to avoid the heat, since cafés and bars rarely open before 8.30 or 9am. The *gîtes d'étape* in France have cooking facilities but very few of the *refugios* in Spain do. (If you do take a camping gaz stove make sure it uses the 200 gram cylinders - smaller ones are available in France but not in Spain.) To economise on weight/space take a tin mug both to heat water in and drink out of.

19. A **tent** is useful in France if you intend to camp a lot (though you can walk the entire route from Le Puy to the Pyrenees staying in *gîtes*) but is not worth the trouble in Spain as rooms are usually available (eg. in bars, cafés) if you are not staying in *refugios*. Campsites in Spain can also be relatively expensive.

In general, travel as light as you can, not just for the weight but because of the constant hills in France and, according to the season, the heat in both countries.

THERE AND BACK

How to get there

Le Puy: by train from Paris to St. Etienne by TGV and then by local train; by coach direct from London to Lyon and then by local train.

Cahors: by train from Paris; by coach direct from London (both are the Toulouse service).

Moissac: by train from Paris (via Bordeaux or Toulouse).

Saint-Jean-Pied-de-Port: by train from Paris to Bayonne by TGV (or by coach direct from London) and then by local train.

Roncesvalles: by bus from Pamplona bus station to Burguete (6pm, not Sundays) and then walk the remaining 3km along the road. In summer the service continues to Roncesvalles and also carries a limited number of bicycles (remove panniers first). (Check carefully in winter/early spring/late autumn, though, as they sometimes only go as far as Zubiri.) In Spain each bus company has its own ticket office (*taquilla*): this route (terminating in Jaurrieta) is operated by "La Montañesa".

Pamplona: by train or coach from Madrid; by coach from London (Zaragoza service).

Madrid: by air direct from London; by train from London via Paris; by coach direct from London.

Other places along the Way (for those who are only doing a section): Figeac is accessible by train from Paris via Aurillac or Toulouse, as is Aire-sur-l'Adour. Logroño, Burgos, León, and Astorga can all be reached by train from Madrid though the coach may often be both quicker and more convenient. Burgos is also on the London-Madrid coach and the Paris-Madrid train routes.

How to get back from Santiago

Air: there are scheduled Iberia flights from Santiago to Heathrow (expensive). Otherwise go to Madrid by coach or train and fly from there.

Train: to Paris. Leaves at 9am every day, arriving Hendaye late evening, in time for the connection overnight for Paris, arriving early the following morning.

Coach: to Paris, direct, two to three times a week, depending on the time of year. Cheaper, comfortable and slightly shorter than the train journey. The journey takes 24 hours and arrives at the Porte de Bagnolet bus station from where you can continue to London. There is also a weekly service direct from Santiago to London.

BEING THERE

Accommodation

In **France** there are four general types of accommodation available along the route: campsites, *gîtes d'étape*, *chambres d'hôte* and hotels.

Most towns, even small, have a campsite, especially those on a river, and many farms along the way offer *camping à la ferme*. Campsites vary in price according to the facilities they offer but as more and more sites are being upgraded there are less simple ones than there were and in many cases it may now be very little cheaper to camp than to stay in a *gîte d'étape* (see below), the only real advantage in carrying a tent being the freedom to stop where and when you want to as campsites are so numerous. Most are closed in winter (ie. from "Toussaint" - All Saints Day, a public holiday on November 1st - to Easter).

It is also possible to walk the entire route from Le Puy to the Pyrenees staying in *gîtes d'étape*, without having to cover enormous distances. These contain simple, dormitory-type accommodation, at least one hot shower and cooking facilities and cost between 25FF and 60FF per person (1997). (*Relais d'étape* is the same except that you cannot cook; anything falls into the category of *refuge* or *abri*.) Blankets are provided so only a sheet sleeping bag is needed. The *gîtes d'étape* (as opposed to other types of *gîte*) are for walkers, cyclists and riders only; there are now plenty within easy walking distance of each other (eg. every 15km or so) as far as Conques though after that they are often further apart (eg. 25km). Many are municipally run (*gîte communal*) and will contain all the above facilities but in other places establishments that call themselves *gîtes d'étape* are in fact only *relais* as they provide no cooking facilities and few opportunities, for example, to wash clothes. These are often run by restaurants, hotels, riding schools or bed and breakfast places that attach a dormitory and showers and provide meals if required but not the rest of the facilities you would expect in a "proper" *gîte d'étape* and may also be more expensive. This does not mean that their standards are low but that pilgrims on a budget should be on their guard. In popular areas it is often advisable to phone the day before, especially at holiday times or on weekends with a *pont* (ie. a public holiday on a Thursday or a Tuesday when people take Friday or Monday off as well) as walking clubs, for example, and other groups, sometimes book (and pay for) the whole *gîte*, even if they do not always fill it; in such cases it is usually possible to sleep there once you are actually on the spot, though good French is normally needed to negotiate. *Gîtes d'étape* may seem too spartan for some people's tastes but they are a very good way to meet and get to know other pilgrims, as are the *refugios* in Spain, especially if you are walking or cycling the entire route. Some are only open from Easter to October. In addition, there is now some pilgrim-only accommodation along the Le Puy route, the beginnings of a network paralleling that to be found on the *camino francés* in Spain and these establishments are indicated in the relevant sections of this guide.

Those who prefer to stay in *chambres d'hôte* (the French equivalent of bed and breakfast in country areas, usually offering an evening meal as well, if required) will also have no trouble as these establishments are becoming increasingly popular. It is usually advisable to phone a day or so ahead. (These are indicated in the text as "CH", not to be confused with the CH = *Casa Huespedes* in Spain which are guesthouses normally offering room only.)

The word *hôtel* in France covers everything from luxurious five-star accommodation to a very basic *pension* or *hôtel de préfecture* and their prices normally reflect the facilities available. French hotels are currently in the process of being reclassified and those that have been done usually have "NN" (*nouveaux normes*) after their star rating. Pilgrims who prefer to stay in hotels will find the local *Pages Jaunes* (ie. "Yellow Pages"), available in most cafés, a useful source of such accommodation, particularly the lower end of the market. A hotel offering a *forfait pèlerin* (or *soirée étape*) has a special rate for dinner, bed and breakfast.

As the availability of accommodation often changes rapidly two sources of up-to-date information will be useful. For the French part of the route as far as Conques the Comité Départemental du

Tourisme de la Haute Loire prepares an annual update (in French) for its own guides but which is for sale separately in their office in Le Puy (12 Boulevard Philippe-Jourde; it also contains information on banks, doctors, etc.). For both the French and Spanish parts of the route the Confraternity of St. James's annually revised guides to (all types of) accommodation are recommended: see bibliography for address.

In **Spain** various types of accommodation are available along the Way, ranging from luxurious five-star hotels (such as the state-run *paradores* established in redundant historic buildings) down to very basic *refugios* set up in schools and church halls.

Hotel usually implies a higher standard of accommodation than that found in a *hostal* which, in turn, normally offers more facilities than a *fonda* (*hospedaje* in Galicia) and, going down the scale, a *posada*. (*Residencia* after either a *hotel* or a *hostal* means it only provides accommodation: neither meals nor breakfast are available.) A number of bars also provide rooms (*habitaciones - camas* means "beds"), so it is worth asking about these, even if there isn't actually a sign or notice to say so. However, a word of warning if you intend to stay in any of these and want to leave early in the morning to avoid walking in the heat: make sure you arrange to pay the previous evening and retain your passport as well as checking, too, how you will actually get out of the building the following morning (ie. which doors or entrances will be locked and how they can be opened) as otherwise you may find yourself unable to leave until at least 9am.

A *refugio* is simple accommodation set up especially for pilgrims on foot or by bicycle (but not for those accompanied by a back-up vehicle) and is *only* for those holding a *credencial* or "pilgrim passport" (see below). (This is to ensure that these facilities are not used by "pseudo-pilgrims", hitch-hikers or other travellers.) *Refugios* are provided by churches, religious orders and *ayuntamientos* (town halls or local authorities) and are being set up in more and more places along the Way, especially since 1989, when the Pope visited Santiago and literally thousands of people made the pilgrimage that year, either individually or in (sometimes huge) groups and in Galicia in particular, in preparation for the very large numbers expected for the 1993 Holy Year when 99,000 pilgrims received their

"Compostelas" (certificates). Some are in large towns, others in small villages, many are unmanned while others, increasingly, have volunteer wardens during the summer months. The facilities offered vary enormously, from those with beds/bunks, a kitchen and hot showers down to those with only a cold tap and in which you will have to sleep on the floor without a mattress. Note, however, that *refugios* are not provided as cheap substitutes for hotels but as alternatives to sleeping rough, places to shelter pilgrims from the elements, therefore you cannot expect anything more from these facilities other than being clean. Some are very large, others very small, some operate in the summer only and in July and August in particular they may be *extremely* crowded since no one ever seems to be turned away. Many are still free of charge but you should always offer to pay and there is usually a box for donations towards their upkeep, especially those run by religious or charitable bodies, such as the excellent "five-star" *refugio* in Santo Domingo de la Calzada. However, since the availability of these facilities varies greatly from year to year details have not been given in the main body of the text though a list of some of the more permanent refuges are given in Appendix E; for up-to-date information it is advisable to join the Confraternity of St. James referred to above and obtain their annually revised guides. Unlike *hotels*, *fondas*, etc., you will not normally encounter any difficulty in leaving *refugios* early and will find too that most other people are doing the same.

Planning the day

Long-distance walkers in Britain usually operate on a "nine-to-five" basis, leaving their accommodation shortly after breakfast and returning in time for an early evening meal. There may be few, if any, places of historical, religious or cultural interest directly on the path, such as churches, cathedrals or stately homes that require a detailed indoor visit (as opposed to historic bridges, fortifications, market crosses and so on that can be inspected fairly quickly from the outside) and those that do normally work "nine-to-five" as well so that combining walking and sightseeing is usually incompatible. Walkers, in the main, tend just to walk (in Britain). In France and Spain, however, not only are there an enormous number of places well worth visiting along the Way of St. James, of outstanding artistic, architectural, cultural or religious interest, but they are also open at convenient times for the walker: as well as 10am to 12pm (or 1pm in Spain) they normally open again from 4 or 5pm to 7 or 8pm. Churches between Le Puy and Conques are usually open all day but elsewhere those in small villages are nearly always locked, unless there is a service going on. However, it is often possible to visit during Saturday afternoons when they are being cleaned in preparation for Sunday.

In July and August in particular it is *extremely* hot during the day, both in France as well as in Spain, with temperatures well up into the 90s°F. In France there is often plenty of shade but in Spain there is very little at all apart from many areas of Galicia. When walking in hot weather it is important to avoid becoming dehydrated by drinking plenty of water *before* you set out as once you realise you haven't had enough to drink it is too late to do anything about it, even if you have supplies with you. It is difficult to do but if you can drink *at least* half a litre of water as soon as you get up (as well as any tea/coffee you may have) you will find the hot weather affects you much less. The best way to avoid walking in the heat is to get up before it is light and set out at daybreak (though not before or you won't be able to see the way). At this time of day it is cool and pleasant, with the added advantage of being able to watch the sun rise as you walk and enjoy the scenery in the early morning light. In this way, even with stops, you should be able to reach your destination by 1 or 2pm, when you can then eat and rest awhile before going out sightseeing/visiting in the (relative) cool of the early evening. It is also a good idea, in large towns and other places of any size, to go for a walk in the evening and check how you will leave, so as not to waste time or get lost the following morning.

Other practical information

Shops (for food) are open till 12 or 12.30pm in **France** and then from 2.30 or 3pm until about 7pm. Those in small villages are usually shut not only on Sundays but often on Monday mornings (and sometimes afternoons) as well, so considerable organisation is needed when following the GR65 since this not only avoids towns but does not always enter the villages it passes - you will often have to leave the route to go shopping.

In **Spain** food shops are usually open between 9 or 10am and 2pm and then again between 5 and 8pm or later. In small villages you may have to ask where these are (though in such places bars often double up as shops as well) and be prepared for them not to be well stocked with what you need: in remote places the lines carried are often only very basic and limited in range. Except for large supermarkets in big towns food shops close on Saturday afternoon and all day Sunday though bakers are often open on Sunday mornings if you can find them: unlike France where they are very numerous and very easily seen in Spain there is usually only one in each village or district, they may not always be marked and may only have a small entrance on the street leading to the large baking area behind.

Public holidays. There are more of these in France (*jours fériés*) and Spain (*días festivos*) than in Britain. In France these are January 1st, May 1st and 8th, Ascension Day, July 14th, August 15th, November 1st and 11th and December 25th. In Spain they are January 1st, Good Friday, August 15th, November 1st, December 5th, 6th and 25th. There are also three others which are taken locally and therefore vary from one area to another as well as (especially in August) the *fiestas* in honour of a town or village's own patron saint and which can last up to a week in some places (Estella, for example). Shops, including those for food (but not bars or bakeries) will be closed on these occasions.

Meals in **France** are available between 12-2pm and 7-9pm. If you are a vegetarian you will probably find life very difficult if you want to eat out. In **Spain** they are much later: 1.30 to 3.30pm for lunch and 8.30 or 9pm until 11pm for evening dinner. However, as most bars in Spain also provide *tapas* (different kinds of snacks, both hot and cold) as well as (in many) *bocadillos* (sandwiches) you need not go hungry if you are feeling ravenous outside regular mealtimes. Breakfast, in *hotels*, *fondas*, etc., is rarely available before 9am though in France you can usually have it from 7 or 7.30am onwards.

Cafés and bars. In **France** these may open as early as 7am in summer along the pilgrim route (check first if you want breakfast before setting out) and may well close by 10pm. In **Spain** they close very late but do not normally open before 8.30 or 9am and in small

Le Puy. View over the town and the Cathedral .
Photo: Maurice and Marigold Fox.
Estaing

villages do not always serve hot drinks all day long. Remember that a *cafetería* (in Spain) is not a self-service restaurant but a bar that also serves things to eat for breakfast (such as cake, sandwiches or hot *tapas*).

Changing money. It is usually possible to change money in post offices in **France**, even in quite small places. There are also an increasing number of cash dispensers (*distributeurs de billets de banque*), including fairly small towns, which also accept Visa, Eurocheque cards, etc. In Saint-Jean-Pied-de-Port there is now one such cash dispenser which will deliver your money in either French francs or pesetas. Bank opening hours are similar to those in Britain. In **Spain** they are only open from 8.30am till 2pm and only on Saturday mornings in large towns. However, there are cash dispensers (*cajeros automáticos*) in all places of any size which accept a wider selection of cards than in France.

Post Offices. In **France** these (*PTT*) are open from 8am in large places, 9am in small, until as late as 7pm, 12.30 or 1pm on Saturdays and many of them have cash dispensers too. In **Spain** they are known as *Correos* and are often open in the mornings only but stamps (as well as envelopes) can also be bought in *estancos* (tobacconists).

Poste restante. If you want to send things to yourself further along the route (eg. maps and guides) or have people write to you you can do this via the *poste restante* system whereby you collect your mail (on presentation of your passport) at the post office. In **France** address the letter/parcel to yourself (surname first), Poste Restante, postal code and name of town. The most likely places you will need will be the following: 43000 Le Puy-en-Velay, 46100 Figeac, 46000 Cahors, 82200 Moissac, 40800 Aire-sur-l'Adour and 64220 Saint - Jean-Pied-de-Port. There is a small fee for each item collected and they are only kept for 15 days before being returned to the sender. In **Spain** this service (the *Lista de Correos*) is free and items are kept for you for a month before sending them back. Address the item to yourself, Lista de Correos, name of town and name of province. If you decide (while in Spain) that you have too much in your rucksack it is considerably cheaper to post it to yourself this way in

Conques. Cathedral. (Photo: M & M Fox)

Santiago than to send a parcel home to Britain.

Telephones. In **France** more and more public telephones operate with *télécartes* (phone cards), except in rural areas. All phone numbers in France consist of 10 digits, with 01, 02, 03, 04 or 05 at the start, according to the region they are in. Please note that if you phone from Britain you do not use the "0", in the same way that you omit it when calling Britain from abroad. The emergency number in France (for all services) is 112.

In **Spain** (which has one of the most expensive telephone systems in Europe) phone boxes usually take both coins as well as phone cards. Most Spanish area codes begin with a "9", which is now included when calling from abroad.

Stamps for pilgrim passports. Modern pilgrims who seek proof of their pilgrimage also carry pilgrim "passports" which they have stamped at regular intervals along the Way (churches, townhalls, etc.) and which they then present to the Cathedral authorities in Santiago to help them obtain their "Compostela". More information about this is available from the Confraternity of St. James.

Snakes have been seen recently on the stretch from Le Puy to Cahors and also between Saint Palais and Saint-Jean-Pied-de-Port. They may not be very common but if you do meet them (usually when it has been very hot for a while) it will be when you are off your guard... (stick useful).

Dogs, their owners nearly always tell you, "won't hurt you", though this is often hard to believe. They may tell you, too, that it is the rucksack that bothers them (and as dogs are reputed to see only in black and white there may be some truth in this, faced with mysterious humpbacked monsters on two legs...) but it is not much comfort when faced with an aggressive one. They live all along the route from Le Puy to Santiago, often tied up in France but frequently running around loose (especially in Spain), hear you ages before you have any idea where they are and are often enormous (though the small ones are, in fact, a greater nuisance, as they have a nasty habit of letting you pass quietly by and then attacking from behind, nipping you in the back of your ankles). A stick is very useful, even though you might not normally want to walk with one - not to hit them with but to threaten. Be warned!

USING THIS GUIDE

Waymarking

The route described in this book follows the GR65 through France and the waymarked *camino francés* in Spain, ending at the cathedral in Santiago de Compostela, ie. in the direction of the (modern) pilgrimage. It is therefore described in one direction only. Those who would like to walk the Way in reverse or return on foot will have no trouble in France as the route is waymarked in both directions but since it is "one way only" in Spain some hints have been included in the text [in square brackets] as the *camino* is often difficult to follow backwards, even if you have already walked the outward journey. It is for this reason that, from time to time, the text contains such seemingly irrelevant remarks as "track joins from back L", redundant for those walking only towards Santiago but helpful for the person going in reverse and faced with a choice of paths to select. Similarly, the reader may wonder, at times, why information about other GRs are given in the description of the French part of the route; this is because all French long-distance footpaths (the *Sentiers de Grandes Randonnées* or "GRs") have the same waymarking system and the walker should be alert to (usually short) sections which the GR65 has in common with, for example, the GR4. When they separate again the walker needs to know

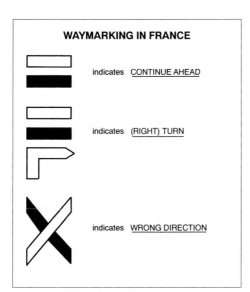

WAYMARKING IN FRANCE

indicates   <u>CONTINUE AHEAD</u>

indicates   <u>(RIGHT) TURN</u>

indicates   <u>WRONG DIRECTION</u>

which turning is the correct one as there is not always an indication next to the waymark.

Waymarking (*balisage*) in **France** is in the form of pairs of horizontal red and white stripes (*balises*), one above the other to indicate that you should continue ahead (see diagram). Turns are indicated by bent red and white arrows, often preceded by broken waymarks to prepare the walker. A useful feature is also the "wrong direction" sign, a red and white cross telling you which direction *not* to take, especially in situations where it is hard to mark the correct option for lack of suitable trees, rocks etc. on which to paint them. In **Spain** waymarking (*señalización*) is in one direction only (towards Santiago) and is in the form of yellow arrows (*flechas*) or flashes (*señales*) which, like the *balises* of the French GR network, are painted on tree trunks, walls, road signs, rocks, the ground, sides of buildings etc., and are normally extremely easy to spot. They appear at frequent intervals and the walker will not usually encounter any difficulty following them, except, at times, in some areas where road construction is in progress. (If, at any time, they seem to have disappeared, wherever you may be, this will be because you have inadvertently taken a wrong turning: retrace your steps to the last one you saw and start again from there, checking carefully.) Some sections in Spain are also waymarked with blue and white metal signs with the picture of a pilgrim in a hat while the beginning part, as far as Viana, has the red and white *balises* of the French GR system as well, as a continuation of the route from Le Puy. In Galicia, in addition, there are standardised concrete marker stones, about the size of old-fashioned milestones, bearing an embossed conch-shell design, the number of kilometres remaining to Santiago and the name of the village, hamlet or spot where they are located. They are positioned at 500m intervals and are not only attractive, providing reassurance that you are, in fact, on the right track (as indicated above, Galicia is criss-crossed with literally hundreds of old "green lanes", involving constant changes of direction in some places) but they are also a useful way of knowing exactly where you are in villages that are too small to bear the usual placename signs. It is apparently planned, eventually, to extend this type of *señal* to the rest of the *camino*.

Maps

Michelin 919 is a single map covering the whole of southern **France** but the IGN (Institut Géographique National) green series is recommended for walkers as the GR65 and its variants are marked on them. The scale is 1:100,000 and only 5 are required (as against 25 in the blue 1:25,000 series): 50(5), 58, 57(4), 63(3) and 69. These are readily available (from Stanfords map shop in London, for example, from The Map Shop, Upton-upon-Severn, or from many general bookshops).

In **Spain**, however, maps are a problem. It is possible to follow the *camino* just with the waymarks and this guide but that would be very limiting. Maps are useful not merely as a means of finding the way when lost but also for situating the walk in the context of its surroundings and for making any diversions the walker might wish to make to visit places of interest within striking distance of the route. At present there are no comprehensive, reliable Spanish equivalents of the Ordnance Survey maps of Britain or the French IGN series. In 1989, however, the Spanish IGN (Instituto Nacional Geográfico), in conjunction with MOPT (Ministerio de Obras Públicas y Transportes) published a map entitled *El Camino de Santiago*, covering the whole of the *camino francés* on a scale of 1:600,000. This is not detailed enough to walk from but situates the *camino* in the context of its surroundings and is readily available (from Stanfords, for example). Otherwise two maps in the Michelin 1:400,000 (1cm:4km) are recommended: 441 North West Spain and 442 Northern Spain. **It is for this reason that detailed sketch maps of the Spanish (but not the French) section of the route are included with this text. A general map is provided, however, to show the route.**

Textual description

Each section begins with the distance walked from the previous one, a description of the facilities available, a brief history, where applicable, and an indication of the places of interest to visit. (Walkers wishing to spend time in any of the larger towns should obtain information leaflets and a street plan from the Tourist Office there.) The text is not divided into stages as in this way the walker can decide for him or herself the distances he or she would like to cover each day. The figures after each placename heading indicate the height in metres where known and, in parentheses, the distance in kilometres from both Le Puy and Santiago. In the case of large towns (Cahors, Pamplona, Burgos, for example) the distances to/ from them start/end in their centres, normally at the cathedral.

Please note that "river" in Spain rarely implies a wide, deep, fast-flowing stretch of navigable water: most, if not actually dried up, are no more than narrow trickles at the bottom of a wide river bed and may be non-existent at certain times of the year.

Abbreviations have been kept to a minimum.

L	indicates that you should turn/fork left,
R	that you should turn/fork right.
(L) and **(R)**	mean that something you pass is to your left or right.
KSO	keep straight on.
UMUR	unmade up road.
FP	footpath.
FB	footbridge.
//	parallel.
km	kilometre,
KM	kilometre marker (found on the sides of all main roads; K is reserved for the marker stones in Galicia).
N	followed by a number (eg. N135) refers to the number of a main road in both France and Spain,
D	to the number of a local road in France,
C	(or the first two initials of the province you are in, eg. LU Lugo) to its equivalent in Spain.
SNCF	is the abbreviation for the French national railway network,
RENFE	for the Spanish one.

Unlike pilgrimages to Lourdes, Fatima or other locations where miracles are sought and help for specific problems requested and where being in the pilgrim destination itself is the most important factor, on the Way of St. James it is the making of the journey itself that is the pilgrim's principal concern, the arrival in Santiago being only a conclusion to the rest of the undertaking. It is not a "map and compass route", though the walking in France is often strenuous and there are a couple of stiff climbs in Spain (over the Pyrenees, for example and up to El Cebreiro as you enter Galicia). Timings have not been given from place to place but 4km per hour, exclusive of stops, is often considered average, especially when carrying a heavy rucksack. However, a comfortable pace may often be more than this - a fit walker may well be able to maintain a speed of 5 to 6km ($3^1/_2$ miles) per hour.

The route is practicable, though not necessarily recommended, all through the year. In winter there is often snow on the Aubrac plateau and nearly always in the Pyrenees and it rains a lot in the Basque country. The weather may be dry over much of the route through Castille and León but as a lot of it is quite high up (Burgos, for instance, is at 2000ft though the area around is more or less flat) it gets very cold, with a biting wind. In spring it rains a lot, especially in Galicia (Santiago has the highest average rainfall in Spain), in Navarre and in all parts of the route through France. If you are not restricted to a particular time of year May / early June or the autumn are best - dry, but not as hot as in summer, and accommodation is also much less crowded. Traditionally, though, as many people as possible aimed to arrive in Santiago for the festivities on July 25th, St. James' Day, **particularly in Holy Years. Many** people still do.

¡Ultreya!

Pinman Waymark

GENERAL MAP OF THE ROUTE - FRANCE

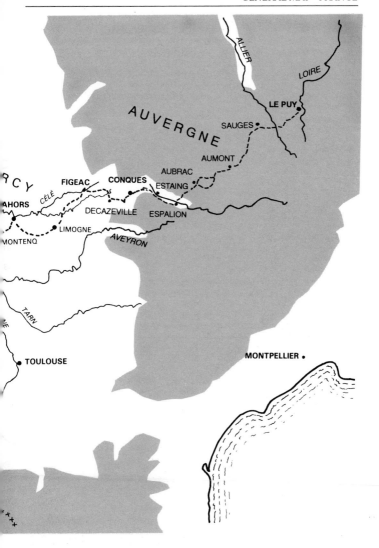

Le Puy. West façade of the Cathedral

The Route

Le Puy-en-Velay 625m (0/1495)

Population 29,000. All facilities. Several hotels, SNCF (trains from Paris via Lyon and St. Etienne or Clermont-Ferrand and St. Georges d'Aurac). Gîte d'étape for pilgrims and walkers in the Maison Saint-François (19pl), Rue Mayol, open all year, Youth Hostel (closed w/ends 31/10 - 31/3) in Centre Pierre Cardinal, Rue Jules Vallès, both in upper part of town. Maison de la Providence (Diocesan Centre), Rue A. Chantermesse, also takes pilgrims. Campsite to NW of town, on island in river. In July-August there is a pilgrim mass in the cathedral at 9am Mon-Sat, 11am Sun.

An ancient town in a volcanic landscape, dominated by rocky peaks rising from the valley floor. One is crowned by the chapel of Saint Michel d'Aiguilhe (the Needle), built by Godescalc, Bishop of Le Puy, after his pilgrimage to Santiago in AD 951 (worth climbing the 267 steps to visit it). Romanesque Cathedral of Notre-Dame, at present being extensively restored, is surrounded by the narrow twisting streets of the old town, with many interesting houses. Inside the cathedral: eleventh-twelfth century cloisters and statue of the Black Virgin. (Black Virgins were once thought to have originated only from Africa but it is now thought that they are also local and "black" because of a life of hard work in the fields and the open air.) Enormous statue of Notre-Dame de France overlooks the town from a rock high above it. Worth spending at least half a day to visit Le Puy. Ask at Office de Tourisme (Place du Breuil) for a walking tour plan of the town. Musée Crozatier. Eglise du Collège, first "Jesuit-style" church in France, thirteenth-century Eglise Saint-Laurent, Chapelle des Pénitents, Baptisère Saint-Jean, Chapel of Monastère Sainte-Claire, Tour Pannessac.

Le Puy has been a pilgrimage centre since the Middle Ages, not merely as a starting (or assembly) point for French pilgrims and the many "feeder" routes and/or those coming from further afield but also in its own right. Pilgrimages to Notre-Dame du Puy began in the tenth century and the shrine has its own "Jubilee" years, those in which the Feast of the Annunciation (March 25th) coincides with Good Friday. The first was in 992 (thus predating the first Holy Year in Santiago, in 1179) and is the third oldest after Jerusalem and Rome. There have been three such Jubilee years in the twentieth century - 1910, 1921 and 1932 - and the next, the *thirtieth, falls on March 25th 2005. Le Puy is also famous for its bobbin-lace making and its (brown) lentils.*

From the main entrance to the cathedral go down the steps and then down the **Rue des Tables** ahead (note old houses with statues in niches at first floor level as you go). Turn L after the fountain (des "Choristes") into the **Rue Raphael**. KSO to the end and continue down **Rue Chenebouterie** to the **Place du Plot**, the traditional pilgrim starting point. Turn R into the **Rue Saint-Jacques** (statue of St. James the pilgrim in niche above chemist's shop on corner of this street and the Place du Plot, plaque of "Amis de Saint-Jacques" on wall on L). Cross **Boulevard Saint Louis** and KSO uphill, climbing steeply, up the **Rue des Capucins**. At the top there is the first clear waymark: turn R and then L after 50m up the **Route de Compostelle**, continuing to climb steadily.

(Note pillar on LH side of road with "limite de l'octroi" at junction with 3rd turning on R.) Good views back over the town. (The route is high up but reasonably shady in this section.)

When you reach the top (modern elastic bandage factory on R) KSO(L) at fork down wide gravelled lane alongside high stone wall on LH side. Lane then becomes UMUR. Good views all round. At the crossing of 5 tracks KSO, passing stem of wayside cross (to your L). KSO, climbing gradually and ignoring turnings to L and R until you reach the road (D589). Turn L along it for 800m to hamlet of

5km La Roche 872m (5/1490)
Junction with GR3, which coincides, going SW, with the GR65 for a short distance.

Turn L off road after first building on L in hamlet. (NB. the waymarked minor road to the R is the northbound GR3.) Follow lane round sharply to R behind houses (ie. more or less // to road). KSO, ignoring turnings and then descend slightly (lane become FP) to join another tarred lane below you and follow this round to the R behind houses.

Just before you reach the road again turn L down grassy track, slightly downhill, which then becomes a FP. KSO, avoiding turns and maintaining your height, as the path winds its way along the shoulder of the hillside, // to the river **Gazelle** in the valley bottom below you to the L. (TV mast on skyline ahead of you.) Path follows low wall on your R for a while (be careful in foggy weather as although it is fairly wide there is a steep drop to your L - you are walking along a ridge here). Path then goes on to open grassland.

When you come to a "T" junction with a farm track (1km later) turn L, descending slightly to small wayside cross on L.

(There are a lot in this area marking the pilgrim routes but though they may seem like the equivalent of our modern waymarks in centuries gone by they were also often used to mark the site of a local shrine or pilgrimage so we cannot just assume they were the forerunners of the present-day balises.)

KSO(R) here at fork (this is where the GR65 and the GR3 separate) ie. the uphill/level track to the R (the GR3 goes L *down*hill here) and KSO on grassy track that then enters small wood before it begins to descend slowly to cross small bridge over stream. KSO again, along tree-lined lane, climbing slowly but steadily until you reach the village of

3km Saint-Christophe-sur-Dolaison 908m (8/1487)
2 bars (1 does food), twelfth-century church built of pink rock, château/seigneurie.

At war memorial, *mairie,* phone box and *PTT* (all on your L on road) turn R along the D31, passing remains of communal bread oven on RH side. 100m later on turn R at small junction down minor road marked "Tallode 0,5km", skirt the *seigneurie's* perimeter wall, go under main road (D906) and KSO(L) on other side. Continue through hamlets of **Tallode** (*chambres d'hôte*) and **Liac** (1km further), turning R at end down walled lane (track ahead of you continues as grassy track) marked "Lic 1km"). Continue to hamlet of **Lic** (lane enters open plateau land) and at end, as lane turns L, turn R at side of building up stony track which then opens out to grassy field and KSO alongside low wall on your L, later with low walls on *both* sides. After 400m turn L down similar lane at right angle junction and cross minor road 200m later. [Variant Bains (2 hotels, SCR, Church of Sainte-Foy de Conques) begins here.] KSO. (Montbonnet visible ahead on hillside ahead of you.) At junction of 5 similar tracks take *2nd* on L (TV mast now ahead of you on skyline) and 200m later fork R. KSO along this lane, ignoring turns to L and R, until you reach the D621 at the end of the village of **Ramourouscle** (1047m) and turn R along it.

In centre of village (junction, fountain, seventeenth-century wayside cross) turn L onto smaller road marked "Montbonnet 2". KSO for 1.5km, ignoring turns, until you reach the

6.5km Chapelle Saint Roch (14.5/1480.5)

Early thirteenth-century Romanesque chapel, the first of many along the way dedicated to the patron saint of pilgrims. It was originally dedicated to St. James, then Saint Bonnet (a local saint) and then, in seventeenth century, to St. Roch. Chapel is normally open.

Continue on road for 500m, passing the Croix des Pèlerins to the village of

0.5km Montbonnet 1108m (15/1480)

Gîte d'étape with camping place adjacent. Bar (does food).

Continue on road, following it through village, uphill, to junction with D589. (Turn R for *gîte*).

Turn L on road and 150m later turn R up gravelled lane by phone box (from here to the Lac d'Oeuf the GR65 and GR40 coincide) which then becomes a walled lane through plateau with fields to either side. KSO, ignoring small turnings. After 1.5km, at clear "T" junction, turn R uphill towards woods, climbing fairly steeply. Just before you reach the top (where the GR65 and GR40 separate, the GR 40 going straight on to the Lac d'Oeuf) turn L at fork onto a more level grassy track, rising gradually before it levels out through semi-shaded conifer woods, continuing to minor tarred forest road. Turn L along it for 20m then fork L down wide FP downhill, into woods again. After leaving woods track continues to descend (view of hamlet of Le Chier ahead), becomes UMUR till you reach the D589. Cross over and veer R down minor road into hamlet of

4.5km Le Chier 1050m (19.5/1475.5)

KSO(L) in centre at tall wayside cross (where road bends round to R) down tarred lane alongside a *coudert* (a sort of village green). Lane becomes walled lane, continuing to descend, with fields on either side. Fork R 200m later down wide FP, descending steadily all the time. Track widens out and as it begins to climb again turn *hard L* down FP, descending steeply into narrow walled lane. This becomes a FP, winding its way steeply down to the valley bottom where it crosses a wooden bridge over the **Ruisseau du Rouchoux**. (NB. this section could be *very* slippery in wet weather.)

Continue on other side, passing in front of houses. Tarred lane climbs gently, passes *gîte d'étape* (on your L) and joins D589 coming from back R. Turn L into village of

2.5km Saint Privat d'Allier 890m (22/1473)

Shops, hotel, campsite, bars, boulangerie, *Tourist Office,* gîte d'étape. *Gothic church, remains of* château.

Continue through village and at end fork R up D301. KSO, cross road bridge over river. 50m later fork R off road up stony track (just before large farm building to RH side of road) - the first of many short-cuts through the zigzags in the road. Go up slope, veer R behind farm and then L up tree-lined walled lane uphill. At top turn L onto very minor road and 200m later, at junction where it veers L to join D301 KSO(R) ahead up FP // to road and then veer R uphill to rejoin road again. Turn R. KSO for 300m then, at bend, fork R up FP into woods which then joins a grassy track coming from back R, // and slightly above road which it rejoins shortly afterwards. KSO on road (tower and chapel visible ahead to L) for 400m to cluster of houses at

2.5km Rochegude 967m (24.5/1470.5)

Tower, tiny chapel dedicated to St. James perched on top of rocky belvedere. Commanding views on a clear day. (Beware of straying too far away from chapel if foggy as there are very *steep drops on two of its sides.)*

To see chapel and tower (remains of a *château*) go up grassy track. To continue turn L after last house on L (facing chapel). Go down rocky FP which descends steadily and steeply (the descent from here down to Monistrol can be *very slippery* in wet weather). When you reach a road (at entrance to hamlet of **Pratclaux**) turn L for 50m then fork L (opposite a RH turn down a "no-entry" road) off road up short walled lane (not well waymarked at start). At top turn L and immediately R onto tarred lane through hamlet. After last house on R turn R down grassy walled lane, cross road at bottom and KSO down another walled lane on other side. Turn R onto road at end (view of tower and chapel behind you) and 30m later turn L down UMUR. 100m later, when it turns L, turn R down grassy lane which becomes a FP, winding its way steeply down to road (again cutting out zigzgags). Turn L and 20m later fork R off road down another steep stony FP. 100m later reach road again and turn R downhill. KSO into

3km Monistrol d'Allier 619m (27.5/1467.5)

SNCF (Paris - Clermont-Ferrand - Arvant - Nîmes), hotel-restaurant, chambres d'hôte, gîte d'étape at Centre d'Accueil (1.5km before village on Le Puy road), campsite by river, café, shop, post office. Romanesque church, former priory of La Chaise-Dieu: cross has carving of pilgrim.

Cross metal bridge over the river **Allier**. (Turn L to visit church, veering R to return to road again.) 220m after bridge fork R down road at side of mill (signposted to "La Madeleine, La Vallete"). Cross bridge over river **Ance** and then KSO, climbing very steeply. (Views over Allier gorge and beyond.) NB. from Monistrol to the separation with the GR412 after Montaure - 6.5km - there are 450m (nearly 1500ft) of ascent.

The road zigzags its way uphill, passing first a stone wayside cross and then a metal one. At metal cross turn *hard* L up stony track to the **Chapelle de la Madeleine** (20m), thought to have been a grotto originally but faced with stone and made into a chapel in the seventeenth century.

Then continue *very* steeply up for another 200m to hamlet of **Escluzels**, veering R after 1st house and then L uphill on road (fountain). KSO uphill on road. 800m later road forks: KSO(L) uphill again but after 150m turn *hard* L up wide forest path, short-cutting hairpins in road. Cross road at top, go up narrow path and cross road again and fork L uphill off road on other side up another forest track. Continue uphill, zigzagging steeply, to

4km Montaure 1022m (31.5/1463.5)

(View over to Rochegude on opposite side of valley.)

When you reach a road KSO(L) ahead (iron cross on R), veering L again at junction shortly afterwards (modern concrete wayside cross on R: this is the junction with the GR412). Continue on road (ie. L) for 300m then turn L onto UMUR. KSO, ignoring turns, climbing gently all the time. (Good views all round.) When you reach the hamlet of **Rosiers** (1.9km, 1066m) KSO(R) on road through village. At a road junction after 0.6km turn R downhill (the GR412 goes on ahead, to Pouzas) to the village of

3.5km Le Vernet de Saugues 1050m (35.5/1460)

Continue through village, turn L (*uphill*) at fountain and KSO(L). 30-40km later turn R down UMUR by iron cross perched on top of large rock. KSO along lane (woods to L, behind fence) through semi-shaded woods. 700m later, at end of woods, track joins from back R. Continue on lane with fields to either side. When you reach road coming from back L at approach to hamlet of **Rognac** KSO ahead, pass iron cross (on your L) and continue ahead uphill. 700m later when road bends round to R by some houses KSO(L) down green lane towards HT pylon. Continue down it, descending gradually all the time until you reach the D589. (Note the unusual wooden sculptures to LH side of road.) Cross the road and descend into

4.5km Saugues 960m (39.5/1455.5)

Population 2000. Romanesque church of St. Médard (and treasury), diorama de St. Bénilde (a local saint), thirteenth-century Tour des Anglais with dungeon, numerous old houses. Saugues was the meeting point of pilgrims coming from the Auvergne via secondary routes and had a twelfth-century pilgrim hospital (now an old people's home near the Chapelle des Pénitents) dedicated to St. James.

Hotels, bars, restaurants, shops, banks, post office. 2 gîtes d'étape, one municipal, one next to CH, Rue des Roches, accommodation (+ meals if required) at Centre d'Accueil, rue des Tours Neuves, campsite.

If you have not already come across this phenomenon before you may be surprised to encounter (from the south of France and onwards) the first of many church and other public clocks (on civic buildings, for example) that strike twice for every hour (and therefore 24 times at midnight...). Since many of them do not have the "ding dong ding dong" prelude to the actual hour strokes that are customary on British clocks the first series is, in effect, an announcement that the hour is going to strike - for the second time - after a couple of minutes' pause. (In small towns and villages in Spain, however, and particularly on civic buildings such as town halls, the "prelude" may consist of a cassette recording of a hymn tune or - not infrequently - the "Westminster Chimes!")

Enter town by **Rue des Cimes**, continue ahead down another street and at junction with 5 roads turn L uphill (**Rue St. Jean**) and then R on **Route du Puy** (main street) into town centre.

Turn L into **Rue St. Gervais** and continue via **Rue St. Médard, Place Joseph Limozin, Rue de la Margeride** (D589 in direction of Le Malzieu) and **Rue Mont du Bouchet** (campsite below you to R). Cross D585 at bottom and then bridge over river **Seuge**. 100m later turn L down UMUR. At road 700m later turn L uphill, forking L at metal wayside cross 0.6km before hamlet of **Le Pinet** (1020m).

KSO on road through hamlet. At last house road becomes UMUR, veering R, climbing gently, towards conifer woods ahead. 200m later KSO(L) at fork. KSO ignoring turns. After reaching a col the track levels out and then descends gently to cross stone bridge over the **Seuge**.

KSO(R) on other side. Track becomes walled lane, climbing gently all the time. Ignore turns to L & R. At the top of a hill 700m later enter

7km La Clauze 1095m (46.5/1448.5)

At junction of 5 tracks at entrance to hamlet ahead on minor tarred road coming from back R. When you meet another (bigger) road coming from back R, near tower, KSO along it through village and continue on road (D335).

At top of hill (5 way junction) fork L ahead downhill on minor tarred road to

2.5km Le Falzet 1134m (49/1446)

Gîte d'étape Continue through hamlet to road, turn L uphill and 40m later fork R up UMUR leading to

1km Villeret-d'Apcher (50/1445)

Fountain. At entrance to village UMUR becomes tarred road, cross D587 (slightly staggered junction) and go down narrow street on other side, veering L, and then turn R downhill to cross river **Virlange** and KSO(R) on other side (path goes alongside fields, following line of HT cables) until you come to a junction with a UMUR: turn R downhill, cross another and at farm building a few metres further on turn L along UMUR. Turn R down wide UMUR just before the farm at

2.5km Contaldès 1143m (52.5/1442.5)

Pass to L of farm, KSO(L) ahead up walled lane, along line of telegraph poles.

[Village across valley to R, with cemetery, is Chanaleilles, 1150m, with shop, café/restaurant and interesting Romanesque church. 1km.]

KSO to **Chazeaux** (800m), turning L and then R at first house, then fork R to R of houses with apse-like protrusion (former oven: there are many such in this region) down cobbled walled lane to road. Cross over and KSO down wide UMUR along valley bottom, climbing gradually.

After crossing a stream veer L uphill through modern gate and then veer R uphill into woods (watch out carefully for waymarks) on stony forest track leading to electricity pylons. In the clearing/firebreak turn L uphill and then, at first pylon, turn L back into woods again, veering L to do a "C" shaped loop which brings you out at the pylons again higher up (road visible ahead). Continue on track to cross river **Virlange** again (twice, by boulder "bridges"), go through another modern gate and veer R to road. Turn L up it and KSO. [RJ: after going through gate make for first pylon to your L.]

Continue uphill, climbing very steeply. Shortly after passing the road (D587) KM post marked "Saint Alban 12, Alt. 1250m" the road levels out and 100m later turn L down UMUR to

6km Domaine du Sauvage 1292m (58.5/1436.6)

The Domaine is visible ahead, some 2km away. If you do not actually want to go there you can continue ahead on the road for 1km as the detour to Le Sauvage and out again is nearly 5km. If so, KSO on road and pick up the GR65 again (still on road) at the exit (to your L) from Le Sauvage (a historic monument, the former Domenerie des Templiers.)

To make the detour: turn L and continue on UMUR. Pass farm buildings and then veer round to R by small lake and continue through woods. KSO to road by ski-chalet St. Roch and then turn L. [RJ: at each of two big "Y" junctions KSO(L) - the other waymarked routes are *pistes* for long-distance skiing.]

Continue along road (D587) passing **Fontaine St. Roch** (site of thirteenth-century oratory) with picnic site and 200m later, at border of *départements* of the Haute Loire and the Lozère (that you are now entering) reach

3km Chapelle-Saint Roch 1280m (61.5/1443.5)

Also known as Chapelle de l'Hospitalet du Sauvage this was a hospital for pilgrims and travellers founded at this col in 1198, originally dedicated to St. James (chapel was next to present fountain). The chapel was rededicated to St. Roch after the Wars of Religion (1562-98) but then fell into ruin. The new chapel built at the end of the nineteenth century was destroyed by a cyclone in 1897 and the present one was rebuilt in 1901. Usually locked but a grille in the door enables you to see inside. Statue of St. Roch with his dog above the altar. Refuge on road (very clean and well kept) a useful place to rest, eat or shelter in bad weather.

100m later, when road bends R, KSO(L) downhill on wide grassy track. (The section from here down to Saint Alban is easy walking.) Continue through semi-shaded woods. At end cross another track and KSO on walled lane. After 2km cross D987.

(Turn L here for 3 gîtes d'étape in La Roche-de-Lajo, 1184m, 1km away to south; return via GR4 the following morning to marked junction indicated in next paragraph.)

KSO on other side, gently downhill all the time. Almost at the valley bottom there is a junction with the GR4 (you can also turn L here for the 3 *gîtes*) and the GR65 and GR4 continue for a short stretch in common. Cross the river **Gazamas** at the bottom and KSO uphill into pine woods. At junction with forest road *gîte d'étape* at Les Faux is signposted to L (10mins away). KSO(L) along wide forest road joining from back R (here the GR65 and GR4 part company again).

KSO, slightly downhill all the time. When the road veers L KSO(R) ahead down grassy lane (not waymarked at start). This leads, downhill all the time, to the D987 (fountain at crossing) in the hamlet of

6km Le Rouget 1017m (67.5/1427.5)

The village takes its name from the red stone in the area. From here onwards the style of building changes and the red tile roofs characteristic of the area up to and including Saugues now give way to grey slate.

Cross road and veer R down minor road which becomes UMUR. At bottom (100m later) KSO(L) on minor road coming from back R and at bottom of hill (end of hamlet) turn R down UMUR which passes under HT cables. When this bends L at farm building KSO(R) down smaller UMUR which leads to the D987 (coming from back R) at entry to Saint-Alban-sur-Limagnole. At junction in front of you veer L down minor road marked "Hôpital" and with football pitch on L. Veer R and then L between and past buildings of regional psychiatric hospital, veering R towards town centre. Go down some steps (L) and turn *hard* L to **Grand'Rue** (shops etc.).

3.5km Saint-Alban-sur-Limagnole 950m (71/1424)

Small town (population 2000) with hotels, shops, restaurants, bars, gîte

d'étape, *bank. Romanesque church of St. Alban in town centre (red sandstone and polychrome brick). Château (various dates) is now part of the regional psychiatric hospital. Campsite at end of town, 500m after GR turn-off. Tourist Office in Hôtel de Ville.*

In **Grand'Rue** turn R in front of church, then L down its side (ie. when facing entrance) and L down **Rue de la Tournelle** to the Hôtel de Ville. Turn L along road to D987 and turn R along it for 400m, turning R at end of town up gravelled lane by sports ground. (Campsite marked 500m further on on road.)

Go up lane through trees, uphill to tall stone cross at top then downhill, ignoring turns, to road in hamlet of

2km Grazières-Mages (73/1422)

Fountain. Turn hard L along road, veer R (at iron cross in front of you) downhill and then veer L to cross river **Limagnole**. Cross D587 and veer R steeply uphill on gravel path through semi-shaded woods, levelling out onto an open plateau at the top. Reach road in hamlet of **Chabannes** (2km) and veer R along it downhill (note stocks on RH side) passing (R) another of the tall stone crosses typical of the Lozère and KSO.

When road veers L at 2nd stone cross (small) KSO(R) down shady lane along line of telegraph poles, then KSO(L) ahead at staggered junction on UMUR coming from road at back L. Continue on ridge (good views), enter woods and descend, gradually at first and then more steeply, down to road, turning L and then R round church in

5.5km Les Estrets 940m (78.5/1416.5)

Gîte d'étape, *phone box, fountain. Formerly a commandery of the order of St. John of Jerusalem, controlling the passage over the Truyère; hence its name - étroits, ie. "straights". Present church dates from 1866, replacing previous one (though plaque on wall refers to "chapelles" being rebuilt); statue of St. Roch inside and lectern has carvings of scallop shell, scrip and pilgrim staff.*

Turn R along road (D7) (church to R) and continue through village (note small stone cross with figure of Christ on LH side) veering L (*gîte* signposted to R) to N106. Cross over and veer R to cross old bridge over the **Truyère** in hamlet of **Le Pont des Estrets** (1km).

Turn L up UMUR between 2 houses and continue steeply uphill. After 1km reach minor road at a bend (iron cross) and turn L downhill into hamlet of **Bigosse**. Veer round to R and KSO(R) along UMUR, undulating along RH side of valley then veering to LH side before veering L uphill along side of woods, climbing steadily all the time. Enter wood and continue to climb uphill (a very long slog up to the D7).

Emerge into small clearing at top and KSO(R) along similar track coming from back L, slightly downhill. Continue ahead, pass (broken) stone cross and then start climbing again until you reach the

4km Route D7 1096m (82.5/1412.5)

Turn L along D7 for 1km, passing disused dovecote (L). Opposite an industrial building fork R down shady walled lane // to road. (Note the prayer and scallop shell on tree to L.) After 1km reach road again at iron cross, turn R down minor road for 400m, rejoining main road again at fire station. Continue down to town of

3km Aumont-Aubrac 1050m (85.5/1409.5)

Small town (population 1050) with former Benedictine Priory and Romanesque church of St. Etienne; restored in 1994 it now has splendid modern stained glass windows. Several hotels; shops, cafés, bank. Gîte d'étape in basement of Relais du Peyre, 9 Route du Languedoc. SNCF (Paris-Montpellier line, also Béziers, Mende, Clermont-Ferrand).

Turn R down some steps into **Rue du Barri Haut**, cross over main road by large iron cross, continue on other side, go down **Rue du Prieuré** and turn L down side of tourist office to church. Turn L uphill (note 1708 Mater Dolorosa in niche at first floor level on L) and go up to **Place du Portail** (Hôtel de Ville).

Here there is a statue of the Bête du Gévaudan, the beast renowned in the area as being responsible for the mysterious disappearance of some fifty people between 1765 and 1768; a lynx killed near Saint-Flour in 1787 was thought to have been the culprit.

Continue ahead on main road (ie. to your R) and then fork R at war memorial. Go under railway line and turn L along minor road alongside it. 200m later fork R up fenced lane leading to side of woods (iron cross to L) and KSO uphill, passing under HT cables.

Turn R at top along road for 300m and then fork L to UMUR (just after town name board). After 150m turn L and then R to go under motorway via (specially placed!) "pilgrim tunnel" (referred to locally as the "Saintjacqueduc"...). Turn R on other side and then L to continue on a level UMUR leading to woods. Continue along it, descending gradually to the **Route de la Chaze** (3.5km, stone cross, 1016m). Turn R along it for 1km (tip of church spire visible) to

4.5km La Chaze-du-Peyre 1040m (90/1405)
Bar/tabac, phone box. Two crosses in square in front of church, one eighteenth-century, the other nineteenth. Church of varying periods with St. James's chapel.

Continue through village on road, passing church and veering R uphill, forking L between drinking trough and iron cross onto minor road signed "Lasbros". After 1km, at junction with D987 (the old Roman road from Lyon to Toulouse, the Voie d'Agrippa, that would have been used by pilgrims in centuries gone by) reach the tiny **Chapelle de Bastide**, begun in 1522 but reworked several times and sometimes referred to as "La Chapelette." Continue on D987 into hamlet of

2km Lasbros 1091 (92/1403)
Fountain, phone box. At end of hamlet fork L down minor tarred road by hamlet's entrance/exit name boards. Continue downhill, KSO(R) at fork and continue uphill, becomes UMUR. Turn L further on to similar track and L again along minor tarred road. 60m later pass junction with GRP "Tour des Monts d'Aubrac". KSO to road junction known as

4.5km Les Quatre Chemins 1174m (96.5/1398.5)
Café. Continue ahead to join D587 for 400m then turn hard L down forest track and R 100m later down track fenced in with barbed wire through grassy plateau land, undulating, with occasional shade.

(In bad weather some parts of the track are very boggy.) Like other areas of the Margaride and the Aubrac this is a paradise of wild flowers in the springtime.

Shortly after track becomes a walled lane you reach a "T" junction with another walled lane to L, opposite cattle pen on R and with grove of trees ahead.

If you want to sleep in the gîte d'étape in Prinsuéjols (1205m, 2km due south, bar/restaurant) you can turn L here and follow the red and

yellow balises *of the GR du Pays known as the "Tour des Monts d'Aubrac". If so, you do not need to retrace your steps the following morning but can take the D73 northwards from Prinsuéjols in the direction of Malbouzou: this road crosses the GR65 further to the west, just after the Ferme des Gentianes.* Otherwise, KSO.

Go through 4 *cledos*, cross road leading to L to **Pratviala** and KSO. Track becomes UMUR (more *cledos*). When you reach a bend in the road (iron cross ahead, the Croix de Ferluc) continue to road (farm to R) and KSO on minor tarred road. 100m later reach crossroads with the D73 at the

4.5km Ferme des Gentianes 1192m (101/1394)

Farm does meals and B&B. KSO ahead, go through hamlet of **Finieyrols** (B&B) and fork R uphill at end (becomes UMUR), wending its way through grassy plateau land strewn with big boulders. KSO ignoring turns. Track becomes grassy walled lane, climbing gradually across the deserted Aubrac plateau. (Splendid views on a clear day.)

At the top of the plateau (1273m, Roc des Loups) KSO alongside wall on L, descending gradually. This is the Grande Draille, a historic drove road, veering R (to become walled lane again) and then L. At "T" junction with gravelled lane turn R and 200m later turn L along minor road at the **Pont sur la Peyrade** and KSO to

4.5km Rieutort-d'Aubrac 1158m (105.5/1389.5)

Phone box. Note two granite drinking troughs and communal oven. CH 2km to L at Marchastel.

[NB. A 20km variant route to Aubrac or directly to Saint-Chely-d'Aubrac - the GR56A plus GR6 and/or GRP turns L here via Marchastel, Lac de Saint-Andéol, Gallo-Roman site Ad Silanum and Pendouliou-de-Fabrègues, 1359m. It is marked on the green series maps but is not waymarked and is an even more deserted route, only recommended in good weather and for experienced walkers.]

Continue on through village, veering R and KSO (1.8km) to junction with D900 at the **Pont de Marchastel** over the river **Bès**. Turn R over bridge and 60m later turn R up UMUR. When you reach a road veer R up it into village of

3.5km Montgros 1234m (109/1386)

Private gîte, auberge (meals, rooms, café).

Continue on road to end of village and at crossroads (iron cross) KSO ahead down UMUR undulating between fields. Cross minor road and KSO uphill ahead. At crossing continue downhill to road (stone cross). Turn R along D900 to

3km Nasbinals 1180m (112/1383)

Hotels, municipal gîte, campsite, equestrian gîte, Tourist Office, pharmacy, bank, boulangerie, épicerie, bars. Eleventh-century Romanesque church in local stone and style (Statue of St. Roch inside). The monument with a pair of crutches on its base is to Pierre Brioude ("Pierrounet", a nineteenth-century bonesetter and manipulator of joints who is said to have treated over 10,000 people a year).

Continue through village, cross D987 and continue, veering L into its centre and then take the D987 in the direction of Aubrac. At the end (at **Le Coustat**) turn first R uphill onto tarred road which becomes stony UMUR through woods. Veer L uphill (becomes walled lane). KSO(R) when you meet UMUR coming from back L, across undulating plateau land in direction of woods ahead.

1km later (at fork marked "Nasbinals 3km, village 4km") fork L along wooded walled lane. At next fork turn R, cross bridge (**Pont de Pascalet**) over the **Chamboulies** and continue uphill. 100m *before* farm building on track you are on turn R over stile uphill up side of field alongside wall (to your L). 100m later cross 2nd stile, following wall as it veers L and 200m later a 3rd stile. Here wall turns L so KSO ahead, uphill, passing to R of and above trees (to your L), joining grassy tractor track coming from back R, uphill all the time. (Tall marker posts at intervals, for bad weather.) Track veers slightly R round brow of hill, following marker posts, to

6km Buron de Ginestouse Bas 1303m (118/1377)

Two small stone houses to R.

(A buron *is a bothy used during the summer months when both the flocks and their shepherds remained up on the plateau until the autumn.)*

Go over another stile and KSP ahead, in direction of small group of woods ahead and 3 small buildings away up the hill to your R ahead (Ginestouse Haut). When you reach a wall go through 5th stile and KSO alongside wall (on your L).

(NB. all these stiles have cledos *next to them but whilst they are easy enough to open they are often very tricky to* shut*!)*

When the wall veers L at woods follow it round and then KSO

above (and // to) woods to your L. Then veer R slightly uphill to follow another wall (again on your L) uphill. Follow wall round to your L, pass between two wooden gates posts.

[The blunt, cone-shaped hill above you to your R is the Trois Evêques, the border of three bishoprics in the old days and today the borders of the départements of the Cantal, the Lozère and the Aveyron, as well as of the old regions of the Auvergne, the Aubrac and the Midi-Pyrenees. From here you leave the Lozère and until just past Conques you are in the Aveyron.]

Go through cattle pen (gates at both ends) and KSO alongside wall to your L. Go downhill slightly, through a *cledo* and then KSO ahead uphill up a very wide walled lane, the Grande Draille again. Continue ahead on this, descending to the road (former sanatorium, now a "colonie de vacances", to R) and 500m later enter village of

3km Aubrac 1307m (121/1374)

2 hotels, restaurant, bars, gîte d'étape *(no shops). Twelfth-century Domerie d'Aubrac, village founded in 1120 by a Flemish knight, Adelard de Flandres, who was attacked there by bandits on his way to Santiago and who almost died there in a storm on his return journey. In gratitude for his deliverance he founded Aubrac as a place of refuge for pilgrims. Church of Notre-Dame des Pauvres is all that remains of the monastery, plus one other building. Tour des Anglais, botanical garden.*

From here to Saint-Chely-d'Aubrac you descend steeply, dropping 500m in 8km (1500ft in 5 miles). The scenery changes after this, the vast open plateau giving way to gorges and many more woods before entering the Lot valley in Saint-Côme d'Olt.

Leave Aubrac along the D987 (west). After 800m fork L off road down wide walled lane (100m before some woods), descending steadily all the time.

(The yellow flowered plant, approximately one foot high, that you see growing everywhere is Gentiane, *whose root is used to make* Suze, *a liqueur.)*

Pass large wooden cross to R and KSO through semi-shaded woodland before emerging into the open and crossing stream (stepping stones). KSO, undulating and semi-shaded, later across open plateau land. Pass enormous wooden cross (on your R) at fork [RJ: fork R] and 100m later fork L down grassy lane when track you are on turns sharp R. 300m later at "T" junction (view of hamlet of Belvezet below and remains of castle perched on top of pillar-like rock) turn L down grassy track which becomes a narrow walled lane winding its way down to foot of "castle". Turn R here (waymarking bad) to road in hamlet of

4km Belvezet 1144m (125/1370)
Turn L along road and then hard R down lane, following wall round to R to lead you into another steep rocky walled lane, descending between fields. At crossing with wide lane KSO ahead, steeply downhill all the time. Cross the **Aude** and continue L on other side, undulating gently for 1.5km, shady all the time, before descending steeply to the road at a farm (**La Vayssière**). KSO on road for 100m, joining another at a "U" bend. Turn L and KSO down to

4km Saint-Chély-d'Aubrac 808m (129/1366)
Small town with hotels, restaurants, campsite, gîte d'étape, shop, Tourist Office, PTT. Fifteenth-century church has statue of St. Roch. From Saint-Chély-d'Aubrac to Saint-Côme-d'Olt the GR65 and GR6 share the same route.

Leave Saint-Chély from the **Place Joseph-Bond** (in front of the *mairie*), turn L down side of the **Ecole Publique** and KSO down narrow street winding its way down to cross the old bridge over the **Boralde**.

(Note sixteenth-century cross on bridge with pilgrim sculpted in its base, with his stick and rosary.)

Veer L, R and then L on other side to cemetery and then turn hard R at "stop" sign onto a UMUR leading uphill behind cemetery, which then becomes a walled lane, climbing steeply to the road (D19). Turn R uphill and 300m later (at L bend) KSO(R) downhill on minor road (signed "Les Combrassats 2") through hamlet of **Le Recours**. 200m later fork R off road down walled lane, which then becomes clear forest track, undulating through woods for 2km. KSO, then track climbs uphill again, becomes FP and rejoins road again. (Note cross just below road.)

Turn R along road (ie. just before hamlet of Combrassats, 919m). KSO(R) at fork at entry to hamlet then turn L behind first building on L down a walled lane, undulating, until you reach a disused farm at **Foyt**. Turn L up grassy UMUR to minor road and then turn R. KSO on ridge (good views), ignoring turns to L and R, descending gradually. After 1.5km pass RH turning to Bessières and 150m later fork R off road to grassy lane which continues along a ridge. KSO, veering L at end, to hamlet of

6.5km L'Estrade (135.5/1359.5)
Turn R along road (handy seat) which becomes UMUR along ridge, descending gradually before veering L downhill through woods and later becomes walled lane between fields.

4km later veer L at fork and then, at junction with forest road, immediately R (ie. a staggered junction) down through woods again, descending fairly steeply till you cross **Le Cancels** (stream - stepping stones). Go uphill for 100m on other side and turn R on D557 (by "stop" sign). 100m later at "U" bend in another road (marked "Castelnau 5.5" to L, "S.Côme 4" to R) KSO ahead between the two down shaded track, forking R shortly afterwards down FP leading to road. Turn L, cross bridge and KSO on road, mainly uphill, for 1.5km to hamlet of

7.5km Martillergues (143/1352)
Turn L down lane after last house on L, downhill, turning R along similar track after 150m. Continue on to hamlet of **La Rigaldie** (1km) and turn L at road. Turn L again 20m later between 2nd and 3rd building on L (view of Saint-Côme-d'Olt ahead to R), veer L and then R at farm building and then R again along lane leading to road (D141). Turn R for 150m to junction by cemetery and then fork R down minor road veering L through tunnel under D587 and KSO up **Rue Mathat** to **Place de la Porte Neuve**.

2km Saint-Côme-d'Olt 385m (145/1350)
2 hotels, shops, restaurants, PTT, gîte d'étape in Tour de Greffe (former prison), campsite, Tourist Office.

Olt is the old name for the river Lot. Medieval town with very few modern buildings. Sixteenth-century church of SS Côme and Damien has twisted spire, tenth-century Chapelle des Pénitents, formerly with pilgrim hospital dedicated to St. James adjoining, Ouradou (pilgrim oratory). Fifteenth and sixteenth-century houses, fourteenth-century château is now Hôtel de Ville, Gothic bridge. Historic information on street plaques: walking tour available from Tourist Office.

Cross **Place de la Porte Neuve**, go under archway and turn L down **Rue du Greffe** to church. Continue (church on your L) through next arch, turn L, cross **Place de la Barryère** and go down

Rue du Teral, veering R at iron cross to cross old bridge over the **Lot**. (Stone cross on bridge.) Turn R almost immediately down minor road marked "Combes".

After 1km along river and after bridge you have a choice between a high-level detour to visit the Vierge Notre-Dame de Vermus, a viewpoint over the whole of the Lot valley with a statue of the virgin on top, worth the climb in splendid weather but not otherwise, or continuing along the road to Combes (waymarked) and thus go directly to the **Eglise de Perse**. If you decide to do this (ie. not visit the Vierge de Vermus) KSO on road (marked "Combes") which goes along the river Lot. Turn L at campsite just outside Espalion to the back of the Eglise de Perse and continue as described below.

Otherwise, to visit the Vierge de Vermus fork L uphill up cobbled walled lane. Go through 2 gates and continue uphill (Font-dels-Romieus, a fountain used by pilgrims, to L uphill), veering R onto more level track and KSO. At meadow to R and 3 ruined buildings start climbing steeply. 300m below the top turn L onto wide forest track (uphill), passing under telegraph poles. At top turn R along grassy lane along ridge, which then descends gradually, veering R at end onto minor tarred road on hill. Turn R along it, undulating along ridge and passing under 2 sets of telephone / HT cables. (Good view over the Lot valley.)

Ignore RH fork and KSO steeply uphill all the time (track now becomes UMUR) and at bend to R KSO ahead (marked "Vierge de Vermus") up FP before descending (ahead) through woods on gravelled lane, turning L down narrow FP 20m later. After passing along LH side of fields re-enter woods and KSO downhill all the time on wider, rocky FP. (To visit Vierge - 15min each way - turn R up steep but clear FP halfway down.) Emerge by house and KSO downhill along gravelled lane. (View of Espalion ahead and *château* on hilltop.) Cross bridge at bottom, behind

5km Eglise de Perse 353m (150/1345)

Romanesque chapel of St. Hilarion (built on site near where he was beheaded by the Saracens in the eighth century) in red stone, former pilgrim halt and priory affiliated to Conques. Very fine carvings on outside but church is often locked.

To visit church: turn L up side of it and enter via cemetery. To continue: KSO ahead into **Espalion**, via the Chemin then **Rue de Perse**, **Rue St. Joseph**, then L and then R into **Avenue de la Gare**, R into **Boulevard Joseph Poulenc** and L into **Rue Camille Violand**.

1km Espalion 342m (151/1344)

Busy town (population 4614) with all facilities and pilgrim bridge over the Lot, built in the reign of St. Louis by the Frères Pontiff (a monastic bridge-building order). Renaissance château (1572) and Musée Vaylet, local museum. Campsite near river. Gîte-type accommodation (no cooking) in VVF (colonie de vacances) 1km outside town on GR65.

Leave town down **Rue Camille Violand** which becomes **Rue Eugène Salette**, pass EDF offices and KSO to very end of road where it becomes a lane after last house on L. KSO then turn L 100m later and then R, before lane goes uphill to become a tarred road leading to junction with D556. Turn R along it (quiet) for 2km then turn L up minor road at wayside cross, shortly before hamlet of Coudoustrimes ahead. KSO (500m) ignoring turns, to the

3km Eglise de Saint-Pierre-de-Bessuéjouls 335m (154/1341)

One of the oldest churches on the route, eleventh century chapel of St. Michel on first floor of bell tower, with ninth-century altar. Good picnic place.

KSO on road then turn R over bridge (fountain to L), R again beside *mairie* and immediately L uphill, passing to RH side of house and continue up narrow FP which zigzags its way *very* steeply up hillside through woods. Continue to climb very steeply (FP becomes wider, rockier / stonier, before becoming a stony track). (Good view of Espalion to rear.)

Shortly before the top it levels out and then joins a road at the top. Turn L along it along ridge for 1km to hamlet of **Griffoul** (wrongly spelled **Brissoul** on IGN maps), veer L at end and 200m later turn R off road onto level earth track (splendid views) which then undulates before becoming a walled lane along ridge. Later on it descends, gradually at first and then steeply. Turn *hard* L at "T" junction and 400m later reach gravelled lane by **Château de Beauregard**.

Turn R downhill for 100m and turn L along minor road, passing church (RH side) of **Trédou** and KSO to hamlet of **Les Camps**. Turn R down minor road, KSO ahead at first junction (down UMUR) and

Church of Saint-pierre-de-Bessuéjouls with ninth-century chapel of St Michel upstairs

turn L at 2nd, which becomes UMUR leading to road. Turn R along it to

6km Verrières (160/1335)

Bar. Do not go into village but at entry fork L down minor road, veering R, then turn L at junction (cross). Veer L and then R downhill, forking R (note building with bell on top to L) to cross bridge over stream. Turn R and 100m later at junction with D100 turn L down it.

500m later, after turning to **La Roque**, fork *very* steeply up hill on stony track, which levels out after a while, becoming FP through

63

woods, more or less // to road below you to R. Descend to the D100 and after 800m reach

2km Estaing 320m (162/1333)

Small town (population 1000) with hotels, cafés, restaurants, shops, Tourist Office. Gîte d'étape, Hospitalité Saint Jacques (small lay community offering lodging to pilgrims), campsite.

Gothic bridge over the Lot. Fifteenth-century château of the Counts of Estaing is now a convent (mass daily). Fifteenth-century church of St. Fleuret has stone cross outside depicting tiny pilgrim.

The GR65 does not go into the town so to visit: turn R over bridge.

To continue: turn L and then immediately R at small chapel on L by bridge (ie. staggered junction), down quiet shady minor road marked "La Roquette". This continues for 3km, undulating along the L bank of the Lot. At junction (La Roquette to R) KSO(L) on same road which then descends to cross bridge over the **Luzanne**.

Turn R along road and 100m later turn hard L up very steep narrow FP through woods, the first of several short cuts in the road's many hairpins. Turn L at top on road again uphill and 20m later, after hairpin, turn hard L up another FP, zigzagging up to road at a cluster of houses in

5km Montégut 400m (167/1328)

Turn R for 20m then L up another narrow FP, which becomes forest track, to road at **Montégut Haut**. Turn L on road and continue uphill, climbing steadily. Pass **Rion del Prat** and then fork L to **Campredon**. At junction with road from back L just before hamlet of **La Sensaguerie** (530m, pump to LH side of road) road begins to level out (splendid views if clear). Continue on road, undulating, mainly shady, then slightly downhill, ignoring turnings. Pass *lieu-dit* **Le Mas**. KSO(L) ahead at R turn to Castilhac and shortly before reaching hamlet of **Falquières** fork L uphill off road up grassy track to woods, which becomes forest track. Climb gradually on and through edge of woods. Cross minor tarred road and KSO ahead down grassy lane, entering woods again, undulating mainly, otherwise climbing steadily.

When you reach a junction at exit from woods (2km after leaving road) turn L uphill (not waymarked to start with), which becomes

Bastide town of Larressingle
The River Nive in Saint-Jean-Pied-de-Port
Photos: Maurice and Marigold Fox

forest road leading to hamlet of **Massip**. KSO on road for 200m then turn R *very* steeply downhill on FP through woods to another road below. Turn L and shortly afterwards turn R along lane through woods which becomes walled lane. Turn L up tarred lane and then KSO(R) along road to hamlet of **Le Radal** (*gîte équestre*, fountain) and KSO for 300m to

11km Golinhac 650m (178/1317)
Shop, café, restaurant, gîte d'étape *(all year), campsite (May-Oct.) Church of St. Martin (statue of St. Roch with* coquilles *inside) on site of foundations of ninth-century Benedictine abbey. (Note cross at entry to village with tiny pilgrim and staff on base.)*

To continue: KSO up road to church, turn L and then *hard* L behind war memorial and immediately R up very minor road, forking L behind houses. At minor road turn R. At crossing KSO down grassy walled lane, veering L to road junction of D42 and D904 (in hamlet of **Le Poteau**). KSO ahead along D42 (marked "Espeyrac 9").

300m later fork R onto tarred lane leading into the woods and uphill on forest track. (There are a lot of wayside crosses in this section.) At road in **Les Albusquiès** turn R and 50m later turn L down hill, L again, veer R and KSO(R) down grassy walled lane downhill continuing between fields to road (1.5km). Turn L and 500m later, at junction, at top of hill, turn R (signed "Espeyrac"). (Good views if clear.) Continue on road, zigzagging down through hamlets of **Campagnac** (593m), **Le Soulié** and **Carboniés** to road junction (D42), turn R, at entrance to village of

8.5km Espeyrac 369m (186.5/1308.5)
Hotel/bar/restaurant, café, épicerie *(behind hotel), fountain/tap by church. Church of Saint Pierre (statue of St. Roch inside).*

Fork L opposite hotel down road leading to cemetery, pass to L of it and continue on FP to cross FB over the river. Turn L on other side up FP winding its way uphill to minor road 800m later. KSO ahead and then KSO(L) at "U" bend in another road. 100m later fork L down grassy track (marked "Sénègres 1.5km"), cross river again by new FB and turn R along D42 for 510m to hamlet of **Celis**. Turn

Dovecote near Lauzerte

R up side of farm and KSO(R) up steep shady FP (becomes walled lane) and continue uphill; pass cemetery and enter village of

3.5km Senègres 506m (190/1305)

Hotel, 3 bars, restaurant, bakery, butchers, superette, PTT *and other shops. Church of St. Martin (statue of St. Roch inside, nice modern stained glass windows) on site of ninth-century priory. Tour carré.*

Turn R up narrow lane to church (shady square at side is a good place for a rest, good views). Pass church, turn L down main street and KSO(L) to end of village. Opposite petrol pumps turn R up narrow FP by electricity transformer, cross road at top and KSO uphill up gravel lane. KSO ahead up another road at top to enter woods, climbing steeply all the time. (This is the Fôret Départmentale de Senègres.) Veer L on UMUR alongside edge of woods (fields to R) and track begins to level out. (Not well waymarked.)

On leaving woods LSO(L) along lane, undulating between fields. KSO till you reach road, turn L, 20m before 5-way junction with D42 and D137. (Large modern wooden wayside cross.)

If you are tired or the weather is bad you can continue straight ahead on the D42, picking up the GR65 again 1.5km later (marked *, not much traffic) after it has done a "loop" and rejoins it again.

Turn R (at junction) along D137 for 750m and at RH bend turn L onto grassy lane along ridge between fields, descend through woods to join UMUR coming from back R and fork L almost immediately afterwards along grassy track through fields to rejoin D42*. Turn R (not much traffic) and KSO (2km) until you come to the junction above the hamlet of

5km Fontromieu 591m (195/1300)

Here the D42 turns L but you KSO along minor road to

1km St. Marcel 570m (196/1299)

Church of St. Marcel (a pope, martyred in 309) but nothing is left of the original Romanesque building except the chapel; the present church was rebuilt in 1561 but only finally finished in 1875. Statue of St. Roch inside, with hat, scallops, stick and gourd, ie. as a pilgrim; stained glass window above door has three scallop shells. There was a leprosarium here in the seventeenth and eighteenth centuries and a Chapelle St. Roch built in 1629, ie. at the height of the plague. This is the original pilgrim route, which

View over Conques

ran along the ridge before descending to Conques in the valley below.

1km later, at a place where several sets of telegraph poles and wires intersect and opposite a modern white building, turn R down a wide lane, descending steeply for 2km, alternating between shady walled lane and rock FP, winding its way downhill all the time. At crossing with bigger track KSO ahead and continue to road at edge of town. Cross over, veer R and continue downhill into

3.5km Conques 280m (199.5/1295.5)
Hotels, shops, restaurants, PTT. Gîte d'étape. The whole town is a historic monument so the balises are very discreet: wooden squares, carved, so watch out carefully for them.

Abbey church of Ste Foy (Saint Faith), its origins dating from the eighth century to the present-day building, is from the eleventh century. Tympanum of the Last Judgement scene on the main doorway is a very fine example of Romanesque sculpture and the abbey also has a medieval treasury. The abbey became famous when the remains of Sainte Foy, martyred in AD 303 and famous for her ability to cure eye disorders, were brought here from the church on the outskirts of Agen (where she came from and was buried) by one Arivisius, a monk from Conques; he had apparently spent several years in Agen (where the saint came from) with the religious community whose duty it was to guard her remains, gradually gaining their confidence until one day an opportunity arose to steal the casket containing them and take them back with him to Conques. Here the relics attracted an enormous numbers of pilgrims and led to the expansion of the church to accommodate them. Conques is a very "touristy" place but try to spend half a day to visit.

From the church, fork L down the **Rue Charlemagne** (paved) and continue downhill, under the **Porte du Barry**. Pass turning (L) up to **Chapelle St. Roch** (perched up on top of hill above to your L) and continue steeply down to the bottom of the hill. Cross the road and continue across old pilgrim bridge over the **Dourdou**. On other side continue on road for 200m then KSO ahead up FP through woods, climbing steeply. Cross road and continue up hill on other side to

1.5km Chapelle Sainte-Foy (201/1294)

Site of a local pilgrimage, chapel built by a spring whose waters were reputed for miraculous cures for eye complaints. View of Conques.

After first bend in track fork R up FP again (watch out carefully for waymark), continuing to climb steadily. Emerge from woods onto open heathland, levelling out a little, and reaching minor road. Turn L and then KSO (at junction with D606 coming from back R). 500m later reach junction with D232 and KSO ahead for 1km to junction with D580 and KSO(R) along it. (*Gîte d'étape* at Noailhac 0.7km.) Continue for 1km to

7km Chapelle Saint Roch 595m (208/1287)

Picnic area. Chapel has statue of saint as a pilgrim.

Continue on road for 500m, uphill, to TV mast (640m). Panoramic views and orientation plan.

*Statue of St Roch
as a pilgrim,
Chapelle St Roch
near Noailhac*

KSO (road descends after TV mast) and at crossroads 1km later KSO on D580. Continue ahead till you are 400m past hamlet of **Fonteilles** then fork L up grassy lane. KSO, veering L along ridge, keeping L along fence all the time, undulating then descending gradually.

Cross a road and KSO (view of Decazeville ahead: the big scar on the landscape to your L is the remains of the opencast coal mine). Go through *cledo* and track then goes through open grassland. KSO(R) on lower of 2 paths and go through 2nd gate ahead, keeping

69

to LH side of fence all the time. 100m later fork L up (and then down) rocky path which becomes FP, winding round side of hill to join UMUR coming from back R. Follow it down to road in hamlet of **Laubarède** and turn L.

Continue on road, passing hamlets of **Fromental**, **La Gaillardie** and **La Combe**. KSO(R) at turning (L) to **Le Madieu** and KSO(R) at next fork 1km later. Continue on road, downhill all the time, until you come to a road with a "stop" sign (bar opposite) in

11km Decazeville 225m (219/1276)

Medium-sized town (population 7000) with the largest opencast coalmine in Europe. All facilities. NB. if you intend to sleep in Livinhac on a Monday buy food here.

Turn L immediately, hard R (**Avenue Laromiguère**, but unmarked at start). Turn R at traffic lights (shop to L) and then 20m later turn L up steep hill (**Route de Nantuech**) which turns R 200m later up *very* steep hill, veering L and climbing continuously. At the top road levels out and at end of village (**Nantuech**) KSO(R) along road joining from L. 100m later turn hard L (uphill again!) and road becomes walled lane, emerging at staggered junction (wayside cross) in a residential area. KSO ahead. Pass cemetery (L) and reach

2km Chapelle Saint-Roch 353m (221/1274)

A parish church, rather than the usual chapel or hermitage dedicated to this saint. Two statues of him inside the church, one in chapel with bread but no hat, the other above the main altar in full pilgrim gear.

KSO on D157 for 1km then turn R down grassy lane opposite farm, veering L and descending steadily all the time, zigzagging down to the D21 opposite the modern bridge over the Lot at the entrance to

2km Livinhac-le-Haut 320m (223/1272)

Café, bakery, shop, PTT, gîte, campsite (with restaurant).

Cross bridge and turn 1st L up long street (**Rue Camille Couderc**, but no name at start), cross a more major road and fork L ahead (**Rue de la République**) to **Place du 14 Juin** (*mairie*, church, café, shops).

Cross square and go down **Rue Camille Landes** to R of **Mairie**. Turn into **Rue du Couderc** and continue to road junction (D627 and D21). Cross over and go down D627 (signed "Capdenac"). 200m later, in hamlet, fork R and 200m later on at farm building KSO ahead up narrow lane to minor road junction (**Peyrols**).

KSO up road, ignoring turns, to hamlet of **Le Thabor** and then turn hard R (NW) down gravelled lane. When this veers R KSO(L) ahead along grassy lane to road junction (marked "Le Poux", "Charnac") ahead. Turn L along D21 and 50m later turn R up minor road (marked "Le Feydel"). 100m later turn L along grassy track (HT pylon ahead L) to farm and KSO(L) along road (**Le Feydel Haut**), mainly uphill, through hamlet of **Cagnac** to join road (D2) coming from back R at entrance to

6km Montredon 396m (229/1266)

Hilltop village with Chapelle Notre-Dame at crossroads (replaces older chapel) and Church of St. Michel on site of former priory. (No facilities.) You are now in the département of the Lot.

KSO(L) and almost immediately fork R uphill to church. Veer L past it and continue downhill on road, turn R again and 200m later, at staggered junction, KSO ahead uphill, then L 100m later (marked "Tournié"), carrying on through hamlet of **Tournié** and KSO ahead at crossroads, downhill.

Turn L at hamlet of **Lacoste**, continue down UMUR and 200m later turn R downhill (*cledo*) on green lane. Turn R at bottom then L onto road and L again at fork. 200m later on at road junction reach

3km Chapelle de Guirande 277m (232/1263)

Romanesque chapel of Sainte Madeleine with late fourteenth-century murals. Gîte d'étape / equestre and camping à la ferme at Le Communal (5mins away).

Turn R (gîte 300m to L).

[NB. from here the GR65 does quite a few "loops" to avoid the road, something made more difficult by numerous tracks in private ownership, so from here to Saint-Félix those in a hurry or with bad weather may prefer to continue on the D2 from the chapel (3km) instead of taking the (6km) "scenic route" via a reservoir and various green lanes, some of which may well be very boggy.]

The GR65 turns R again 100m after the chapel up a minor road to hamlet of **Guirande**. At "T" junction turn R down lane lined with oak trees, which then turns L onto UMUR at small "aerodrome". KSO(L) along side of fields downhill to road. KSO then turn 1st L downhill by wayside cross in hamlet of **Le Terly**, leading down to reservoir (*plan d'eau*).

Cross it by a causeway, KSO ahead on other side, passing to L of farm, and continue ahead, downhill along line of trees. 300/400m later turn L down similar track. Continue on road (in hamlet of **Bord**) and turn R. At end of hamlet veer R down grassy lane, then L, then R onto fenced-in lane leading to road in hamlet of **La Cipière**. KSO(R) along it to road (D2) and after 300m turn hard R at junction (V9) along road for 1km to

6km Saint-Félix (238/1257)

Romanesque church of Sainte Radegonde has Adam and Eve with tree and serpent on its eleventh-century tympanum. Later stained glass window of St. James.

Fork L after church (behind restaurant - not always open), passing between buildings onto a narrow FP. Turn R along tree-lined lane to road. KSO(R) along it, KSO at crossroads and go through garden of private house (a *gîte de France*) and KSO ahead up FP to minor road. Turn R and KSO uphill to road in hamlet of **La Causse**. Turn L and 80m later fork R (opposite fire hydrant) down lane leading to D2 (1.5km). Turn L and continue on road for 1.5km.

[To visit the thirteenth-century church of Saint-Jean-Mirabel KSO ahead when reaching D2 (ie. instead of turning L): church is 300m ahead.]

At brow of hill (place marked on map as **Bel-Air**) fork L down walled lane to road. Turn L for 30m then R marked "Les Crouzets" and "L'Hôpital") and 300m later turn R up green lane. Emerge onto gravel lane. KSO(R) to D2 by junction, turn L and then L again to D210 (leading to Lunan, 1km, whose church of St. Martin is a historic monument, 200m). Turn R down tarred road which becomes UMUR, descending to crossing of paths, the

4.5km Carrefour des Sentiers 327m (242.5/1252.5)

Turn R up green lane, rising slowly up to road. Turn R for 150m to D2 then turn L (view of Figeac ahead). 100m later fork L, KSO(L) at fork and 800m later turn R down walled lane (dovecote to L).

[This is the junction with the GR65A. If you do not want to go into Figeac but intend, for example, to go directly to the gîte at La Cassagnolle, you can either follow the GR65A (waymarked) or take the road via Fumat, both options picking up the GR65 again at the Aiguille du Cingle (an obelisk).]

At field at end turn L down walled FP, skirting it, and KSO.

Cross UMUR and KSO downhill to D2 and turn L down to junction with N140. Cross it (carefully) and 20m later turn L up green lane and then R along road, uphill, / / to N140 (to your R below). KSO(L) along road coming from back R and descend to cross railway line. Continue down **Rue de Londrieu**. Turn L along **Allées Victor Hugo**, then R and either KSO and cross bridge over the river to visit Figeac or turn L immediately down **Avenue Jean-Jaurès** to continue on GR65.

9.5km Figeac 194m (252/1243)

All facilities. SNCF (Paris, Aurillac, Toulouse), 2 campsites but no gîte. Busy town on river Célé (population 10,500) with network of restored medieval streets (ask in Tourist Office for walking tour leaflet), worth half a day's visit. Former abbey church of Saint Sauveur, consecrated 1093, with ambulatory characteristic of pilgrim churches. Churches of N-D du Puy and Saint Thomas. Formerly an important pilgrim halt with six hospitals (one still exists). Musée Champollion (Egyptology), Musée du Vieux Figeac, Gothic Hôtel de la Monnaie, Maison des Templiers.

To continue: turn L down **Avenue Jean-Jaurès**. 150m later turn (2nd) L up street (marked "Cingles Bas") alongside high wall, veering R then L under railway line. Turn R and then fork L uphill. Road becomes UMUR / forest track through woods, climbing steadily up side of hill and veering L, passing TV mast to reach war memorial, an *enormous* concrete cross, with the names of the 145 people deported on May 12th 1944. Picnic area with view over town of Figeac.

Continue ahead on road, mainly uphill, for 1.5km to 2nd monument (obelisks marking limits of eighth-century Benedictine Abbey, another picnic area): this is the place where the GR65A variant meets up with the GR65 again.

To continue on GR65, turn R (the waymarks ahead are those of the GR65A). 200m later KSO(R) along D922 and 100m later fork R down wide road past factories and marked "Malaret". KSO along level road on ridge, ignoring turns to L and R. (On the skyline you can see the water-tower in Faycelles as a reference point.)

Continue along road, passing **Malaret**, passing above Buffan and just after a crossroads KSO to

5km La Cassagnolle 311m (257/1238)

Birthplace of Louis the Pious, son of Charlemagne and second Roman emperor. Gîte d'étape.

KSO(R) at fork and continue on road, KSO(L) at junction in Ferrières (modern stone cross). KSO(R) at next junction (note dovecote to R). Join road from back L. Cross D662 and continue into village, veering R uphill to church in

4km Faycelles 319m (261/1234)

Bar in summer, chambres d'hôte.

Continue head L, past church, KSO(L) up walled lane, turn L on road (D21). Good view over Lot valley.

KSO(R) at junction.

(Note caselles *in this area. Also steeply pitched barns, 2 stories, with grassy "drive"/ramp leading up to 1st floor entrance.)*

Continue on D21 for 2km till just past RH turn for Ayrens (hard R), then fork L down shady lane for 300m to road. (200m ahead on L is La Planquette, a *gîte d'étape* and campsite.) Turn R almost immediately down FP and at end turn R onto D18 just before its junction with the D21 in hamlet of

3.5km Mas de la Croix 327m (264.5/1230.5)

This is where the GR651 starts, the (waymarked) variant route along the Vallée de la Célé: see Appendix A.

a) *for GR651:* KSO along D21 to **Beduer** (0.8km, shop, bar).

b) *for GR65:* fork L by bus shelter down minor road, pass above château and then, at small crossing (iron cross) turn L up narrow walled lane which then becomes a minor road. When it bends R downhill turn L down a (wider) walled lane and KSO, ignoring turns, as it wends its way downhill (*lavoir* to R) and then up to minor road.

Turn L and immediately R uphill at junction (marked "Surgues") then turn L down UMUR 120m later and KSO, ignoring turns. When it becomes a walled lane (farm of Combes-Salgues to L) KSO. At crossing of paths 100m later turn R along another walled lane.

KSO, ignoring turns, to road (D38). Turn L for 250m down UMUR. KSO. In a grassy clearing where UMUR forks L fork R up grassy lane. KSO ahead at crossing and continue uphill to road in hamlet of **Le Puy Clavel**. Turn R and 100m later turn L down grassy

Dolmen near Gréalou

UMUR. KSO to road and turn R uphill to D19. Cross over and KSO (iron cross to L).

[NB. in this area the footpaths are often broken by roads/staggered junctions/short stretches on road, hence the complicated instructions.]

Turn L after waterworks building, then R (*épicerie-tabac* to L) and arrive at the church in

9km Gréalou 374m (273.5/1221.5)
Hotel/bar/restaurant. Romanesque church of Notre-Dame de l'Assomption. There are a lot of dolmens in this area.

Turn R at church, pass cemetery (R) and continue on UMUR. At junction with road KSO ahead on UMUR along ridge, continuing along open heathland to small stone cross (thought to be the oldest such cross in the region). Opposite a dolmen veer L down green lane alongside wall.

Go through *cledo*, continue down to road (D82) and KSO on other side down walled lane, ignoring turnings. KSO ahead at junction and continue until you reach a road. Turn R and then at a "T" junction turn R again to hamlet of

4km Le Verdier 316m (277.5/1217.5)

a) If you want to take the variant route through the woods to Cajarc (the GR65A, waymarked with a diagonal white "bar" through the red and white *balises*) KSO on here on road.

b) to continue on GR65 turn R into hamlet and KSO on road, uphill for 500m, to crossroads (iron cross). KSO ahead (marked "Chemin des Vignes"), continuing to climb until you reach another road. Turn L and 150m later fork L up UMUR and KSO through fields, track then becoming a green lane. At crossing KSO ahead (level) and continue to road. Cross over and continue on other side on UMUR which becomes walled lane, descending till you reach a "T" junction with ruined building on L.

Turn L along UMUR and KSO, ignoring turns, uphill to road. Cross it and continue ahead down green lane, descending to join road coming from back L. KSO(R) for 20m then KSO(L) (at bend to R in road) down walled lane. This becomes tarred lane, descending all the time.

150m after road joins from back R turn R along green lane under the cliffs (Cajarc below to your L). This becomes a stony track that descends continuously in a straight line until you reach a field at the bottom. Turn R alongside a wall on a grassy path and then KSO along minor at end and turn L onto D922.

The GR65 does not enter Cajarc. To visit town KSO. To continue, turn R immediately (ie. after turning L onto D922).

6km Cajarc 160m (283.5/1211.5)

All facilities, campsite (on GR), gîte d'étape. Town situated in a "circus" of chalk cliffs. Pilgrim bridge over the Lot built in 1320 and a hospital existed in 1269. Chapelle de la Madeleine (only the chancel remains), known as "Chapelette de Cajarc" today, the chapel of former thirteenth-century leprosarium. NB. after Gaillac the causse *begins, with no food or water until Cahors, except in Limogne, so stock up on both before leaving Cajarc.*

Having turned R off D922 continue past campsite (R) and continue on UMUR, following railway line. Just before *2nd* tunnel under railway turn R uphill, before a house, up FP zigzagging back up to D922 (above you to R under cliffs). KSO(L) ahead and then KSO(L) again at junction with "Chapelette" (on L) and huge wooden cross (on R). Picnic area.

KSO(R) almost immediately and KSO(R) at fork after 1km and descend to 5-way junction. Take 2nd R (brickworks to R) then join D19 coming from back R. (Church in Gaillac up on cliff top ahead of you.) Cross suspension bridge over the Lot and turn L on other side, continuing uphill on road to entry to

4km Gaillac 180km (287.5/1207.5)

At RH bend on entry to village fork L steeply up short FP and KSO(L) up minor road, KSO(L) at fork and continue ahead on level grassy lane. KSO(L) on track from back R and enter woods, uphill, veering L. KSO(R) at fork and then fork R again (ie. centre of 3) almost immediately, continuing on stony UMUR.

(Watch out carefully for waymarks as there are no distinguishing features in the causse and no views through or over the trees, which are not very tall and mostly old and untended.)

Turn L at crossing near brow of hill and KSO ahead along track coming from back L. KSO along track coming from back R and fork L almost immediately afterwards. Two tracks join from back L: KSO, mainly uphill. KSO(R) at fork, then ahead at crossing. Eventually you reach the top and the track levels out before descending slowly, joining a wide UMUR coming from L after passing under electricity cables as you leave the woods (farm of Mas de Couderc visible below to L).

KSO(R) for 400m then take 2nd turning hard R just after passing under telephone cables, downhill. Turn L at next crossing and KSO to hamlet of

6km Mas del Pech 339m (293.5/1201.5)

KSO in front of former chapel to road (D79). Cross over and continue on minor road (marked "Mas de Matthieu" and "Mas de Parrache"). Turn R at "T" junction down tarred lane and then KSO down narrow walled lane. At "T" junction after 1km turn R down wide walled lane, KSO(L) at fork, veer L and KSO until you reach a minor road (1km). (*Lavoir* L, pond and waterlilies R). Turn R.

Continue through hamlet of **Mas des Bories** (note dovecote to R), passing wayside cross (L) and KSO on road for 1km, downhill. Turn hard L at road junction up shady green lane into woods. After 800m at "manhole cover" turn R down FP along side of fields (there is the hum of traffic on the road in distance all the time so this is not

Traditional **lavoir** *near entry to Limogne*

as quiet as you might expect), across the bottom to UMUR and turn R downhill to road 200m later (well on L). Turn R uphill to hamlet of **Mas de la Teule** and L at wayside cross. Follow road round for 300m then turn R (at LH bend in road) onto green lane which then veers L to become a forest track through woods.

Turn L at junction, KSO to road (D143) and turn L along it to hamlet of **Mas de Palai**. Fork R onto smaller road and then hard R onto another and KSO(R) and KSO(L) at iron cross down another walled lane. KSO, ignoring several turns to L and R for 1km approx, then fork L downhill to D911. Cross over and continue down walled lane. At road in hamlet of **Mas de Bassoul** turn R and then immediately fork L. KSO (L) at junction and reach D24 (by huge iron cross and enormous *lavoir*). Turn L.

The GR65 does not enter Limogne. To visit the town KSO on D24. To continue: take 2nd road on L after *lavoir*, down walled lane.

8km Limogne-en-Quercy 300m (301.5/1193.5)
Small town with SCR. Hotel on GR outside town. Gîte d'étape next to PTT. Campsite on edge of town (on D911).

Reach minor road. KSO ignoring turns, cross D19 (hotel on L) and 100m later turn L down wide walled lane, semi-shaded, for

2km, descending gradually to road just before farm in **Ferrières**. Turn R and continue uphill, then fork L at junction with wayside cross. 150m later KSO(R) down walled lane (another farm to L) and 500m later, as you begin to descend, turn R through a *cledo* onto FP through trees.

(Watch out carefully for waymarks in this section: it is easy to be lulled into a rhythm and forget to pay attention...)

100m later go through a 2nd *cledo* and turn L along narrow walled lane.

After 500m cross road and continue on wider walled lane on other side. After 1km reach another road coming from R (turn R for *gîte d'étape* at Pech Olié - 900m.) Continue on road for 75m then continue straight ahead, taking LH of 2 green lanes at LH bend in road. 200m later turn L into similar lane and KSO for 1.5km to junction with minor road. Turn R (on road, not *hard* R on UMUR) and after 200m reach

6km Junction with GR65B (307.5/1187.5)

The GR65B, waymarked, is 7km long and takes you straight to the start of the section on the Cami Ferrat (old Roman road) 1.5km after Bach, passing through the village of Varaire (café).

To take the GR65B - KSO.

To continue on the GR65 - turn R along walled lane for 400m, turn L along road for 200m and fork R up lane. Cross D52 and continue ahead on minor road, meeting the GR36 coming from back L 100m later. Veer L past hamlet of **La Plane** (1km) and KSO(L) down wide UMUR, ignoring turns, for 4km until you reach a farm at

5km Les Bories Basses 310m (312.5/1182.5)

Continue on minor road. Just after farm the GR65 (KSO) and GR36 separate (turn R). KSO for 1km, ignoring turns, to village of

1km Bach (313.5/1181.5)

Village takes its name from a German family who settled there in the eighteenth century.

Turn R on road (D19, marked "Caussade"), cross D22 and 600m later fork L down a grassy lane. 900m later turn R at a junction with a similar track coming from your L (and the point at which the GR65B rejoins the main GR65). This is the **Cami Ferrat**, an old

79

Roman road. KSO (quite literally!), ignoring turnings, for 7.5km, crossing successively, the D42, the *ruisseau des valses* (a stream that is often dry and where, briefly, the track ceases to be level), the D55, reaching the D26 in the hamlet of **Mas de Vers**.

(The GR65 follows the Cami Ferrat ("iron path", due to its originally being paved) for 15km altogether. Like all Roman roads it leads in more or less a straight line and linked Caylus with Cahors. It was not much used by pilgrims in the past, though, due to its not always being well maintained and to its solitude, lending itself readily to ambushes and not having easy access either to food or lodging.

There are not many distinguishing features in the cause *it passes through and few buildings to either L or R. It is level, in the main, and most of it is either shady or semi-shaded, with woods and/or fields to one side or another. At weekends you may meet people on mountain bikes but otherwise it is a very solitary route, though not as far from habitation, as a glance at a map will reveal, as you might suppose as you walk along.)*

500m before Mas de Vers a gîte d'étape / équestre *is indicated, 7min/ 500m to L, "chez Richard".*

9km Mas de Vers 252m (322.5/1172.5)

Cross D26 (stone cross at junction) and the **Cami Ferrat** continues on other side as a minor road. Cross another minor road and the **Cami Ferrat** then becomes a UMUR. Cross D10 and KSO, descending, gradually to minor road 1km later at a large *lavoir* (good place for rest/shelter).

Turn L along road and KSO to a junction with a minor road leading to Le Pech. Turn R and at 1st bend KSO(L) ahead down grassy lane. (For *gîte* at **Le Pech** continue on road uphill for 1km.) 1km later turn L down similar lane, 100m later turn R onto gravel lane and 50m later reach D49 and turn L along it for 400m. Turn R onto D6 and KSO uphill for nearly 1km.

At bend in road between deserted house and modern industrial building turn R up a FP, a short-cut to a walled lane 100m above you: turn R along it. 500m later turn L downhill at fork. At valley bottom fork L uphill into woods and KSO to road (C4) at entrance to village of **Flaujac-Poujols** (football ground to R) and KSO(R) along it for 20m. Fork L down tarred lane which becomes UMUR (pebbled surface with big lumps is very uncomfortable to walk on), semi-shaded, through woods. KSO, descending steeply to valley bottom and turn R along track coming from L.

After 150m you reach a road (D22) but turn *hard* L along a UMUR (*not* along road) and then KSO(L) at fork. Track leads slowly uphill up valley and then veers L to become a FP leading up to a gravel lane, 2km later, at **La Quintade** (a group of three well-preserved buildings). Turn R and 100m later at top of hill (the *lieu-dit* **La Marchande**) reach the D2.

Turn R and KSO(R) (marked "Les Hauts de St. Georges") and 75m further on turn L at wayside cross down grassy lane. This leads back to the D2 shortly afterwards: cross over and continue on other side down minor road (marked "Chemin de Cabridelle") which then becomes a UMUR, veering L to open grassland and continuing along a ridge (the **Mont St. Georges**).

2km later (radio mast to L) track begins to descend. Join minor road coming from back L and KSO. After passing a 2nd radio mast (on L) you can see Cahors below for the first time as you begin to descend steeply. Turn R downhill at "T" junction, zigzagging down to a railway line (on your L) which you then turn L to go under when you reach a more major road which becomes the **Rue du Barry** in the **Quartier St. Georges** in

17km Cahors 122m (339.5/1155.5)

All facilities. SNCF (Paris-Toulouse-Port Bou), campsites, YH in Foyer des Jeunes Travailleurs, 20 Rue Frédéric Suisse (near mairie). Foyer des Jeunes du Quercy, 129 Rue Fondue-Haute, run by nuns, also puts up walkers/pilgrims.

Large town (population 21,000) surrounded on three sides by the river Lot. Important pilgrim halt and a good place for a rest day. Cathedral of St. Etienne with cloisters, several interesting churches and secular buildings. Pont Valentré (finest fortified bridge in Europe), museum. Ask in Tourist Office for a town plan with walking route.

The GR65 does not enter the town centre.

a) *To visit Cahors:* after turning L under railway line turn R at traffic lights at end of **Rue du Barry** into the **Place de la Resistance** (at side of main road), go up steps (L), cross over main road and cross the river **Lot** by the **Pont Louis Philippe**. Continue ahead along the **Boulevard Gambetta** to **Place Aristide Briand** (*mairie*, Tourist Office). To continue (and pick up the GR65) turn L shortly afterwards down **Rue Wilson** which leads you (crossing railway line via an underpass at the end of this street) to the **Pont Valentré**. Cross the bridge and pick up waymarks by turning *left* at end.

b) *To continue without visiting the town centre:* cross road at traffic lights and then fork L between road and campsite (**Camping St. Georges**) past a modern hotel (R) and continue along what was formerly the towpath alongside the **Lot**.

(The path is now tarred, with a fair amount of traffic - it is only very slightly longer to go through the town centre), under the railway bridge, past the Fontaine de Chartreuse (L) (on a Gallo-Roman site, an underground river still providing the town's drinking water.)

Just *before* you reach the **Pont Valentré** the GR65 turns sharply L, *very* steeply uphill up narrow FP with steps (and handholds where the steps have worn away).

The steep section is not very long but if you have a large/heavy rucksack, if you are not very agile, if you don't like scrambling or if the weather is wet (and therefore slippery) you may prefer not to take this route but proceed as described below.*** (Or if you are spending a day in Cahors and have time you may like to try the steep option without a rucksack: the views from the top are splendid on a clear day.)

The FP zigzags its way uphill (watch out carefully for waymarks) and then levels out a little. It passes the top of a water treatment tower and then becomes a UMUR. Follow it until you reach a minor road at radio masts. (Very good views of Cahors and the Pont Valentré as you climb.)

1km Croix de Magne 223m (340.5/1154.5)
A very large cross, visible from the town near the Pont Valentré.

Turn R and follow this road to crossroads (bus stops to R) and turn L.

***If coming along the old towpath continue past the entry/exit to the **Pont Valentré** and immediately afterwards fork L down a road closed to traffic from this end, the **Route de Lacapelle** (ie. *not* the road to your R with *balises*; these are the waymarks for the GR36) and at a "stop" sign 50m later turn L onto the D27 and follow the orange waymarks of another (equestrian) route. 200m later, at junction marked "Croix de Magne" (to L) turn L (road is no. C1, the **Côte de la Croix de Magne**) and KSO for 1km. Just after 2nd bus stop the GR emerges from the road on the L (the **Chemin de la Croix**

de Magne) at a crossroads. The GR turns L here onto the road you are on so you simply KSO.

After turning L turn L again 100m later (road bridge to R) and follow road down to N20, ignoring turnings, and running / / to it. Go through the tunnel under the N20 at bottom of hill.

Veer L on other side and turn L (ie. over tunnel) and KSO on this road, ignoring turns (occasional shade, not too much traffic) for 1.5km then, at bend to R in road (between houses nos. 171 and 181) KSO(L) ahead up hill up UMUR (**Chemin de la Combe Nègre**), which then becomes tarred. Reach outskirts of

4km La Roznière 200m (344.5/1150.5)
Turn hard L immediately (don't go into village - church ahead). 150m later KSO(R) at wayside cross and continue on ridge. After last house KSO ahead along FP which descends gradually and then steeply to UMUR, turn R along it downhill to minor road, turn L along it to reach the D653. Turn R along this for 100m and then fork L to D7, cross bridge and then turn R up UMUR uphill into semi-shaded woods (*causse*).

This climbs steadily and then levels out, undulating. After 3km reach minor "T" junction near houses, turn L, cross D7 and KSO(L) uphill up road into village of

5km Labastide-Marnhac 257m (349.5/1145.5)
Phone box, fountain behind church. Camping à la ferme *near entrance to L.*

[To visit Saint-Rémy, 30min, a pilgrim hospital built in 1286, turn R after church, a variant GR, waymarked. To return to GR65 either retrace your steps or take the D67.]

To continue: KSO, pass church (L), *mairie* (L), join D7 and KSO(L) along it. 100m later fork L onto UMUR (note *caselle* on L). At crossing of UMURs 500m later KSO. (Turn L for variant GR65 via **L'Hospitalet**.)

KSO(R) at fork by restored house (**Maison Gâteau**), KSO(R) at next fork and KSO, ignoring turns, part fields, part *causse*, to "T" junction with another UMUR. Turn L and 200m later reach minor road (3km).

Turn R (L turn is the variant GR65 coming from L'Hospitalet). KSO at crossroads. KSO along ridge, road becomes UMUR after

1km (this is the old Hospitalet-Lascabanes road). After 3km, still on ridge, turn *hard* L at a junction onto another UMUR, veering R. Fork L just before inside of "U" bend at minor road. Cross over and fork L (ie. not straight ahead) down UMUR. Track joins from back L at opening on plateau: KSO ahead. KSO ignoring turns.

When you reach another road (iron wayside cross L) cross over and KSO(L) ahead, diagonally, along UMUR. KSO. When track begins to rise slightly fork R at junction to grassy track veering L and then R downhill into wide bowl-like valley. When green lane joins from R KSO(L) along it and downhill (becomes tarred) through hamlet of **Baffalie**. Turn R downhill at junction (Lascabanes and church ahead).

100m later at bend turn L down grassy lane between fields. Turn L at end (*lavoir* on R) onto minor road, turn R 200m later skirting large château-like property and enter

13km Lascabanes 180m (362.5/1132.5)

Turn L at *mairie* onto main street and at end of village turn R (marked "St. Pantaléon 6") and then R again to church (picnic table). Turn L onto minor road (marked "St. Géry / Sabatier") and 300m later (at bend) KSO ahead up UMUR and then uphill into woods, along walled lane (note *caselle* to R) till you reach a minor road. Turn R along it for 1km to a junction with the **Chapelle Saint-Jean-le-Froid** on the LH side.

(The chapel is always open, a good place for rest/shelter.) Fountain 100m behind it. (Fête and Mass in Occitan last Sunday in June.)

Turn L at chapel and continue ahead, pass to R of farm and veer R uphill on UMUR. Continue ahead ignoring turns on UMUR, through fields. At crossing with other UMURs turn L uphill, through woods and then fields. At water tower turn R, cross UMUR and reach D37.

Turn R along it for 400m then fork L onto UMUR along ridge between fields, ignoring turns to L and R. After 2km approx. fork L at small hill in front of you and 200m later reach D4. Turn R.

[For the variant GR65 avoiding Montcuq - shorter, waymarked - take 2nd L onto minor road marked "Barnac" and then turn R immediately through fields. This rejoins the main GR65 1.5km south of Montcuq, just before the D28.]

600m later turn R onto minor road marked "La Mothe, 0.7",

veering L (to become // to D4) along ridge. KSO(L) ahead onto UMUR at RH bend in road, descending gradually down to village of Montcuq, arriving in square opposite a church.

9km Montcuq (371.5/1123.5)

Small hilltop town dominated by twelfth-century keep. Hotel, SCR.

To visit town: KSO.

To continue: turn L along D28, cross bridge and 50m later fork L uphill up tree-lined lane. Continue at top on open track through fields and at wide UMUR turn R and then L along D28. [Variant rejoins main GR65 from L here.]

150m later at RH bend KSO(L) down minor road, descending gently and then turn R onto FP a few metres after road enters woods. Pass entrance gates to **Château Charry** (L) and KSO, down to D28 again. Cross over and KSO on other side, downhill down green lane. Turn R at bottom along minor road to Berty (4km), forking L 100m later (marked "Carros, 0.6").

After approx. 1km turn L down UMUR through fields, cross the **Tatuguié** (stream) by metal footbridge and continue ahead alongside fields, veering R, L and R again (small lake to R) uphill (slippery in wet weather) to road in hamlet of **Bonal** (1km).

KSO(R) along road (Montlauzan ahead on hill). 600m later turn R at junction and continue on road (note topiary wayside cross to L) ignoring turns to

7km Montlauzan (378.5/1116.5)

You are now in the *département* of the Tarn et Garonne. The GR65 does not enter the village so do not turn hard R at top of hill but KSO downhill instead, to the D45. Turn L along it for 100m then turn R up path alongside vines at first, then continue on FP to L of hedge, uphill all the time into woods.

Emerge briefly onto open plateau (more or less level with Montlauzan church behind you) then re-enter (semi-shaded) woods. KSO, ignoring turns. After 2km reach minor road at bend and KSO(R) along it. KSO at junction (L turn to **Al Casse**) and then KSO(R) down UMUR (at LH bend in road), alongside long wire fence. KSO for 1km until you reach another road, cross it, and KSO ahead along FP under trees, veering L (view of Lauzerte behind wooded hill) and then winding its way down to a minor road.

Turn R and 200m later, opposite farm (lake ahead to R below), turn R along grassy lane which then turns R alongside fields and then veers L uphill to farm.

At top *fork* R downhill (ie. not straight ahead) down walled lane, continue ahead alongside fields, veer L and then R, downhill to road. Turn R and at roundabout continue ahead, up D2 uphill.

Halfway up hill turn R up steep grassy lane. Turn R at top then immediately L up UMUR, hard L at top onto road. Turn R, veering L into

5.5km Lauzerte (384/1111)
Hotel, SCR, Tourist Office, gîte d'étape.

Bastide hill town dating from twelfth century. Medieval houses, two churches (St. Barthélmy and Eglise des Carmes).

From the market place go down the **Grand'Rue** to the lower town (shops) and turn R onto **Route de Moissac**. After bend by cemetery turn L downhill down grassy track (watch out carefully for waymarks) leading to road. Turn L ("no entry") then join D953 for 100m before turning R down D81 (marked "St. Jean").

Take 2nd R uphill (marked "Péries") and KSO(R) up tarred road which becomes green lane (lake to R), leading uphill (at times steeply) through woods (2km). (Good view back to Lauzerte at top.)

At road turn L for 300m to the (much photographed) "pigeonnier du Quercy", a dovecote, and 20m later turn R downhill on UMUR to small Romanesque church in valley bottom.

3km Eglise Saint-Sernin (387/1108)
KSO(R) uphill and 100m later turn R along minor road (lake below to R) and 200m later fork R along grassy lane along side of hill, leading down to minor road near farm. KSO(R) veering L. At junction KSO ahead on another minor road and reach D57.

Turn R along it for 1.3km and then (opposite UMUR to R) turn L up wide grassy lane leading along side of woods. Follow line of trees, veering R uphill to minor road by house (**Mirabel**). Turn L for 300m then turn L on road at top of hill. Fork R 100m later before bend down lane between hedges leading downhill through fields; turn R, L and L again (ie. round three sides of a square) and KSO on grassy track to valley bottom.

1km (after leaving road) turn R over stream and continue uphill on muddy track veering L to farm. KSO(L) on minor road to

5.5km Auberge de l'Aube-Nouvelle (392.5/1102.5)
Hotel/restaurant. At junction 100m later turn R steeply uphill to road, turn L along it (D22) for 1km to

1.5km Dufort-Lacapalette 206m (394/1101)
Café (closed Tues.), shop, post office.

Fork L onto D16 (towards Moissac) and after 1km turn R onto minor road to **Saint-Martin**. Turn L after 1.5km, passing church (to R), Ferme-Séjour at La Baysse (R, CH) and descend to D16 again.

Cross over, continue on LH side for 50m and after bridge continue on / / track, sometimes below, sometimes level with, D16 for 1.4km. Turn L opp. farm up minor road and 100m later turn R (road becomes grassy track), veering L and then R alongside trees. 300m later turn L uphill up FP through woods for 500m to top of hill. Turn R onto track coming from L and 200m later reach minor road. Turn R along it and KSO along ridge, passing farm at **Carbonières** (R), and continue to church and hamlet of

9.5km Espis 152m (403.5/1019.5)
Continue along ridge, ignoring RH turn before Le Mole, after which road begins to descend. KSO, going downhill to cluster of houses at

2.5km Gal de Merle (406/1089)
At junction at bottom of hill (HT pylons) KSO(R) ahead, cross footbridge over stream and 100m later reach D957.

Turn L. If you are in a hurry KSO on road (noisy) into Moissac.

Otherwise: be careful, as there is the standard route into Moissac and a variant, both with the same waymarks.

a) For the standard route take the *5th* turning R (**Chemin des Vignes**). This leads you, after some 1.5km, to the **Avenue du Chasselas**. Turn R along it for 100m then R again along **Chemin de Ricard**. Turn L at end, cross level crossing and 100m later turn R, going along **Faubourg Ste Blanche**, **Rue Général Gras**, **Rue Malaveille** and then turn R up **Rue de la République** to the abbey.

b) For the "scenic route" (ie. the variant), which has very good views though you may not feel like it at the end of a long day, take the *4th* R turn up the "**C39 de Malengane**". KSO for 1.5km and then turn L steeply uphill just before house no.643 (waymark missing) beside orchards for 150m to a minor road. Turn R and continue uphill again and onto a ridge, the **Croix de Lauzerte**. After 1km road begins to descend, KSO ahead at junction down the **Côte St. Michel**, descending steeply down grassy track (plenty of seats) and a tarred road to the old section of the town by the public library. Pass to the R of it (the abbey is behind it).

2.5km Moissac 76m (408.5/1086.5)

All facilities. Population 12,000. Hotels, SCR, SNCF (trains to Agen, Bordeaux, Montauban, Toulouse). Gîte and campsite 1km south of river.

Major pilgrim halt from the Middle Ages onwards. Abbey church of St. Pierre, former Benedictine monastery founded in the seventh century with impressive cloisters; first built in 1100 they contain 116 columns and 76 capitals, 46 of which tell Bible stories or the lives of saints. Musée St. Jacques is in the former church (of St. James). Centre d'Art roman (Romanesque art) in former convent buildings to north of railway line near Abbey. Try to spend at least half a day to visit the town.

To leave Moissac: from Abbey either:

a) Go back down **Rue de la République**, KSO down **Rue Jean Moura** (alternative street-name in Occitan is **Carriera Sant-Jacmes**) to **Place St. Jacques** and church (St. James). Turn R into **Boulevard Alsace-Lorraine** and 100m later turn L to cross the (metal) **Pont St. Jacques** over the canal. Turn R and continue along the **Quai Magenta**, go under road bridge, KSO along **Quai Ducos** and then the **Promenade Saint Martin** (on LH bank of canal all the time), picking up waymarks again.

b) from Abbey - turn R into **Boulevard de Bieubre**, continue into **Avenue Pierre Cahabrie** (SNCF to R), cross **Avenue Gambetta** and then road bridge over the canal. Turn R along the **Promenade St. Martin** as above.

Continue along the canal towpath to a lock.

3.5km Ecluse de l'Espagnette (412/1083)

After that you have a choice:

a) The main GR65 crosses the canal at the bridge and, presumably to vary the long, flat (though not uninteresting) walk along the canal, goes up along a ridge, visible ahead of you, before coming down again in **Maulause**: strenuous but with good views over the

*Moissac, Abbey Church.
Fortified porch-tower
and south façade with
portal of the Apocalypse*

"lake" where the rivers Tarn and Garonne meet. The GR comes down briefly into **Boudon** *(village, shop)* before climbing up again. After Maulause (9km) you continue along the towpath as indicated in b) below.

b) The *variante* continues along the L bank of the canal towpath and is described here.

Neither of these options is the historic route: this crossed the Tarn in Moissac and continued via St. Nicholas de la Grave, thus missing out Auvillar, but the construction of the Autoroute des Deux Mers in the early 1990s necessitated considerable rerouting of the GR65. Both options are waymarked with the normal balises (as opposed to the variant form with a white bar for the towpath alternative). The towpath is shady, quiet in the main (especially after Maulause), slightly shorter and suggested as a change after the constant ups and downs of the route till now and because there are no significant "sights" on the higher level option.

Continue on the LH bank of the canal, pass a second lock 3.8km later (**Petitbezy**), go under the D26 road bridge and pass a brick bridge at the beginning of **Maulause** (2km, *bar/restaurant, shop in village itself*). Picnic tables on RH bank by the 2nd (concrete) bridge. At another similar bridge turn R onto the other bank of the canal and continue, passing another lock, to the road bridge at

12.5km Pommeric (424.5/1070.5)

Bar, shop, twelfth-century church in village, accessible by FP to R shortly before you reach the bridge.

Go under bridge and turn R immediately up a FP which takes you up onto the road and then R again to cross the bridge over both canals.

(Auvillar is visible on the hill ahead of you; campsite (Capelanois) on LH side of road after crossing bridge.)

KSO ahead (marked "Espalais 3"), KSO at crossroads and veer R just before entry to village of **Espalais** (3km, shop). Continue to end, pass church (R, seats) and turn L to cross road bridge (carefully) over the **Garonne**.

Turn L on other side, fork R, pass Romanesque **Chapelle Sainte Cathérine** (R) and zigzag steeply uphill. At large renovated *lavoir* (R) turn hard L uphill, passing *gîte d'étape* (R) and enter the **Place de la Halle** in

5km Auvillar 108m (429.5/1065.5)

SCR, hotel, gîte d'étape, Tourist Office.

Small town on hilltop with circular medieval market hall, very well restored, in arcaded square. Church of Saint Pierre, museum.

Continue ahead along **Rue de l'Horloge**, passing under arch, and KSO ahead uphill (**Rue de la Sauvetat**, the D11 to Bardigues). Turn L at top of hill, turn L onto minor road (marked "Hautes Peyrières") just before town exit boards. Veer R at last house down grassy track leading downhill, then slightly up, 500m later, to D11 again, by bridge over stream. Turn L, go under motorway and continue on D11 to

3.5km Bardigues (433/1062)

Bar/restaurant by church.

Continue on D11 for 350m then turn R down minor road and continue on plateau for 2km to a "T" junction. KSO *ahead* down UMUR which becomes FP (overgrown to begin with) which leads in more or less a straight line downhill, pass farm (R) and via a tarred road to D88 (1km). Cross over, veer R and then turn L over bridge over the river **Arrats** and KSO on road for 1km to

4.5km Saint Antoine (437.5/1057.5)

Small village with no facilities except the gîte d'étape (ask in mairie)

which takes its name from the religious order of the Antonins, who set up a hospital (the present château) for people suffering from ergotism, a disease also known as "St. Anthony's fire"; this was very prevalent in the Middle Ages, contracted by consuming cereal products (eg. rye bread) contaminated by the ergot fungus and resulting in a gangrenous condition of hands and feet. There was a similar such hospital further along the pilgrim road to Santiago shortly before Castrojeriz. You are now in the département *of the Gers.*

Continue through village, KSO ahead at crossroads onto minor road (the D953 veers L here), uphill. After 1.5km at farm (L, views of castle at Flamarens ahead) KSO ahead downhill down lane. Cross field, then stream, continue up on other side and KSO on minor road up to village of

4.5km Flamarens (442/1053)
Castle (twelfth to fifteenth century) a historic monument, being restored but can be visited during July and August (10am-12pm and 2-7pm, except Tuesdays).

Turn R at "stop" sign (D953) and then immediately L to church. Go down path to R of castle to road and KSO(L) 1km later (at place known as **La Patte d'Oie**).

[To go to Miradoux, 3.4km, shops, bars, PTT, pharmacy, large church with single nave, turn L along D953. You can pick up the GR65 again either by FP from the Château de Fieux or by taking the D23 to rejoin it just after the farm at Mayens.]

KSO ahead and 100m later, opposite the **Ecomusée de la Paysannerie à Flamarens** (museum of local history and customs, open July / August) fork L down grassy track veering to L of pond, downhill. 300m later *fork* L and then *turn* L downhill alongside a long line of poplars.

After 300m turn R through fields towards small wood and turn L on other side of it, downhill. Cross stream and go up again to minor road and turn R.

(As far as the Château de Fieux the route is constantly "stepped", as you link one parallel minor road with another.)

200m later turn L down road to farm, KSO ahead on grassy track veering R at end to road. Turn L along it and after 300m turn L down UMUR (view of Château de Fieux ahead), turn R at end of road and turn L at "T" junction after farm (**Tulle**).

The undulating countryside in this region consists mainly of cornfields and hundreds of acres of sunflowers, all lined up like battalions of well-trained soldiers who turn their heads towards the sun en bloc, according to the time of day...

At D119 turn L for 400m then R up minor road towards the

6.5km Château de Fieux (448.5/1046.5)

The château, *privately owned, was built in the nineteenth century but in a mixture of older styles: Gothic, Renaissance, Tudor, Baroque ...*

Part way up road (at red "Propriété privé" sign) fork R and continue on / / grassy track between newly planted hedges. Turn R near buildings and then veer L uphill to electric transformer.

[From here you can also turn L to go to Miradoux (2km), along track below castle for 1km and then turn L (at lieu-dit *Sentis) and then turn R into village.]*

Continue downhill along path lined with fruit trees and veer R at end to minor road. Turn L and then turn R (after **Mayens**, farm) onto D23 to

3km Castet-Arrouy (451.5/1043.5)

The GR does not go into the village itself but turns R 100m beforehand onto grassy track. (**Pilgrim information boards in 5 languages at turn.**)

To visit church, (with newly restored nineteenth-century paintings), KSO for 100m into village: free guided tours daily May-Sept, 10am-12pm, 3-7pm. (Covered picnic area opposite church and drinking water in cemetery opposite.)

To continue: turn R off road onto grassy lane with fields to L and R, seemingly in more or less a straight line for 1.5km then (view of Château de Fieux to R) turn L along line of trees. Pass farm, turn R onto minor road (D245) and at bend turn L between fields into woods (**Bois de Lagrave**).

The "hides" you may see here are palombières, *used in the pigeon-shooting season so be careful in the autumn.*

KSO on other side, UMUR becomes tarred road before a farm (**Gajeannet**) and reach D218 (**stone wayside cross**). Turn R (downhill and then up) for 1km and then turn L at crossroads. Veer R and at bend (by enormous maize-drying frames and a farm, **Lombirac**) you reach the

5km Junction with the GRP "Coeur de Gascogne" (456.5/1038.5)
Gîte d'étape *at the Ferme de Busquette is 200m along the GRP to your R.*
If you want to go straight to Le Romieu (ie. missing out the "loop" to
Lectoure) you can continue straight ahead (R) here (the waymarks are red
and yellow).

To continue on the GR65 veer L, go through farmyard, turn L
down grassy lane through fields, veering R to continue alongside
line of trees. Contine to the N21, cross it (carefully) and continue on
other side on minor road, up and downhill and then up to

3.5km St. Avit-Frandat 191m (460/1035)
Bar, telephone.

At top of hill turn L, veer L uphill to church and continue along
RH side of church. Pass cemetery (L, note old crosses set in outside
wall), fork R and continue towards the **Château de Lacassagne**.

The château *is a historic monument, which includes a unique replica*
of the Great Council Chamber of the Knights of Jerusalem in Malta (visits
possible).

Turn hard R just before it, downhill, and then veer L along valley
bottom. Turn R onto UMUR and immediately L by houses onto a
minor road, leading uphill. Continue on plateau at top and KSO to
D248. (Lectoure visible in the distance.)

Cross over and KSO for 1km. At RH bend before farm (**Gayon**)
KSO ahead down grassy lane, descending to cross stream (**Bournaca**)
and continue ahead uphill again. KSO again (uphill) at crossing
onto tarred road.

At top of hill turn R along road for 600m then turn L, at
Jouancoue (farm) down minor road alongside orchards. Veer L
down side of farm at bottom (**Clavette**) and continue ahead, downhill,
down walled lane. Join another track coming from back R and
descend to minor road at valley bottom by houses. Turn R and then,
after 400m opposite houses, turn L steeply uphill on grassy track to
road by **Tour du Bourreau** (fourteenth-century executioner's tower).
Go up **Rue Barbacane** ahead and enter

7km Lectoure 186m (467/1028)
Population 4000. All facilities. 1 hotel, gîte d'étape. *One of the oldest*
towns in the Gers. Cathedral of SS Gervais & Protais, seventeenth/
eighteenth-century Hôtel de Ville, ramparts, many interesting old houses.

(Lectoure is also a spa town.) Ask in Tourist Office for walking tour leaflet.

To visit: turn R to cathedral etc.

To continue: cross **Rue Nationale** and go down **Chemin Saint Clair** (to R of public garden opposite), go down steps and turn R in front of the **Maison de Retraite** (note eighteenth-century Ancienne Tannerie to L). Pass thirteenth-century **Fontaine de Diane** (L), KSO(L) ahead down narrow street that turns L in between walls (a *carrelot* in Gascon) leading to N21.

Turn L for 100m then go down minor road (**Chemin de la Tride**) between the N21 and the D7, downhill. Turn R at bottom along D36 for 100m then turn L, go over level crossing and immediately turn R along minor road / / to railway line. Just before *2nd* level crossing (to R) turn L onto D7. Cross the **Pont de Pile** over the river **Gers** and 100m later, before another bridge, turn hard R, veering L along wide grassy lane between hedges (semi-shaded).

Fork L at junction with similar track, reach the D36, cross it and KSO on minor road on other side. KSO(L) at junction and KSO, continuing on grassy track after tarred surface ends at a farm. Halfway up hill pass to other side of hedge and KSO.

Just before farm turn L onto UMUR, veer L 100m later up to road in hamlet of

4.5km Espasot 160m (471.5/1023.5)

Turn R (useful stone seat) and KSO for 2.5km along ridge (very little shade).

100m after a crossroads (camping and CH Le Nanton St. Jacques signposted to R here) with a stone cross (a *croix de justice*, picnic area with info. board) fork R down grassy lane. Track joins from back R, KSO. Pass another small stone cross on pedestal (R) and KSO. Cross UMUR, KSO. After 1.7km turn L at road into

4.5km Marsolan 171m (476/1019)

Remains of hospital St. Jacques at entrance to village. Shady square behind church good place to rest/eat (covered area adjoining if wet). Phone box.

Enter by *mairie*, pass to R of church and continue downhill to cross D166, continue on other side, KSO at crossing 200m later then KSO(L) at bend onto grassy track leading up through fields. Pass small lake (L) and continue up green lane to minor road at bend (2.5km). KSO(R) along it and when tarmac stops at last house KSO

Chapelle d'Abrin, former pilgrim hospital

along grassy track along ridge (good views) before descending to continue ahead (in more or less a straight line all the time) through fields. KSO.

Join minor road coming from back R just before a farm (**Bertsuguières**), pass farm of **Montravail** and turn R down UMUR (downhill) 100m *before* the

5km Chapelle d'Abrin (481/1014)
Former commandery of the Knights Hospitaller of St. John of Jerusalem (now a private house), pilgrim halt at meeting of two routes (the other came from Rocamadour and Moissac via Agen).

Pass lake (R), KSO(R) uphill at fork and KSO. After 800m at top of hill (UMUR bends L) KSO ahead downhill along green lane, through fields and uphill into woods. Turn L at top of hill at "T" junction, leave woods, reach road at bend and turn R for 80m. Turn L along UMUR. Opposite farm (**Le Double**) turn *hard* R alongside woods onto another UMUR and descend gently to La **Romieu**, veering R at entry, then turn L at "T" junction and immediately R along the **Rue Surmain** (to visit town) or L along D41 to continue.

5km La Romieu (486/1009)

Bar/restaurant, café, shop, PTT, gîte d'étape. Tourist Office (May-Sept).

The village takes its name from the romieux *(ie. pilgrims) who passed through it on their way to Santiago. Like Condom and Lectoure, La Romieu also has an enormous church for its size, an indication of its former importance. Fourteenth-century Collegiate (built by Clement V, one of the Avignon Popes) is well worth a visit.*

To leave: turn L on D41 then turn R down grassy lane (100m after *road* turns to R) through fields. Turn R at bottom and 150m, later turn L towards **Château de Maridac** and veer R alongside it 300m later down green lane and KSO to road. Turn L (ignoring 1st RH turn) uphill. Turn L at top and immediately R down UMUR, veer L before farm and then KSO(L) downhill on grassy track to valley bottom. Cross stream (**ruisseau d'Auvignan**) and continue uphill ahead.

[In this part of France, as in Castillian Spain, you can often see quite far ahead to where you are going as the landscape is very open.]

At the top of the hill (hamlet of **Quiot**, stone wayside cross) continue down UMUR on other side of road then 200m later *turn* R (and then *fork* R) down green lane. Cut through minor road at "S" bend, KSO over bridge along green lane, fork L at junction and KSO to top of hill, passing to L of farm (**La Baraille**) and veering R on road to

6.5km Chapelle Sainte-Germaine 168m (490.5/1004.5)

Twelfth/thirteenth-century chapel, all that remains of former monastery dedicated to a local saint. The church is open when the cemetery is.

Continue on road to hamlet of **Baradieu**, turn L by pond and 400m later turn R down UMUR to **Moras** (restored farm). Pass to R of it (lake to R), veer L, cross stream (stepping stones) and then turn R immediately along hedge and KSO alongside lake (**Bousquetara**). Follow tracks as it veers L uphill, pass (on L) farm of **La Fromagère** and 1km later, at top of hill, cross D204 and continue downhill on other side, veering L, to D7 (1km).

Cross over, turn L and 50m later turn R down minor road. Just before hamlet of **L'Espitalet** (to L, after bend) turn R down grassy lane alongside hedge (view of Condom cathedral ahead). 500m later turn R onto road and 200m later, after **Rue Roucoutoucou** on R, turn L at side of houses down grassy bank, cross footbridge over river **Gèle** and fork R down FP alongside a very high wall (the

Couvent du Carmel de Prouillan).

[The GR65 and GRP part company here: GRP turns L, waymarked in red and yellow.]

Turn L at corner and then R down **Rue du Carmel** and R down **Avenue Victor Hugo** into

9.5km Condom 81m (502/993)

Population 8000. Typical Gascon town situated on a spur between the rivers Gèle and the Baïse, centre of the Armagnac industry. All facilities, several hotels, Tourist Office, gîte d'étape in Centre Salvandry.

Cathedral of Saint Pierre, churches of St. Bathélemey de Pradeau, St. Jacques and St. Michel. Musée de l'Armagnac, cloisters (now the mairie).

The GR65 does not enter the town itself but skirts it along a ring road, probably no shorter than going into the centre, before crossing the river **Baïse** to leave it.

To enter town: cross boulevard and go down side of church (**St. Barthélmy du Pradeau**) in front of you (**Rue Dutoya**), continue down **Rue Gambetta** (pedestrianised) and turn L into **Place St. Pierre** (cathedral). From there continue along **Rue Chorron**, cross **Place du Lion d'Or**, continue ahead down **Rue des Armuries**, fork L down **Rue Roques** and turn R over the **Pont des Carmes** over the **Baïse**.

To continue without entering the town: at the end of the **Avenue Victor Hugo** turn L along **Boulevard Clemenceau**, continue along **Boulevard St. Michel**. Pass church of **St. Michel** (R), cross **Place Lucien Lamargue** (ie. the D930) and continue down **Rue Gavarret** and then turn L along the **Quai Buzon** (all very noisy as there is a lot of traffic) and then turn L over **Pont des Carmes**. (The building on L at end of bridge, now a theatre, was formerly a Carmelite convent.)

Turn L immediately after crossing bridge along upper (RH) of two FPs alongside river, the **Chemin de la Digue**. This passes behind the church of **St. Jacques**, which originally had a hospital attached to it.

(The statue above the blocked-up doorway on the street side is not St. James but St. Joseph, a dedication made in recognition of the latter's help in alleviating the sufferings of plague victims in that quarter of the town, La Bouguerie.)

Shortly after the church of St. Jacques veer R to the D931, cross it, continue on banked up FP and then turn L down a minor road at the fork with the D15 (the **Chemin Capots de Teste**, the area in which there was a second Hôpital St. Jacques, as well as two other non-St. James hospitals plus leprosaria). The minor road takes you through a residential area, veers R to go under a railway bridge and then turns L immediately to the hamlet of **Ciprionis**.

At top of hill KSO(R) at 1st junction and KSO(L) at 2nd. KSO, passing **L'Inquiétitude** (a farm).

(The linguistically-observant walker/pilgrim will already have noticed Montravail, and Monrepos elsewhere, with Monplaisir still to come...)

Continue, passing other farms, for 2km, ignoring turns, and much more up than down. At "S" bend in road at top of (present) hill: KSO(L) ahead along green lane, uphill to plateau. UMUR joins from R. KSO (view of Larresingle to R ahead) and 200m later reach road in an area known as Le Carbon.

5km Le Carbon 179m (507/988)
To visit Larressingle, a tiny fortified town, completely walled, turn R along road at Le Carbon. This was the fortress of the Bishops of Condom in the Middle Ages and is well worth the 15min detour (in each direction) to visit. To return, however, you need not retrace your steps again but, via a minor road to the SW you can pick up the GR65 where it crosses the D278, just before the Pont d'Artigues, turning R to cross it.

If you prefer not to visit **Larressingle** KSO ahead down green lane, downhill for 1km. At crossing with another track veer L and then R to skirt small pond and veer L down FP through woods (in effect continuing in a straight line from where you broke off). KSO will you reach a road (D278), cross it and 100m later cross the

3km Pont d'Artigues (510/985)
Originally a Roman bridge over the Osse, with five arches. In the Middle Ages the Commandery of the Order of Santiago had a pilgrim hospital here and there was also a church of Notre-Dame by the pilgrim bridge but nothing remains today.

KSO to crossroads and turn R for 600m then turn L by HT pylon up grassy lane alongside trees (to your R) for 1.2km. [KSO for **Beaumont**, 1km, whose château can be visited in summer.] Turn R on minor road and L at "T" junction 500m later (at R turn to Routges).

Church of Routges is 100m ahead of you off road, the oldest church in

the region. Note the small door on the side of the church: this was used by the Cagots, an outcast population.

KSO ahead along ridge at staggered crossroads (D254) and KSO for 1km more. 300m after passing hamlet of **Laserre-le-Haut** KSO(L) at fork to **Le Glesia** (former gallo-roman site) and 200m later KSO(L) down green lane. 1km later at **Pages** UMUR becomes tarred and 200m later at bend (fountain) KSO ahead up green lane under trees, veering L. 1km later pass **Château de Lasalle-Baqué** and KSO(R) along D113. Turn L at junction with cross (D15) then immediately R along D113 again into

9km Montréal-du-Gers 135m (519/976)
Shops, café, restaurant, hotel, Tourist Office, PTT.

Small town (population 1200) with thirteenth-century bastide, arcaded market place, thirteenth-century church, several interesting old houses, museum, ramparts. Galloroman villa at Seviac (2km, worth visiting) also has gîte d'étape.

Enter town down **Rue Aurenson**, turn L into square and go down RH side of church and then turn R along **Boulevard des Remparts**, veering R and then turn *hard* L downhill, hard R immediately to the D15 and hard L onto a minor road. KSO. After crossing bridge road becomes a UMUR (veering L uphill): KSO(R) and KSO, ignoring turns, for 800m to a road. Turn L along it then, at farm (**Ribère de Bas**), fork R down UMUR (marked "Barrière de Ribère").

KSO for 1km along the bed of an old railway line, cross metal bridge (Château de Montaut to L) over a UMUR and then ahead L 30m later and L again under bridge (ie. in order to do a "right turn"). KSO for a few hundred metres then veer L uphill to road. Turn L and 100m later turn R up track leading between vines, continuously along line of trees to L. Veer L to UMUR coming from L, KSO along and 200m later turn L through more vines. Continue on road after 200m by farm and 150m later KSO ahead along grassy track following line of telegraph poles alongside vines (to R).

Pass farm (L) at road coming from R, KSO ahead along a UMUR, then veer R alongside woods (L) at minor junction. KSO for 600m to road (D29). Cross over, continue alongside vines (L) for 200m, cross road leading to farm (Bédat) and continue alongside more vines to the D31.

Cross the D31 and KSO ahead (slightly staggered to L) on minor tarred road. 400m later turn L alongside vines, continue on FP and then on green lane (tower visible ahead) to cemetery (drinking water) in village of

9km Lamothe 167m (528/967)

Thirteenth-century guard tower. From Lamothe to Nogaro the walking is all fairly flat and easy, if not all that interesting.

Turn L and then hard R downhill past church (shady porch) to valley bottom and turn L along former railway line (tracks removed). KSO for 7km, mainly shaded, to the D931 at the entrance to Eauze (huge factory to R), turning R into the town. KSO into the **Place d'Armagnac** and the church.

7km Eauze 142m (535/960)

Population 4300. SCR, hotel, PTT, Tourist Office. Gîte d'étape (pilgrims only) above Tourist Office.

Former Galloroman capital (Elusa) and Roman colony. Benedictine priory founded in tenth century and attached to Order of Cluny. Church of St. Luperc (a local saint) built by the Benedictines, finished 1521, using rubble stone from Roman sites mixed with local brick. Two seventeenth-century confessionals. Icons on long centre panel behind altar are modern (1977), by Nicholaï Greschny (Tarn artist). Numerous old houses, including Maison de Jeanne d'Albret, Museum (with treasury of 28,000 Roman coins), Andalusian-style bull-ring (Arènes Nimeño II).

To leave: from church turn L into **Rue Robert Daury** (pedestrianised) and continue ahead down **Avenue des Pyrénées** (D931) for 500m then turn R down **Allée de Soumcidé**, veering L and continuing on wide grassy lane ahead by last house.

KSO, cross UMUR and KSO veering R towards a farm at a road (2km from Eauze). Turn L uphill and 200m later KSO ahead at crossroads (marked "Pennebert"). At RH bend in road by farm KSO ahead down green lane, KSO(R) at fork and continue downhill. Turn R and then L alongside edge of large field, turn R at bottom corner along edge of two more fields (stream below to R in trees), veering R at end and then turn L to cross FB over **Bergou** (stream).

KSO ahead up RH side of next field, passing to other (RH) side of hedge half way up and continue up old sunken tree-lined lane. Cross UMUR by ruined farm (**Angoulin**, R), cross minor tarred road 200m later, KSO ahead along grassy lane, veer R up side of field amd at crossing of tracks turn L in front of vines to road 100m later.

Turn R, pass farm (**Riguet**) and 400m later turn L (opposite end of a line of woods / / to road on other side) between vines. Veer L uphill alongside hedge and continue on green lane to junction at top of hill.

7km Ferme de Peyret 160m (542/953)

For *gîte d'étape* in old school in Sauboires, 800m further, turn R. Otherwise, to continue, KSO along green lane. KSO(R) on track coming from back L and go downhill between vines. Pass several lakes (a fish farm) to L and turn L onto the D122. KSO for 2km to

4km Manciet (546/949)

Shops, Café des Sports with rooms, rural bull-ring for courses landaises *(cattle races). La Bonne Auberge is on site of former commandery (with Hôpital St. Jacques and chapel) set up by the Spanish Ordre Hospitalier de Santiago (ie. Knights of Santiago). Church of Notre-Dame de la Pitié has "viewing kiosk" and prayer desk accessible from the street when church is closed.*

After the level crossing the GR65's waymarks lead you R to continue immediately on the N124. If you prefer you can cross this and go up steps to ramparts by war memorial and turn R down the **Rue Centrale** (church, shops) and rejoin the N124 300m later at a "stop" sign, continuing ahead (L) along it.

After 1km (opposite former Manciet railway station, now a used car dealers) turn L along D153 (to "Cravencères"). 700m later (just before bend) turn R up UMUR for 1km, passing farm (**Bel Air**) and then turn R onto tarred road. Turn L along D522 for 500m then, at crossroads, take *2nd* LH fork, passing to R (not L) of house and continue downhill, ignoring turns, to cross the **Midouzan** (stream).

KSO ahead through field, cross irrigation dyke and turn R alongside it, then L (at a bigger one), veering L. Turn R uphill up LH side of woods, fork R to walled lane for 100m and then turn L onto tarred road.

100m later (at end of first field of vines) turn R up track alongside hedge (to L). Veer L at end towards woods and go downhill to R of them to road. Turn R, cross stream (**Saint-Aubin**) and continue for 1km to crossroads (note discoidal cross). Cross over, pass between houses, go down grassy bank and then tree-lined lane. KSO(R) at minor road and reach D522 200m later. Turn L along it into

9km Nogaro 98m (555/940)

Population 2000. All facilities, hotels, campsite, gîte d'étape (on GR leaving town), Tourist Office, bull-ring.

Small town taking its name from "Nogoarium" (a "place planted with walnuts") and established in the eleventh century. Romanesque church with former Hôpital St. Jacques nearby.

The GR65 does not enter the town so *to visit:* KSO after level crossing. *To continue:* turn R down **Avenue de Damiade** (the N124) then L after sawmill down **Avenue des Sports**. Pass *gîte* and campsite (R) and veer L, turn R along edge of football field and turn L (estate of new houses to R) at minor road leading 200m later to D147. Turn R for 150m then fork L onto minor road (**Chemin de Miran**) for 1.3km to D143. Turn R for 700m then turn L (just before houses) down minor road.

KSO for 2km, downhill through woods, cross the **Jurone** (stream) and road becomes UMUR. Continue to **Laverie** (a farm) on road. Turn R then veer L downhill for 1km, veering L along stream, until you reach the N124. Turn R and cross the

6km Pont sur l'Izaute (561/934)

In the section between Nogaro and Aire-sur-l'Adour there is a lot of road walking but with very little traffic apart from tractors (and the N124).

KSO on N124 for 600m then turn L down tree-lined UMUR. KSO for 2km to farm.

(Note buildings with colombages, *Tudor-style woodwork typical of the Landes region and already encountered elsewhere.)*

Pass between buildings and continue (now a road) for 500m to D152 in the hamlet of

4km Lanne Soubiran (565/930)

Turn R for 500 along D152 and then turn L down minor road at small crossroads, veering R. 500m later KSO(L) along minor road coming from back R. Pass lake, veer R alongside woods and at sharp LH bend turn R along green lane (ie. 2nd of 2 RH turns), veering L into woods, downhill, veering at bottom towards field. However, just *before* the edge of the wood turn hard R along grassy lane. KSO, then shortly after passing 2nd of two *miradores* (platforms some 70-80ft high up in the trees used by hunters for spotting game/birds, these two with impressive old-style ladders to reach them), KSO(R) at fork. Veer R and then L along edge of wood and continue to road (1.5km). Turn L and then R 100m later on (more) minor road. Pass one farm and just before a second turn R downhill on minor road and then L 500m later at crossroads.

Turn R and then 200m later, just after passing to RH side of small wood, turn R down grassy track, veering L and then T slightly downhill and through fields. Fork L at group of trees 300m later and KSO. At crossing of tracks (farm over to L) turn *hard* R alongside vines (L) (1km from road).

Continue ahead (hedge to R, also disused **Ferme Micoulas**) towards woods. Pass alongside RH side of woods (vines to RH side now) and then turn L to enter woods. 100m later reach minor road, turn L and 150m later reach D169. KSO(L) along it for 150m to farm

6km Tapiot (571/924)
Turn R beside farm and continue down green lane, veering R downhill. Turn L at "T" junction at bottom (pond to L) along bottom of field (always muddy), enter woods and KSO for 1.5km to farm (**Manet**). Pass to R of buildings and turn L onto minor road then turn R onto another 200m later. KSO for 2km. At "stop" sign turn R onto track alongside railway line and KSO for 2.5km. Turn L over level crossing and after 250m reach the

6km Route D935 (577/918)
Cross the road (carefully) and KSO on other side on minor road which becomes UMUR. KSO. Veer R behind woods and KSO. After 750m turn R at HT pylon alongside irrigation ditch and then immediately L to cross it by a FB (machine shed on other side). Turn R towards farm (**Laguillan**), veer L in front of it and then turn L along its access road to "T" junction.

Turn R for 500m to just before farm (**Lacassagne**, 2.5km) and then *hard* L onto minor road. Pass in front of another farm (**Baqué**) and KSO to D107. Turn L over metal bridge (Barcelonne campsite to L before you cross it), the

4km Pont sur l'Adour (581/914)
Turn R on the other side onto the D39 towards Aire-sur-l'Adour leaving the *département* of the Gers and entering the Landes just

before the entry to the town.

[NB. the first turn on the L (waymarked) is the old GR65, now a variant. It does not enter the town itself but takes a high-level detour, joining up with the present route on the N134 on the outskirts, just before you turn R onto the D2.]

To go directly to the gîte d'étape (in the Centre de Loisirs, Quartier de la Plaine): turn R down the **Chemin de la Plaine** 150m after the pavement begins at entry to town.

To go into the town and continue: turn L 200m after pavement starts at entry to town down **Rue du Jardin Publique** (marked "Stade, Piscine"). Pass park (L), Cathedral (R), eighteenth-century *mairie* (R) and continue ahead along **Rue Labeyrie** (note brick building on RH side of street, former religious courts of justice and the nineteenth-century octagonal Halle aux Grains to R) and then, at beginning of **Avenue des Pyrénées**, fork L up **Rue Félix Despagnet** and the **Rue du Mas**, passing the **Eglise de Sainte-Quitterie** (L, 1.5km).

2km Aire-sur-l'Adour 81m (583/912)

Population 6200, all facilities. SNCF (trains to Tarbes), buses to Pau/ Agen, Dax/Tarbes, Mont-de-Marsan/Pau, campsite by river, gîte d'étape, several hotels.

Ancient town in two parts: the river, Cathedral of St. Jean Baptiste, twelfth-century but altered several times, mairie, and nineteenth-century Halle aux Grains; and the "Mas d'Aire" or higher town with the brick built Eglise de Sainte-Quitterie built on site of Benedictine monastery. (To visit: guided tours only, in French; ask at 12 Rue du Mas.)

From the Eglise de Sainte-Quitterie continue to end of **Rue du Mas**, KSO ahead along N134 for 200m (**Avenue des Pyrénées**) to roundabout (bar, shop in petrol station). Turn R onto D2 (**Rue Nelson Mandela**) and then L 150m later opposite school down **Rue Georges Fraisse** then L again along **Rue du Jardinet**. Turn R at end onto minor road leading down to a large reservoir (this is not yet indicated on maps).

Continue (L) ahead along edge of lake for 1.5km and near end veer L to D 456. Turn R, cross bridge and 200m later turn R onto UMUR, veering L uphill alongside woods to hamlet of **Bégorre** and continue on road. 300m later turn L at crossroads, KSO for 1km then turn L onto wide UMUR between fields.

There are very few distinguishing features in this region, flat, with large-scale agriculture. Due to remembrement - *the regrouping of small, uneconomic portions of land into larger, more viable units - this whole area now consists of geometrically laid-out fields with irrigation channels and few hedge boundaries.*

200m later turn L onto similar track and KSO for 2km to D62. Turn R (huge cement works to R) then L immediately onto UMUR.

Veer L after 1km then turn R. (Church and village of Latrille 500m to L.) Cross D375 and KSO for 3km to hamlet of

13km Matot 185m (596/899)

Turn R opposite wayside cross onto minor road which becomes a green lane and follow it for 2km, turning L at "T" junction and immediately R onto minor road, crossing bridge. Continue to D11 in hamlet of

2km Pontet 188m (598/897)

To go to Miramont-Sensacq (church, hotel, bar/restaurant, gîte d'étape, shop) turn R along D11 (water tower in distance). Afterwards rejoin GR65 by turning south on D134.

To continue: cross road and continue ahead, veering L at farm (**Jamboué**) and then turn R onto UMUR. 200m later turn L along UMUR and 300m later (pond to R) fork R at junction. Continue for 700m further to **Lion d'Or** (house on R) and shortly afterwards turn R. After 1.3km, before you reach the D134 (at **Jamboué-de-la-Lande**), turn L at "kink" in UMUR down wide grassy track between crops and 200m later veer R to road. Turn L and then immediately R opp. farm onto minor road.

Turn R, pass 2 farms, road becomes green lane, descending gradually to valley bottom. Veer L to cross stream by FB, enter woods and 200m later KSO ahead along track coming from back L 150m later KSO ahead along UMUR coming from L. Cross bridge and at road turn L (to continue) or R (to visit church).

7km Eglise de Sensacq 149m (605/890)

Eleventh-century church formerly dedicated to St. James. Contains total immersion font (for infants) in NW corner. Tap in churchyard. Completely enclosed porch, vestibule style, with some benches (useful for rest).

After visiting church return to junction (L) and KSO, following road round, through hamlet of **Pibot** to D111 (1.5km). Turn L and

KSO for 1.5km more to

3km Pimbo 190m (608/887)

One of the oldest Bastide villages in the Landes, founded c. 1268, with collegiate church of St. Barthélmy on site of monastery founded by Charlemagne. Fountain (drinking water).

The GR65 does not go into the village but turns *hard* L at entrance (by wayside cross L) down road (view of Arzacq-Arraziguet ahead on skyline), turning *hard* R 200m later down UMUR leading to valley bottom. Turn R down minor road at "T" junction, cross the river **Gabas** (ivy-covered house on L has tap with drinking water outside and notice indicating that there are still 924km to go to Santiago ...). KSO at crossroads and after 2km reach crossing with D32, in **Boucoue**. Turn L (note style of church, L) for 2km to junction and KSO ahead along D946 for 1km. Fork R uphill and at top follow road round to L into town, veering R. (Turn L in square for *gîte d'étape* - pilgrims only - in Centre d'Accueil.)

6.5km Arzacq-Arraziguet 231m (614.5/880.5)

SCR, 2 hotels, Centre d'Accueil takes pilgrims. 2 main squares, side by side.

Bastide town founded by "les Anglais" in thirteenth-fourteenth centuries. Arzacq was in France at that time, not in the Béarn, then a separate country. (Note names of rivers in the area: Luy-de-Béarn and Luy-de-France.) Arzacq used to mark the boundary between France and then (then independent) Béarn country.

To continue: KSO ahead (1 square to L, other to R) along small street (unmarked) to R of bank, turn L 100m later down walled lane then turn L alongside large artificial lake. Just before the end (and before a deserted house) fork R onto grassy track leading around end of lake and along other side of it, turning L 300m later uphill into woods. Continue to road (400m) and turn R.

KSO for 2.5km (road becomes UMUR), descending to bridge over the **Luy-de-France**. Turn L by watermill and 400m later turn L to church in

4km Louvigny (618.5/876.5)

Modern church of St. Martin replaces original church belonging to château formerly existing above the village in hamlet of Lou Castet: the remains of castle (dungeons) and church demolished earlier this century. One stained

glass window in new church contains coquille *and pilgrim staff and gourd.*

Continue on road to R of church then turn R uphill 200m later up steep lane to hamlet of **Lou Castet**. Turn L at "T" junction and fork R *down road* (not *up* UMUR) at junction (Moundy). KSO along road for 300-400m, turn *hard* R down UMUR between fields and then (Garos church visible ahead L on hilltop) fork L along earth track. At road turn L and continue steeply uphill to hamlet of **Daouby**. Turn L along D275 for 50m then fork R down green lane, descending through woods and then alongside large field (woods to L) to valley bottom. Go along UMUR to road (1km from Daouby) and turn R.

At junction almost immediately afterwards watch out carefully for the waymarks. The GR65 turns L here, leading through woods, past **Bignote** (a farm) to the village of

5.5km Larreule (624/871)

Formerly an important pilgrim stage with church of St. Pierre, partly Romanesque. (The name Larreule *means "La Règle" (ie. monastic rule) in Gascon, a name found elsewhere, near Maubouget on the Arles route and in La Réole on the Vézélay route.)*

However, the junction after Daouby is also misleadingly waymarked to "Uzan, Larreule" to the *right*. You can go straight to **Uzan** (eg. if you are in a hurry or in bad weather as the descent to Larreule is very steep) by turning R at the junction, ignoring turns, and KSO for 1km. Turn L at "T" junction by farm and L again at municipal tip (*déchetterie*). 200m later at junction turn R (or KSO for 1.5km to visit Larreule) to Uzan along D49 for 1km.

Pick up GR65 again 500m later when it joins the road from a wide track coming from back L (but *not* waymarked) just before a 2nd bridge (over the **Luy-de-Béarn**). 100m later turn L (at bend) down green lane, veering R and 400m later (waterworks building to L) turn R along minor road leading to church in

3km Uzan (627/868)

Church of Sainte-Quitterie, Fontaine Sainte Quitterie on other side of road (a saint very revered in the area).

With the church to your L veer R uphill. Turn R at war memorial (phone box) then L (marked "Géus"), veering R at large wayside cross. (Note "pebbledash" buildings, both old and restored.) 300m later turn R onto another minor road.

KSO for 1km, turn L and follow road round, over bridge, veering R uphill and into village of **Géus**. Turn L alongside *mairie* and 500m later at farm (**Lacassourette**) road becomes UMUR and 200m later KSO ahead, at bend, on grassy lane. KSO for 1km until you reach a road.

> *Turn R:* - to visit the church in Pomps (St. James, with statue).
>
> - to visit Château de Morlane, fourteenth-century castle, restored and furnished: take PR and follow *yellow* waymarks.
>
> *Turn L:* - to continue (the waymarking is confusing in this area) and then turn R at junction to enter

5km Pomps (632/863)

Church of St. Jacques (with statue of the saint), seventeenth-century, château *with octagonal tower. Bar/restaurant, shop.*

To continue turn immediately (ie. 1st) L (even if waymarked with an "X") and KSO, pass junction (ignoring confusing waymarks) and KSO to D945 (1.5km).

Cross over and 200m later, after houses, fork R down UMUR which disintegrates to FP (often overgrown but easy enough to follow as it goes in a straight line all the time), veering R at end, after 1km, to D269 by bridge over the **Lech**. Turn L and follow road round to L and then up to the village of **Castillon**, visible 2km away in front of you on top of the hill.

4.5km Castillon 198m (636.5/858.5)

Hospital for pilgrims and travellers in eleventh century, Church of St. Pierre.

Turn L at church and then, at junction, KSO ahead down minor road which becomes a green lane after farm (Lacoume). Rejoin road (D269) again after 800m and KSO(L) ahead for 1km. Turn L (**Chemin de Benicet**) and KSO for nearly 1km to the D276. Turn R and 250m ahead of you on the LH side is the

2.5km Chapelle de Caubin (639/856)

Restored Romanesque chapel on the site of the remains of a former Commandery of the Knights of St. John. Garden opposite (picnic tables)

contains a sculpture recalling the passage of pilgrims en route to Santiago.

Continue on road, uphill, into

2km Arthez-de-Béarn 211m (641/854)

SCR (no hotel), campsite near sports stadium.

A very long town along a ridge (nearly 2km from one end to the other), originally developed around the Augustinian commandery whose monastery was destroyed in the Wars of Religion. Several interesting old houses, ramparts. Note transition towards Basque-style architecture.

Enter the town along the **Route de Caubin** and continue along the **Rue de Begoue** to junction with traffic lights. KSO ahead (D275), KSO along **Rue du Bourdalet** and **Route de Gouze** for 4km to hamlet of **Bataille** and fork R (to "Marcerin"). Fork L down hill (N117) and 600m later turn L onto UMUR (before going under the HT cables) and 100m later turn R along another UMUR leading to D275 again 750m later.

Cross over and continue ahead on UMUR. KSO for 2km, forking R downhill at fork to N117. Turn R and then immediately L onto D275 ("Maslacq 2"). Cross the railway line, the **Gave de Pau** (river) and the A64 motorway and KSO to village of

8.5km Maslacq (649.5/845.5)

Shop, hotel, gîte d'étape.

Turn L (C9, Lagor) and then L again opposite château onto the D9. 300m later cross bridge over the **Géü** and turn L onto a minor road. 500m later you can either continue on the road or turn L to take short cut through the fields which brings you out just before the suspension bridge over the **Gave de Pau**. (If you continue on the road KSO(L) 300m later at fork.) Take 2nd UMUR ahead at a bend (just before the suspension bridge to your L) and KSO more or less // to river then veer R uphill through woods to the crossing near the

4km Chapelle de Notre-Dame de Muret (653.5/841.5)

Neo-Byzantine oratory, 1936, on site of eleventh-century sanctuary. To visit: turn hard L for 300m.

To continue: KSO to D9 (200-300m).

(The "monster" in the valley below you to the L is the Usine de Lacq, one of France's biggest nuclear power stations, but resembling lighted candles on a giant industrial birthday cake...)

Cross over, turn L behind house and then R 100m later down

minor road to valley bottom. KSO over bridge at fork. KSO(R) at next fork, continue to farm (**Haut-de-la-Coume**). Pass between buildings and continue on grassy track at edge of wood (field to R). Follow edge of woods round to L, enter woods, cross stream over FB, go through (electric) fence and turn R, following it uphill to UMUR (leading to a farm on your L, **Larqué**). Turn R along UMUR and 150m later at crossing turn R along road, leading down and then uphill. At top (a ridge) cross another road and go straight downhill on other side, veering R and then L to

8km La Sauvelade (661.5/833.5)

The Church of St. James the Great is all that remains of the monastery, originally Benedictine, founded by Gaston IV of Béarn in 1128, and later Cistercian. It was sacked by the Huguenots in 1569, restored after 1630 and then sold at the time of the French Revolution. Statue of St. James. Gîte d'étape *next to abbey.*

Turn L along D110, past *mairie*, for 1km then fork R up minor road (D110 continues L). KSO, continuously uphill, for 3km. At the very top, opposite a large restored house, turn R along a road coming from the L. Continue on ridge for 600m then fork L and 300m later turn L, downhill to cross the **Saleys**. Continue uphill for 1.5km to a "T" junction with a road running at right angles along a ridge (former school to R, small water tower in front).

At this point you may find waymarks leading you not only L (the option described here) but also R and forking R. Turn L along the ridge for 1.5km then turn R down a minor road. (Splendid views over to the Pyrenees in clear weather.) KSO for 3.5km, downhill through woods and then along the level. Veer R near the end, cross a bridge and turn L along a minor road into

10km Méritein (671.5/823.5)

500m later, at church (R) turn L for 50m then L again down a minor road, with fields to either side, for 1.5km. Cross another road via a tunnel underneath it then KSO to junction with the D111. Turn R, cross bridge over river, continue and cross **Avenue de Mourenx** and KSO on other side (**Rue de la Batteuse**) between former petrol station (L) and ramparts (R).

Turn R (*PTT* now on your L) and continue down **Rue St. Germain**, turning L into **Place Carrérot** to the **Eglise St. Germain** in

2km Navarrenx 125m (673.5/821.5)

Population 1,500. All facilities. Hôtel du Commerce, gîte d'étape (mairie), campsite by river.

First town in France to be fortified with Italian-style ramparts (sixteenth-century): ask at Tourist Office for town plan with walking tour. Church of St. Germain finished 1562 but a Protestant temple till 1620 when it was reconverted to a Catholic church. In former times Navarrenx also had a significant Cagot population, many of whom became prominent public figures.

To continue: from church and **Place Darralde** KSO(L) ahead down **Rue Saint Antoine** and down to cross the bridge over the **Gave d'Oloron** (river).

Turn R onto D115 on other side of bridge for 250m then turn L down gravelled road (towards TV/radio mast) and turn R 300m later onto D936. 100m later turn L into

2.5km Castetnau-Camblong (676/819)

(Castetnau = *"villeneuve"* in Béarnais, Camblong = *"le champ long".*) *Seventeenth-century church, note Béarn-style houses. Bar/tabac.*

Fork L uphill and then turn hard R. Pass church and 100m later turn L down minor road to "T" junction (approx. 600m) with wayside cross. Turn L onto UMUR through forest, descending to cross the **Pont de Camblong** over the **Lausset** (1km).

100m later turn R at crossing of tracks and KSO, reaching woods uphill (800m). At top, by *mirador* (at your feet!), turn hard R (back downhill again, a manoeuvre necessitated by not being able to go through private land). Track joins from back R - KSO and cross wooden bridge over the **Harcelanne**. 150m later reach minor road. Turn L for 1.2km then turn R up grassy track, forking L 50m later.

Veer R uphill, through fields, veering R again to become UMUR and reach "T" junction (1.5km). Turn L, descend to cross the **Cassou dou Boué** (small river), pass to R of large shed and then veer L uphill on stony track to a crossroads with the D115 (1km after stream). Turn R then immediately L (marked "Château de Mongaston") onto minor road and go downhill for 2km to bridge over the **Apaure** (picnic tables). KSO ahead. 400m later pass entrance road (L) to

9.5km Château de Mongaston (685.5/809.5)

Castle built in the thirteenth century by Gaston IV of Béarn, destroyed by

fire 1929 and now restored by its present owner. (Visits May 1st - October 30th except Tuesdays, 2.30-6pm.)

Continue on road and 500m later turn L in hamlet of **Cherbeys**. After 150m turn R through farmyard to road bridge over river **Saison**. Turn L over it immediately and then fork R on other side down a slope onto minor road veering R to village of **Licnos** (birthplace of Saint Grat, bishop of Oloron). Turn L at junction, then R at wayside cross, veer L and then R to cross bridge over river **Borlaas**. KSO, cross the D23 and KSO ahead on minor road for 1.8km, slightly uphill, passing pig farm.

Just after farm to R (**Bouhaber**) and before LH bend KSO ahead up grassy lane. KSO(L) at fork, go through gate into meadow and continue straight ahead towards some vines below. Go down track to R of them, pass to R of house and go down tarred lane to D11 (500m). KSO(R) along it for 1.2km to

7km Aroue 109m (692.5/802.5)

Gîte d'étape, bar/tabac in petrol station. Romanesque church of St. Etienne has twelfth-century bas reliefs with Santiago Matamoros in linten in sacristy doors.

Continue on D11, passing **Château de Elgart** (built in the nineteenth century but in Renaissance style, now an agricultural training centre) and turn L at crossroads 200m later by large wayside cross, onto minor road. KSO for 1.5km, veering L at farm entrance, then turn R down narrow gulley-like lane (slippery in wet weather). 50m later turn R down narrow lane between hedges (*very* muddy, even in summer) for 300m to farm (**Oyhamburia**), pass to R of it and continue on UMUR (farm's access road) for 400m.

Turn L uphill up FP at corner of woods, veering L, and then go downhill. Veer L to cross stream by FB, cross field and 100m later climb up 3 steps over wall into cemetery of

4km Eglise d'Olhaïby (696.5/798.5)

Simple Romanesque church of St. Just. (Large covered porch is a good place for rest/shelter.)

Leave by gate, continue on tarred lane for 150m then KSO(L) along minor road for 1km, ignoring turns (road becomes UMUR after 1km). KSO, turn R at fork and veer L to farm (**Jaurriberria**). Pass to L of it and continue uphill on wide lane onto plateau

(**Archelako**), turning L at top and then L along tarred lane. 2.5km later (ie. after Jaurriberria) turn R at "T" junction to

4km Ferme de Benta (700.5/794.5)

If you want to go to Saint Palais (7km, Donapaleu in Basque), the capital of the Basque province of Basse-Navarre, KSO at farm on minor road to Quinquilemia, continuing through Uruxondoa and Béhasque-Lapiste, turning L onto the D11 to Saint Palais at Quintalena. (Population 2000, all facilities, hotel, campsite. Musée de la Basse Navarre et des Chemins de Saint Jacques de Compostelle, next to Mairie.) If so, you can pick up the GR65 again at Hiriburia by taking the D302 south and either continuing on the road or taking the turning L onto the Vézélay route.

Otherwise, *to continue:* turn L (farm to L) down minor road, downhill. KSO, ignoring turns, for 1km then turn R along D242 for 1km. Turn L along C2 ("Larribar 1.2") for 1km then veer L at *frontón*, L to church, cross bridge over D933 and then KSO down minor road *(bar/tabac to R at bend).*

4km Larribar-Sorhapuru 89m (704.5/790.5)

Bar/tabac. Veer R between 2 farms and continue downhill to cross 4 arch bridge over the **Bidouze**.

(Note shrine to R with small statue of St. Jacques behind glass in a stèle *and also watercolour of church under glass.)*

At a "T" junction turn L onto grassy track, enter woods and track becomes FP with rocky "steps", becoming narrower as you climb. When it levels out, veer L and path becomes wider. Go through "gate", continue along narrow FP between hedges, gradually widening out, and reach road at farm.

2km Hiriburia 151m (716.5/788.5)

A few metres to the R, where the routes from Paris, Vézélay and Le Puy are thought to have met, the Société des Amis de Saint Jacques have erected a small monument. You can also go to Saint Palais from here (and continue straight from there to Saint-Jean-Pied-de-Port): follow the Vézélay route, marked with coquilles *(see the monument's "feet" - if you follow the direction pointed by those marked "Ostabat" you will also see where you are going next: up the clear track uphill in front of you, the "Chemin de procession" leading to the chapel).*

To continue: continue ahead for 100m then cross the D302 and turn L up the "Chemin de procession" leading to the **Chapelle de**

Soyarza, 300m.

This is a modern building replacing a much older oratory dedicated to Notre-Dame. Adjoining the chapel is a covered rest area with pilgrim book. Superb views all round from the top on a clear day.

Continue downhill on the other side on wide UMUR, veering L alongside woods. 800m later, 100m past modern shrine (L) turn R down clear grassy track, veering L to join UMUR coming from back L. Veer R then L downhill to village of

3km Harambeltz (709.5/785.5)

Site of former Benedictine priory-hospital of St. Nicholas. The 1000 year old chapel remains and has an eighteenth-century altarpiece and statue of St. James but belongs to the families in the village and is not a parish church. It is difficult to visit though the door (but not the grille) is often open, enabling you to see inside. Note interesting old houses in the village.

KSO(R) down main street, pass to L of church, KSO ahead under trees at LH bend, veering R and then L downhill immediately on FP veering R at bottom to cross stream. On other side track is wider: KSO up it, ignoring turns till you emerge from the woods at a "T" junction with a UMUR (1.5km). Turn L and go downhill, veer L at bottom then R and follow road round ignoring turns. Pass **Lagunatona** (group of houses) and at crossroads KSO. 200m later fork L down grassy track which becomes walled lane into village of

5km Ostabat-Asme 124m (714.5/780.5)

A small village today but in the past it was an important gathering point for pilgrims coming from or along different routes. In the Middle Ages its hospitals and inns could accommodate up to 5000 pilgrims but today only the Maison Ospitalia remains and is now the gîte d'étape. Bar/shop.

Turn R, pass *gîte d'étape* (R) and continue uphill, veering R and then turn L along main street through village, veering L and then fork R onto tarred lane. KSO ahead at crossroads. Road becomes UMUR at farm (**Berrautia**). KSO, go through gate and KSO on track descending between hedges. At junction with similar tracks and large wayside cross KSO (more of // to road below all the time). Veer L to pass between farm buildings and KSO(L) ahead shortly afterwards to minor road leading, veering L, to D933. Turn R along it for 600m to

3.5km Larceveau-Arros-Cibits 160m (718/777)

Hotel, pharmacy. From here to Saint-Jean-Pied-de-Port you are following the D933 along the valley all the time, mainly on old lanes, on one side of the main road or the other.

Just before road junction (with roundabout) with the D918 turn R up minor road, veering L to continue / / to D933 below. Just before the hamlet of **Chabarra** (main road now 150m to L) KSO at crossroads and go through hamlet, passing to R of large house and continue ahead on lane between fences. Turn L at minor road and 50m later turn R onto green lane.

Join minor road coming from L and KSO(R) ahead, veering L in hamlet of **Bastida-Choko**. 300m later, before RH bend uphill continue ahead on grassy track to cross stream and then turn L alongside it, returning to D933 again. Turn R along FP alongside but above road and in hamlet of **Utziat** (there was a hospital for pilgrims here in the twelfth century). KSO ahead along minor road in front. Veer R and almost immediately turn L through gateway, to continue alongside hedge to your R. (You are now / / to road again.) Follow the hedge, pass inside the edge of a wood and then above vines before returning to the D933 again (1km). KSO along road for 300m to a roadside cross (R), the

5km Croix de Galzetaburu 262m (723/772)

This cross (1714, the name means "tête du chemin") was placed at this crossing of Roman roads where pilgrims from secondary routes joined the Via Podensis. It has Christ on one face, the Virgin and child on the other and two inscriptions on its base: a Latin hymn and a Basque text indicating that you are halfway between the Soule and the Labourd, two of the three Basque provinces in France.

Turn L down a minor road leading to the village of **Gamarthe** (1km). At the end, after a wayside cross, fork L down UMUR, go along side of one field ahead, turn L along its end, go through gate, over footbridge and turn R alongside irrigation channel. Turn L at end of field along fence (and watch out carefully for grass snakes in hot weather), turn L again at corner and 100m later cross stile. Turn R along track, veer L uphill, pass to L of farm (**Biscaya**) and turn R on road and immediately L along another minor road. KSO for 1km, KSO at crossroads and 200m later turn L up small tarred road, veering R. KSO for 1km till it descends and reaches a sharp fork just

115

before a (2nd) cattlegrid (*passage canadien* in French).

Turn *hard* L uphill, veering R, road becomes UMUR after a while. Then, after 1.5km, at top of hill, you have a choice:

a) Turn R over stile and go down through the woods to the main road shortly before **Saint-Jean-le-Vieux**, bringing you out near the farm at **Apat-Ospitale** (originally an abbey hospital founded by the Knights of Malta in 1186).

The Romanesque chapel of St. Blaise survives but is now a garage. This route is not recommended in wet weather. If you take it, watch out carefully for the waymarks. At the time this book was prepared some sections were extremely overgrown and difficult to negotiate.

Turn L along the D933 to the main square in Saint-Jean-le-Vieux.

b) Slightly longer (but not much traffic), an alternative route is waymarked in yellow. KSO ahead on the wide UMUR, which becomes a road, following it downhill in a large "C" shaped loop all the time, ignoring turnings. Pass through the village of **Bussunarits**, join larger road coming from L just in front of eleventh-century **Château d'Apat**, cross bridge, veer R to crossroads and KSO ahead on smaller road. Veer R near end and emerge on the D18, turning R to church and main square (and returning to GR65) in

8km Saint-Jean-le-Vieux 212m (731/764)
SCR, hotels, campsite.

Pilgrims originally went straight from Saint-Jean-le-Vieux to St. Michel (the route described in Aimery Picard's twelfth-century guidebook). The deviation via Saint-Jean-Pied-de-Port developed from the thirteenth century onwards. Church of Saint Pierre, an example of a typically Basque church, with galleries on two levels around three sides of the nave. Until the fourteenth century it was affiliated to the Augustinian Canons in Roncesvalles. Musée archéologique.

With your back to the church turn L at LH far corner of square onto a minor road, KSO(R) at junction and KSO(L) at fork. Turn L at crossroads and 300m later turn L back to D933. Turn R for 100m and then turn L down tree-lined road and then R 200m later down minor road between fields, leading through the **Quartier de la Magdeleine** (campsite to R).

Pass *frontón* (L) and turn L down side of church of **Sainte Marie-Madeleine** (the present building in pink stone replaces an earlier one). Cross the river **Laurhibar** and KSO, uphill to crossing with D401 (Route de Caro). Cross over, KSO up **Chemin St. Jacques**, go through the **Porte Saint-Jacques** and down the **Rue de la Citadelle** to the church (L) in

4km Saint-Jean-Pied-de-Port 180m (735/760)

Population 1400. All facilities, several hotels, gîte d'étape, campsite. Tourist Office, SNCF (to Bayonne).

This is "Saint John-at-the-foot-of-the-Pass", a small border town on the river Nive, capital of the Basque province of Basse Navarre with an ancient cobbled haute ville. Several places of interest: Citadelle, overlooking the town, with its system of ramparts (being restored); access either from the top end of Rue de la Citadelle or by staircase (escalier de la poterne) leading up from the footpath along the river by the side of the church - worth the climb on a clear day. Prison des Evêques, Musée de la Pelote, fourteenth-century Eglise Notre-Dame-du-bout-du-pont ("Our Lady at the end of the bridge", part of the former priory-hospital). Pont Romain, the different portes (Saint Jacques, d'Espagne, for example). Note architecture of Basque-style houses with often ornate wooden overhangs at roof level, balconies. If you have time to spare the Tourist Office has a booklet of waymarked walks in the area.

Traditionally pilgrims entered the town by the Porte Saint Jacques at the top of Rue de la Citadelle and those who have followed the GR65 will have done the same. After that there were two routes to Roncesvalles. The older one, following the course of the river Valcarlos, is now the modern road (D933 in France, N135 in Spain). This route is a little shorter (20km) and is not so steep but is on the main road nearly all the way. However, if the weather is very bad or visibility poor, you may prefer to take this. The other, high-level Route Napoléon was the one he took, following existing tracks already used by shepherds and pilgrims for several centuries. This leads over the Pyrenees via the Col de Bentarte and the Porte de Cize, continuing along the path of the old Roman road from Bordeaux to Astoria, and is normally accessible without any trouble (ie. too much snow) from May to October. It is 26km long and is a spectacular route on a clear day. It was also the one favoured by pilgrims in centuries gone by because, although it was much more strenuous, it was also exposed for most of the way, and they were thus less likely to be ambushed by bandits than on the densely wooded route through Valcarlos. If you are a fairly fit walker allow at least 7h actual walking (excluding stops); if not, allow much longer,

MAP 1

especially if it is very windy (when it will always be against you).

However, start early in the day whichever route you take (eg. 6.30am in summer or as soon as it is light), not only to avoid the heat but also being high up later in the day when the light is fading and you are tired. If you choose the *Route Napoléon* take enough food and water *with you, including (both routes) the following morning's breakfast.*

A. VALCARLOS ROUTE

From **Rue de la Citadelle** go through the **Porte d'Espagne** (passing the church on your L, *fountain*), cross the bridge over the river **Nive**, go up the Rue d'Espagne but then turn R into the **Rue d'Uhart**. Continue along **Place Floquet** (under the *jardin publique*), through the rampart gateway and then, after 20m, bear L when you see a signpost to "Arnéguy 8. Frontière d'Espagne". Follow the road up to the border at Arnéguy on the French side, cross it and enter

8km Valcarlos 365m
Border town on the Spanish side, with shops, Tourist Office and bank (not always open). Church of Santiago contains a life-size representation of Santiago Matamoros.

Continue along the road as it climbs up and up.

Between Arnéguy and Ibañeta you will see yellow arrows and also the red balises of the French waymarking system leading you off the route at intervals, to short-cut some of the many bends, but these are not at all easy to follow once you are off the road, in very dense forest.

Follow the road up and then, when it reaches the top, continue downhill to the

10km Puerta d'Ibañeta 1057m
Continue as described from "4km Puerta of d'Ibañeta (759/736)" on page 123.

B. ROUTE NAPOLEON

The Route Napoléon is, in fact, the variant version of the GR65 as between Saint-Jean-Pied-de-Port and the Vierge d'Orisson (12km, 1095m) there are two paths (both waymarked): the GR65 as such (a walkers' route, avoiding the minor road) and the Route Napoléon or historic route which is described here. This has now become the D428, a tarmac road until just before the Col de Bentarte, but is very quiet with very little traffic.

[The Route Napoléon is also practicable on a mountain bike if you are prepared to dismount occasionally, eg. after Honto on the short-cut section and near the border but there should be no problem with a sturdy machine. Touring bikes could also manage it if they did not take the short cut at Honto but remained on the road and if their riders were prepared to dismount along all the non-tarred sections - some 7-8km. On a clear day it would definitely be worth the effort.]

Both routes go down the **Rue de la Citadelle**, past the church of **Notre-Dame-du-bout-du-pont** *(fountain)*, through the **Porte d'Espagne**, cross the bridge over the river **Nive** and continue on up the **Rue d'Espagne**. However 100m later they separate, the main GR65 turning *right* up the **Chemin de Mayorga** (waymarking in red and white).

(If you check your route out the evening before you leave you will see that it is easy to distinguish the two alternatives.)

The GR *variante*, ie. the Route Napoléon, continues *ahead* here, up the **Route Saint Michel**.

This is clearly waymarked with both yellow flashes and/or arrows (these flechas amarillas *will continue all through Spain too) as well as with cockle shells and is easy to follow as you continue up the D428 all the time, ignoring turns, apart from a few occasions (indicated in the text) when you short-cut some of its many "hairpins".*

Continue up the **Route Saint Michel** for approx. 100m, bear L at a fork and after 20m you will come to a junction with the **Route Maréchal Harrispe**. Take this (ie. bear R off the Route Saint Michel, which bends round to the L).

There is a sign here saying "Chemin de Saint Jacques de Compostelle. Route des Portes de Cize. Summus Pyrenaeus de la Voie Romana". (Fountain on L.)

KSO and after approx. 500m there is a small junction and the road name changes to Route Napoléon.

Follow the road as it winds (mostly) up and (sometimes) down, past small roadside farms. At fork bear L. KSO following road all the time (but keep turning round from time to time to admire the view - after this there is nothing as steep until you climb up to **El Cebreiro** and enter Galicia). At this level there are still trees to provide some shade. Pass a "T" junction (**Maison Etchébestia**, 302m), and KSO. Watch out for occasional vehicles. 100m further on, road forks at massive tree (good place for a rest) - keep R (fork to L goes down to village of Saint Michel).

50m after passing the hamlet of **Honto** (540m) the road veers R but the GR65 bears L up a grassy track (the old road), leaving the modern road for a while (to rejoin it later) making a short cut via the old, steep route that zigzags between walls/banks at first and then on open ground.

The waymarks are mainly painted on rocks on the ground in this section but if you have difficulty in seeing them (eg. in snow) you can spot the place where you will meet the road again (a) by a tap on the RH side of the road and (b) by 2 small houses L and R of the road - the one on your R is called Arbol Azopian.

The path joins the road again (at 710m) after 8-9 "hairpins".

[NB: if you are walking *to* Saint-Jean-Pied-de-Port, ie. going back, leave the road to your R after the tap on your L, dropping down by a drystone wall and walking alongside it. This turn is well marked on a large rock at RH side of the road before you leave it.]

From here you can see over the mountains to the east towards the Col de Somport, Mont d'Aspe etc., snow-covered (peaks) for much of the year.

KSO on road, ignoring tracks to either L or R. When you see a farm building off to the L where a stream crosses under the road, the road veers round to the R and shortly afterwards, after 3-4 more hairpins, the road flattens out and you reach the

12km Vierge d'Orisson 1,095m (747/748)

A small statue of the Virgin Mary in a prominent position at the side of a road junction and in a level area, brought there from Lourdes by shepherds. Panoramic views and a good place for a rest (not too long). At the Vierge d'Orisson you are halfway in time (but not in distance) between Saint-Jean-Pied-de-Port and Roncesvalles. It is still 6km to the border and the route still climbs, though less steeply now, up to the Col de Bentarte, after which it is nearly all downhill. The temperature may be cooler as you climb higher but the sun, if it is out, will still be as hot.

Be careful to take the R fork here (the LH option leads you back down again!) and continue on road (having taken R fork) and KSO at road junction (with the D128 (R) to Arnéguy). At 1177m pass the "remains" of **Château Pignon** (L). Ignore a turn to L after 300m and also a fork to R after 300m (to a farm 100m off road).

Continue on road until it begins to veer round to L, at which point the *camino* leaves the road (at 1240m) up a clearly-marked grassy track with a wayside cross (erected in 1990 on the RH side of the road with an inscription in Basque - "I am the way ..."). This path takes you towards the pass above you on the rocky summit of **Leizar-Atheka** (1300m). Since the road veers L you are in effect continuing more or less in a straight line, although you actually walk off the road to the R.

(The road itself continues for another 3km to the border at the Col d'Arnostéguy, more or less on the level, before it comes to a dead end. However, if you get caught unexpectedly in foggy weather you can continue along this road and then backtrack along the border fence until you reach marker no. 199 and where the terrain is slightly shaded: see below.)

Climb up between the two very large rocks, after which the path begins to descend. Pass border marker stone number 198 (1290m) and then follow the border fence (above the forest below you to the R) to marker no. 199 (1344m). 120m after this you cross a cattle grid through the fence into

4km Spain (751/744)
You may find remains of snow here, even in early June.

The grassy track veers round to the R, past a tumbledown house (L) at the **Col de Bentarte** (1330m). Continue along path through beechwoods. Pass sheep pen and hut (with tap) on R. Do not take R fork here but KSO back into the woods again (well waymarked).

When you come out of the woods again the track falls away to the R (good views) but KSO (ie. don't fork R here). 10m further on track forks left but KSO (ie. take R fork). (Over to your L you will now be able to see the TV mast on Monte Orzanzurieta, 1570m.) From here the path winds (mostly) up for 1-2km to meet the road at the

4km Col Lepoeder 1440m (755/740)
From here you have the first, plunging, view of the rooftops of the abbey at Roncesvalles down in the valley below, the village of Burguete and, on a clear day, right across into the province of Navarra.

There are in fact two routes down to Roncesvalles, one via the Puerta de Ibañeta and the other, very steep, via the Calzada Romana (old Roman road), which drops down to the monastery directly, straight ahead, passing

to the L of the hill known as Don Simon. This has been re-waymarked recently and is now the "standard" route. Both are described here.

a) For the "short sharp" route KSO ahead (following the marker stones) at the **Col Lepoeder** to the road, cross it and descend, forking L, into the woods. This is well waymarked so watch out carefully for the yellow arrows and the red and white *balises* as there are no distinguishing features to orient yourself. It descends very steeply all the time, describing a "J" shaped loop, straight down to the abbey, dropping over 500m (1500ft) in only 3.5km. At the bottom turn R to enter the abbey from the west (ie. the back, fountain). Cross diagonally through a courtyard and pass in front of the church.

b) The alternative (and recommended for people with bad knees) is to follow the road, which you join by taking a short path R off the road you are on after the Col and follow it down (there are a few short cuts through its hairpins) to the

4km Puerta d'Ibañeta 1057m (759/736)
This is where Charlemagne had got to when he heard Roland blow his horn, too late to go back to help him. A bell used to toll at the original chapel to guide pilgrims in bad weather. A modern ermita *(chapel) was built in 1965 to replace the earlier ruined chapel of Charlemagne, with a sign in French, Spanish, Basque and Latin inviting pilgrims to pray to Notre-Dame de Roncevaux. There is also a modern monument to Roland (Roldán in Spanish) of* Chanson de Roland *fame.*

From here you can walk through the woods for the last 2km to Roncesvalles, gently downhill. The track is waymarked: go down to RH side of small building to L of road just after you reach the chapel. Shortly before you get to the abbey you are joined by a track coming from the L, after which you enter the rear of the monastery *(fountain).* Cross diagonally through a courtyard and pass in front of the church.

2km Roncesvalles (Orreaga) 925m (761/734)
Shop with guidebooks etc., hotel-restaurant, monastery-run posada, *youth hostel. Walker pilgrims may stay in the refuge in the old hospital building after obtaining their* credencial *or "pilgrim passport" from the vice-abbott.*

Augustinian monastery and hospital founded early in the twelfth century. Set in the "valley of thorns" in the foothills of the Pyrenees it has

Puenta la Reina. Pilgrim bridge over the River Arga (photo: Simon Derry)

a long tradition of looking after pilgrims (it fed 25,000 a year during the seventeenth century). Collegiate church, chapel of Santiago, fourteenth-century royal pantheon containing the thirteenth-century tombs of Sancho the Strong and his wife Doña Clemencia of Toulouse. Museum with religious paintings and sculpture, treasury.

The whole section from Roncesvalles to shortly before the outskirts of Pamplona is shady in the main and so can be walked comfortably even in July/August unless you are unusually affected by the heat.

Leave the monastery by the main entrance (KM47 on the N135), and turn R immediately onto a FP // to the road by an information board. (Fourteenth-century pilgrim cross on L on way out of the village.) Continue along a path shaded by trees, more or less // to road to begin with and then moving further away, gently downhill. KSO. 2km further on, after passing through a 2nd gate, turn L onto a track coming from the R and rejoin road at K47 at the side of the HQ of the Guardia Civil. Turn R onto road [RJ: turn L here] and continue for 500m to

2km Burguete (Auritz) 893m (763/732)
Hostales, *another house with rooms, 2 bars, 2 restaurants, bank, pharmacy.*

Basque village with splendid eighteenth-early nineteenth-century houses with armorial devices on either side of the main street.

KSO down main street past modern church of **San Nicolás de Bari** and **public garden** and turn R 100m later along the side of the bank building. Go down track and cross lane. KSO ahead over footbridge over stream and continue on UMUR. Veer L onto other UMUR coming from R and KSO.

After going through gate and crossing stream fork L slightly uphill into woods. At end of field fork L and KSO, climbing steeply uphill. Go through fence at top, cross track and KSO ahead downhill on UMUR (shady). Emerge on road (just below modern church of **San Bartolomé** and tower of the *Biblioteca Pública* on the other side of the road) into

4.5km Espinal (Aurizberri) 871m (767.5/727.5)
Shop, 2 bars, panadería, *restaurant.*

Basque village founded in 1269; houses with armorial devices above doorways.

Turn R on road through village. After passing fountain (on L) turn L at house no. 19 (called **Aunta Mendi**) onto minor tarred road uphill. 200m later KSO(L) at fork onto UMUR. 100m later fork R onto FP leading into the woods, uphill all the time, via steps, to the top. (View to rear over foothills to TV mast at Monte Orzanzurieta and Col Lepoeder.) Fork R at top, turn L through gate and continue R along gravel lane and then KSO alongside fence along side of field. Go through gate at end and under trees and cross the road (carefully) at

2km Alto de Mezquiriz (Puerta de Espinal) 922m (769.5/726.5)
A new trilingual stèle *invites the pilgrim, in French, Spanish and Basque, to pray to Notre-Dame de Roncevaux.*

After crossing the road do *not* go straight on through the gate and up the track, even though it might seem the most obvious path to take, but turn L instead, before you reach the fence, down a small FP, leading downhill, via a gate, into the woods. This veers R at fork into semi-shaded woodland, undulating and short-cutting many of the hairpins on the road below you to the left. FP takes you down (gate at end) to lane coming from the R. Turn L along it, reaching road 60m later at bend and then turn R off it up old, tunnel-like path, shaded overhead, which then becomes a lane. Turn L at fork with another lane coming from T and continue downhill to road at bridge over stream. [RJ: turn L and then take L of two forks.]

Turn R and continue on road for 100m then fork R down FP (which becomes a lane) behind crash barrier at next bend when road starts to climb again. Emerge on old main road in village of

4.5km Viscarret (Biskarreta) (774/721)

Small village with shop, bar, the end of the first stage of the Way of St. James as outlined in the Codex Calixtinus. *(It began in Saint-Michel-le-Vieux, 3km south of Saint-Jean-Pied-de-Port.)*

Turn R, cross main road (church above you to L) and continue to end of village. Turn R and then L down track which then reaches road 200m later. Continue ahead, passing small cemetery (on your L) and go downhill on FP to L of road, // to it to begin with. Rejoin road, continue along it for 200m, fork R down FP (which becomes green lane) and KSO into village of

1.5km Linzóain (775.5/719.5)

Church on hill to L is a good place for a rest, shady, with good views. From here to the Alto de Erro the route climbs uphill and then along a wooded ridge.

Follow road through village past *frontón*, veer L (fountain), then turn R uphill under footbridge over road and KSO upwards. 400m later cross minor gravel road and KSO(L) ahead (slightly staggered crossing) up stony lane which then becomes a FP, uphill all the time.

Veer L onto wider track coming from back R and then fork R onto FP. (In this section the red and white *balises* are more frequent than the yellow arrows.) Emerge at fork of track and gravel road and fork L up track with *camino* "milestone" marker at start. Shortly afterwards cross gravel road and KSO ahead down shady lane.

It was in this section that Roland (Roldán in Spanish) eventually decided - too late - to blow his horn to summon help from Charlemagne and his army, as related in the Song of Roland.

At junction with (walkers') signpost ("Linzóain 5.7km, Erro 2.850, 0.30h, NA40 and NA40) turn R and take LH of two forks downhill, following line of HT pylons. 300m further on reach the road (C135) at

4km Alto de Erro (Puerta de Erro) 801m (779.5/715.5)

Cross the road (the stone construction opposite covers a former well, much used by pilgrims) and KSO through more woods, ignoring turnings to L and R. After 1km pass to the L of an old building: this is the **Venta del Caminante** or **Venta del Puerto**, a former pilgrim inn (*posada del peregrino*). Continue downhill, watching out carefully for the waymarks (view of Zubiri ahead with its large magnesita factory). Follow the track as it gradually loses height, descending to the old medieval bridge over the **Arga** in

4km Zubiri 526m (783.5/711.5)

Bar, restaurant (both may have rooms), shop, bank, panadería.

The name Zubiri means "village with the bridge" in Basque. The bridge itself was known as "el puente de la rabia" because, so the story goes, any animal that crossed it three times was cured of rabies. The large building immediately to the R before you cross the bridge was a former hospital, possibly a leprosarium. From Zubiri to just before Arre the camino *follows the valley of the river Arga, crossing it (and back again) a couple of times.*

If you want to go into the village cross the bridge (fountain on other side, next to church). Otherwise, turn L along path just before it (waymarked). Go up hill and down side of large house down lane, cross stream by footbridge and KSO on other side, veering round to R. At "T" junction with gravel road near factory turn R along it downhill, then L on a tarmac road to pass to L of factory (ie. it is on your R). Road climbs and when you are level with the last factory building fork R onto a track // to both road and electricity cables (between the two). (You are now above and // to the river Arga in the valley below you to the R.)

Towards end of factory workings and at junction with another track coming from back R go downhill steeply (steps) following line of electricity cables. Cross road at bottom and KSO ahead. Cross stream and KSO down FP (// to and between two sets of electric cables) which then leads uphill between banks to emerge at side of house in hamlet of **Ilarratz** (2.6km) Turn L (fountain) and then R down minor tarred road. At bend in road (signed "Eskirotz 500m") KSO(L) uphill to hamlet. Fork L at end along walled lane with fields below it to your R. KSO. Pass battery hen farm as track becomes UMUR and KSO to minor road. Cross it, go up short flight of steps and KSO on FP through field which continues alongside another and then between banks. Track climbs up and down, joined by another from back L shortly before you reach a minor road at entry to village of

5km Larrasoaña (Larrasoaina) (788.5/706.5)

Fountain (no shop).

Village founded as a monastery, later donated to Leyre, formerly with pilgrim hospitals. Church contains statue of St. James.

To enter village turn R, cross bridge and then turn L at church. To continue: turn L onto road and follow it to hamlet of **Aquerreta** (1km, fountain). KSO(R) down green lane at house with armorial device (1747). KSO downhill, cross minor tarred road (slightly staggered junction) and KSO ahead on lane. Track takes you in and out of woods above, but // to all the time, the main road below you to the R. Path then descends steeply (section with steps) to continue close to and // to river, passing weir (R) shortly before reaching modern bridge over the **Arga** at

4.5km Zuriáin 495m (793/702)

Cross bridge and veer L onto main road (N135). Continue along main road for 300m and then turn L down minor road signposted to "Illúrdoz 3". Cross bridge over the **Arga** back on to the LH bank again and take R turn at bend in road almost immediately afterwards. Continue on path to village of **Irotz** (2km). Veer R round side of large white house, pass in front of church (to your R) and KSO on concrete road. Cross medieval bridge back over the river again to village of **Uroz**. Turn L onto FP // to road (and between road and river). Continue to village of

3km Zabaldica (796/699)

Church contains statue of St. James but is usually kept locked so to see it you will have to ask for the key at a nearby house. (To visit it turn R in middle of tarred road for 20m and cross main road.)

Continue for 200m on FP then rejoin road (N135), cross over and fork R uphill up FP just before road KM9 and the old road bridge over the **Arga**. Track continues // to river, high up.

(From here you can see the village of Huarte in the distance to your L and the Romanesque Ermita de la Virgen de la Nieve over on the hill on the opposite side of the river.)

The octagonal Romanesque church at Eunate is a pilgrims' burial place
connected with the Order of St John of Jerusalem
The eleventh century bridge at Puenta la Reina, attributed to Doña Mayor,
wife of Sancho the Greater of Navarre

The town of Logroño with its bridge over the River Ebro
A fountain by the Cathedral at Burgos.
The man is retrieving coins from the water

Continue to village of **Arleta**, pass to RH side of church and KSO. KSO to dual carriageway, cross road by tunnel and veer R uphill on road on other side. This then veers L and leads, after a few hundered metres, to the bridge over the river **Ulzama** (a tributary of the Arga) at

3.5km Trinidad de Arre (799.5/695.5)
Immediately after the bridge, on the R, is the Basilica de la Sanctísima Trinidad, where there was also a small pilgrim hospital in former times and a refugio today.

Turn L after crossing the bridge (fountain on R) and enter

0.5km Villava (800/695)
Suburb of Pamplona.

Go along main street for 1km past public garden (L) and bar (R) to crossroads with traffic lights. Continue straight ahead along a tree-lined *paseo* (note elaborate Basque-style school of agriculture on R) and enter suburb of

1km Burlada (801/694)
Shops etc.

When you reach some traffic lights with a Michelin tyre dealer (R) and the **Villa Josepha** with a large, tree-filled garden (L) *do not* continue straight ahead to cross the river by the road bridge but cross the road and turn R along the **Calle Larraizar** with a school on its R, past a block of flats, to the main road. Cross this and KSO on other side along a minor, tree-lined road, the **Camino** or **Carretera Burlada**, for 2km, ignoring LH fork at first "kink" in road.

At a bend in the road you will get a good view of Pamplona cathedral and then note (L) two houses with their facades decorated all over with scallop shells embedded in the stucco.

When you have almost reached the river (fountain on R by school) a minor road crosses the one you are on. Turn R and then almost immediately L over the **Puente de los Peregrinos**, the old pilgrim bridge over the river Arga with a recently decapitated statue of St. James on a small column at the far end. Cross the public garden straight ahead towards the town walls, following waymarks, cross road at traffic lights diagonally R and KSO to walk between the inner and outer sets of ramparts. At the gateway KSO up the **Calle del Carmen** into the old quarter of

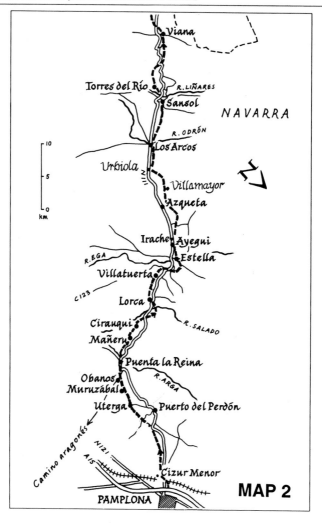

2km Pamplona (Iruña) 415m (803/692)

Population 200,000. All facilities. RENFE, buses to Burguete, Puenta la Reina, Estella, Logroño. Tourist Office: Calle Anumada, near the Plaza del Castillo.

The end of the second stage of the Camino de Santiago in Aimery Picaud's guide. A fortress town situated on rising ground in the middle of a broad valley, Pamplona (Iruña in Basque) was the capital of the ancient kingdom of Navarre and is the capital of the modern autonomous región of the same name. It is probably most famous today for the festival of San Firmin during the first two weeks of July with the "running of the bulls" but it also contains many places of interest (the Tourist Office produces a useful leaflet for a walking tour of the city) and it is worth spending at least half a day here. Gothic cathedral with outstanding cloisters, churches of San Sernin, San Domingo, San Nicolás and San Lorenzo. Museo de Navarra, Ciudadela (fortress area, now a park). Pamplona has many public fountains.

The route is waymarked through Pamplona with blue and yellow plaques bearing the Council of Europe's schematised "path of the stars" motif. (The direction to take is the one in which the "point" of the cluster is facing.) However, although you will see these plaques elsewhere along the camino *they are often only for decorative and not route-finding purposes.*

To visit the cathedral: turn off the **Calle del Carmen** at a small square with a statute.

To continue: KSO along the **Calle del Carmen**, turn R into the **Calle de Mercadores**, continue to the **Plaza Consistorial** (Ayuntamiento), turn R into the **Calle San Saturnino** and KSO ahead to the **Calle Mayor**. At end, KSO, passing to L of a public garden. At the crossing of **Avenida Piu XII** and **Avenida Jaconera** veer L to parkland surrounding the **Cuidadela** and follow the flagstone path (waymarked). When it turns in front of the **Cuidadela** veer R across the grass to the road. Cross this and continue down the **Calle Fuente de Hierro**, which leads downhill under the road bridge across the campus of the University of Navarre and then becomes the **Camino de Santiago**.

Continue ahead along a minor road signposted to "Cizor Menor", crossing the bridge first over the river **Sadar** and then the river **Elorz**. KSO. When the modern road forks to the L, fork R, KSO and either cross the railway track (carefully) or go up steps to road (both options join up 100m later). Continue ahead and this path then becomes the pavement along the main road to the L, which it then joins. KSO to top of the hill to the village of

4km Cizur Menor 483m (807/688)

Bars, restaurant (but no shop), fountain in public garden (R).

Restored Romanesque church on R of main road, remains of the twelfth-century commandery of the Knights of St. John of Jerusalem and the old pilgrim hospital on L. From here onwards there is very little shade.

Continue downhill on road and 100m later fork R down FP down LH side of the *frontón* and veer L (KSO) to road which becomes UMUR.

(Ahead of you is the Monte del Perdón (1.037m) and a line of forty modern windmills along a ridge to its R, providing Pamplona with its electric power.)

Join tarred road coming from L and KSO. 100m later (road bends R) KSO(L) on UMUR. When this bends to R after 200m turn L up clear FP through field under electric cables leading towards the church and village of **Guenduláin** visible straight ahead of you on small hilltop. 200m later cross minor tarred road and KSO ahead uphill again.

KSO, ignoring LH turn at junction by line of four large trees. Shortly before a group of eight trees UMUR bends L: KSO(R) on earth track ahead. At junction with UMUR (small lake / reservoir to L) turn L up hill. At next crossing 60m later KSO towards windmills on skyline. (Good views of Pamplona to rear.) Continue uphill to

6km Zariegui 570m (813/682)

Fountain. Continue straight on through village (Romanesque church on R) between houses and then ahead on a UMUR (towards the windmills all the time). 500m after village ignore L *turn* but take L *fork* at "Y" junction 20m later, steeply uphill (isolated tree on RH side of path near top is a good place for a rest but in evening sun only). KSO.

Splendid modern fountain (though not necessarily working) on your L at a spot named Gambellacos. Legend has it that a pilgrim making his way up to the Alto del Perdón, exhausted and overcome by a terrible thirst, was accosted by the devil, disguised as a walker, who offered to show him a

hidden fountain but only on condition that he renounce God, the Virgin Mary or St. James. The pilgrim refused but then St. James himself, disguised as a pilgrim, led him to the hidden fountain and gave him water to drink in his scallop shell.

Reach the road at

5km Alto del Perdón 780m (818/677)

Panoramic views ahead to Puenta la Reina and laid out in front of you, like a map, are the villages you will pass through next: Uterga, Muruzábal and Obanos. At the crossing with the road there is now the "Parque Eólico del Perdón", constructed in 1996, a picnic area with cast-iron "cut-out" sculptures of pilgrims on foot and horseback, plus two donkeys and a dog. The inscription reads donde se cruza el camino del viento con el de las estrellas *("where the path of the wind crosses that of the stars"), a reference to the* camino de Santiago *and the Milky Way.*

Cross over the road and go down the other side, watching out carefully for the waymarks, to valley bottom. Join track coming from back R and KSO(L). Cross small river (with a long line of trees along its bank) and go uphill again into village of

3km Uterga (821/674)

Fountain, bar (unmarked). KSO through village and continue along quiet road to

3km Muruzábal (824/671)

Bar, fountain.

Go through village and as you are leaving it turn R diagonally, just before a large roadside cross (R), walking along the edges of fields. Join road coming from L and KSO. Fork R at top of hill into village of

2km Obanos 414m (826/669)

Bank, restaurant, panadería. *Ermita San Salvador, where the route from Roncesvalles is joined by the one coming from Arles over the Somport pass. A short detour is recommended from here to the twelfth-century church at Eunate, 3km away on the Monreal/Las Campañas road. It is an octagonal building surrounded by a series of arches and was used as a burial place for pilgrims.*

Enter the village by the **Camino Roncesvalles**. KSO to **Calle San Juan**, turn R into the **Calle Julian Gayarre**, L down a tree-lined with a school (L) to church (public garden on its R). Continue diagonally through archway and KSO, following road as it bends to R passing *frontón* (fountain opposite) then the **Ermita San Salvador** (L). When the road becomes a rough track at the side of a farm (R) KSO above vines (to L) and follow it down to the main road.

Cross over, turn L down FP through allotments and then alongside wall and fencing // to road all the time. Rejoin road by hotel. Here there is a modern statue of a pilgrim to mark the junction of the *caminos francés* and *aragonés*. Turn L along the N111 for 300m to

2km Puenta la Reina (Gares) 346m (828/667)

Population 2000. All facilities. Buses to Estella, Logroño and Pamplona.

The town gets its name from the eleventh-century pilgrim bridge over the river Arga. This was built at the command of Queen Urraca, daughter of Alfonso VI and with its six arches remains unchanged today. It is also one of the most interesting on the camino. *Church of Santiago (with statue of St. James the pilgrim inside).*

Turn L at *refugio*, a two-storey building on the corner run by the Padres Reparadores, with an arcaded verandah outside, and then turn R in front of the seminary, passing between it and the **church of Santiago** (R). KSO down the **Calle Mayor** until you get to the old bridge over the **Arga**. Cross it and turn L on to road. Cross main road (near modern bridge) and fork L onto minor road, // to main road. When this veers R, back towards the main road, at large wayside cross (picnic area, fountain), fork L onto UMUR, which then becomes a cart track, running // to the river. Continue along it for 1.5km and then, when you see a modern (water or electricity) tower across on the other side of the river to your L, you will see a turning off to your R onto a wide track. Take it, go uphill, forking L shortly afterwards to a ravine and then follow it (now a FP) uphill again, turning R after a flight of steps onto a wide earth track leading steeply uphill. Pass site of former thirteenth-century **Monasterio de Bargota** (fountain, picnic area and orientation plan on main road above you to R) and continue on UMUR // to road until you enter village of

4km Mañeru (832/663)

Note medieval crucero *(wayside cross) at entrance, moved when the road was widened.*

Fork L down road (marked "Yesos Pamplona", leading to gypsum factory to L) and continue downhill, fork R over bridge, cross trangular "square" and continue ahead along the **Calle de la Esperanza** into the **Plaza de los Fueros** (and the Casa Consistorial; note houses with *blazones*). Turn L at end then R to continue on **Calle Forzosa/Camino de Santiago** and continue through fields. (View of Ermita de Aniz on the hillside above you to the R.) Pass cemetery (on your L). KSO(R) when track joins from back L shortly afterwards. Continue on this, forking L at fork and then turn L at "T" junction and R immediately afterwards onto FP between hedges, walls and fields leading to hilltop village of

3km Cirauqui 498m (835/660)
Shop, bar, fountain in public garden. (Bar 100m to R on main road.)

Very well-restored ancient village with Gothic church of San Roman. The route through Cirauqui is a bit complicated with all the turns indicated by the yellow arrows but, basically, you go round the base of the village in a clockwise direction and then continue the straight line you started on entering.

On entering village continue ahead between houses, turn R and then L up steps and continue ahead (staggered junction) up unnamed street ahead under arch in tower and up to top of street (steep). Turn L at top into the **Plaza** and go *under* arch ahead (with stone seats, a nice cool place to sit/rest) and out the other side, turn L downhill and then R down **Calle del Mediodia**, 2nd L downhill, veering R to join road coming from back L. This becomes a track. Follow it (tree-lined) downhill onto old paved Roman road which leads you over the river on the old bridge and continue till you reach the main road again, at a roundabout/turning area.

Cross the road and turn L a few yards later onto earth road which continues // to main road below to your L. Follow it as it undulates through fields, passing bridge on site of Gothic bridge and medieval route on line of Roman road.

After reaching the brow of a hill (view to main road ahead) turn R down FP by HT pylon, downhill, veering L alongside edges of fields. Continue on this to junction with minor road to your R marked "Monasterio de Alloz" and "Embalse de Alloz" (a reservoir). Turn R on road, follow it under modern aqueduct and after houses on L turn L through two green gates onto a path which goes over an old bridge.

This crosses the river Salado ("Salt River"), one of the many rivers that Aimery Picaud warned pilgrims neither to drink themselves nor allow their horses to, or they would die immediately. He also relates how he saw two Navarrese sitting there, sharpening their knives in preparation for flaying any pilgrim's horses who had the misfortune (as did his own) to drink there.

Follow the path from the bridge and it will lead you *under* the modern road. On the other side turn R up an old road and follow it to village of

7km Lorca 483m (842/653)

Bar (unmarked, w/ends only), fountain, rooms.

Go through village past church (on your R) and down main street to road. Continue along it to top of hill and then turn L and then R along path alongside cornfields and / / to road. Follow track to village of

4.5km Villatuerta (846.5/648.5)

Cross old bridge and veer round to L uphill to church (good place for a rest, good view; fountain with drinking water *behind* church). Continue in front of church, veering R. At road fork R and join main road 50m later (opposite the Ega Pan bread and cake factory). Turn L along it (2 bars 30m to R next to car wash) and 20m later cross over main road and go up lane at RH side of first house to L of bread factory. Veer L behind it and go uphill under electric cables.

Follow this path uphill past farm building and fields and as it starts to descend turn R along a FP on an embankment above an olive plantation (partial view of Estella ahead). KSO, veering L all the time, round and above fields. On level with allotments FP becomes a green lane: KSO downhill, surface becomes concrete, winding its way up and down alongside high wall/embankment (welcome seat to R at top of hill by junction) descending to join minor road. Enter Estella on main road at bend in river Ega. [RJ: turn L up road marked to "Servicio Provincial de Incendios" (fire station).]

4.5km Estella (Lizarra) 426m (851/644)

Population 13,000. All facilities. Hotels, buses to Pamplona, Puente La Reina, Logroño. Tourist Office: Calle San Nicolás 3.

Estella (Lizarra in Basque) is the end of the third stage of the camino in *Aimery Picaud's guide and contains several interesting Romanesque churches: San Pedro de la Rua, with very fine cloisters, San Miguel (now restored), San Juan Bautista, Santa María Jesús del Castillo, San Sepulcro. The Palacio de los Reyes de Navarra is a rare example of a secular Romanesque building, with some well-known capitals, including Roland and the Moorish giant Ferragut.*

The yellow arrows through Estella are very confusing as they take you on (more than one) tour of the town's main "sights". It is suggested that you obtain a walking tour leaflet from the Tourist Office to visit its many places of interest and proceed as follows to enter the town and then continue your journey.

Turn R along main road but on entering the town do *not* follow "centre city" traffic signs over road bridge over river but fork R, past sign "Estella" in tiles on a building in front of you and then turn L over a (very) steep humpback bridge. Turn R on the other side to the **Plaza San Martín** *(fountain).*

To leave Estella carry straight on along **Calle San Nicolás** (ie. behind Palacio). KSO and pass under archway at end of street to a road junction (church on your L). KSO on this (main) road, which divides after 300m. Cross over to the RH side and take the R fork, up an UMUR next to a petrol station and go up hill behind large hypermarket. Bear R at a factory and KSO to village of

1km Ayegui (852/643)

Just *before* you reach a square (**Plaza San Pelayo**, houses, flats) at the very top you can *either* a) turn L for the **Monastery of Irache** (visible ahead) *or* b) turn R to miss it. Both *caminos* join up again after the Hotel Irache (ahead on the main road).

a) Turn L in square and then R downhill to road. Cross it and veer L up lane to twelfth-century church and **Monastery of Irache** (500m).

This was one of the first Benedictine houses in Navarra (it can be visited). It had a pilgrim hospice attached to it which was famous all along the pilgrim route. Fountain and shady picnic area, Museo del Vino.

Opposite the monastery an enterprising bodega (vintner) has installed a Fuente del Vino (wine fountain), two taps with red wine, one with water, with instructions not to abuse the facility, offering pilgrims the opportunity to drink a glass and thus fortify themselves for the journey ahead. (Caution on hot days ...) The message reads: ¡Peregrino! Si quieres llegar a Santiago con fuerza y vitalidad, de este gran vino echa un trago y brinda por la Felicidad.

KSO ahead up lane. 150m later, at houses, you again have a choice:

i) KSO ahead. This path (waymarked but not described here) continues through the countryside to the LH side of the main road, via **Luguin**, rejoining the other further on in the village of **Urbiola**.

ii) turn R alongside houses to road opposite hotel. Cross over and behind hotel rejoin option b).

b) At the square (flats, houses) KSO ahead down very clear track (you can see it laid out well ahead of you) which brings you out by the **Hotel Irache** on the main road. After the hotel (ie. with road to your L), by a complex of chalets, veer R along earth road, cross another and continue ahead to go through tunnel under the road.

This next section is fairly shady and takes you along a gated track through undulating woodland (conical mountain visible ahead).

KSO on clear track, ignoring turns.

When you reach a minor road (at gates) cross it and fork L off road on other side, veering R on FP under trees. At end of woods (gate) FP continues through fields. Join a wide track coming from R and continue to village (visible ahead), entering by big white house to R of church.

5km Azqueta (857/638)
Continue through village on road (*fountain* and seats on RH side) to junction with main road near tunnel (to back L). Fork R downhill to farm and turn L uphill behind last building onto earth track uphill through fields, later becoming a FP. When you emerge into a field of vines (and tip of Villamayor church spire is visible ahead) veer R along side of the field, uphill, turning L 100m later along field track, emerging from field to your R. Pass a restored building that looks like a double-arched church doorway but is in fact a medieval fountain and continue to village of

2km Villamayor (859/636)
Continue to church (Romanesque) and turn L downhill, cutting down path to cut out zigzags. KSO a short distance and then turn R along a clear UMUR leaving the one you are on (and which leads down to the main road ahead) at right angles.

The walking in the section between Villamayor and Los Arcos is easy (though watch out carefully for waymarks) and very pleasant in either very early morning or late evening light (though give yourself enough time to reach Los Arcos). There are no villages except Urbiola, no shade, no roads and almost no buildings at all along the way; woods over to the L and, later, large rock formations ahead to R.

Turn L between two groves of trees, uphill, and continue diagonally through field. Turn R at top on lane by houses, veering L to road at village of

2km Urbiola (861/634)

Fountain by church, bar (not always open) 200m back at crossroads to L.

Cross over and fork L down concrete road and fork R down earth lane by cemetery (on hill).

(Luquin, the end of the LH variant from Irache, is 500m away on other side of main road, and the two join up here.)

KSO, rejoining road by small white house on L. Turn L on UMUR and KSO, ignoring turns (1st L leads to main road), 2nd R, uphill by 2 buildings on hillside signposted "P. Cazadores". Take *third* turning (a short-cut) onto earth road just before ruined building (a former chapel?) on small hilltop to R, returning to UMUR after 200m. 150m later, at top of hill, turn L down earth road (marker stone tells you there are 5km left to Los Arcos...) towards range of small hills which then turns R 100m later.

After 1.5km turn L onto track joining from R, just before a ruined chapel on a hill in front of you. 1km later KSO(L) along track coming from back R. KSO, ignoring turnings, to Los Arcos (visible only 1.5km beforehand).

10km Los Arcos 447m (871/624)

Population 1500. 2 hostales (one with bar), shop, bank, bars, bar/ restaurant, pharmacy. Refugio in old school on R after crossing bridge outside town walls. Buses to Estella, Pamplona and Logroño. Fountain.

Now only a small town with an arcaded square but formerly very much larger. Church of Santa María with Gothic cloister and interesting choir stalls in flamboyant Gothic interior. Several houses with armorial devices on facades in the long Calle Mayor.

Enter the town from the north past farm buildings. Turn L at fork and go down the full length of the **Calle Mayor** till you reach a small triangular "square" at the bottom. Turn R to **church** *(fountain)*. KSO (church on L) through archway ahead, cross road and then bridge over river **Odrón**, past public library (R). KSO taking R fork uphill past cemetery (R), **Capilla de San Blas** (L), electricity substation (L) into open countryside.

From here you will be going more or less // to the road and on a clear, non-hazy day you will have a good view of Sansol 6km away in the distance. There is very little shade at all in this section but the walking is easy, through fields and vineyards, and is well waymarked.

Ignore turn to L, KSO and then turn R (just after the track goes into a dip) alongside a banked-up field. Carry on along the bank between 2 fields and when you meet another track crossing diagonally KSO (ie. R fork). KSO along this track, gently downhill into fields. After 1km it is joined by another coming from the R. KSO. Cross a bridge over stream and KSO. When you reach a minor road turn L and follow it into village of

6km Sansol 505m (877/618)

Small hilltop village with very few modern buildings. Food shop inside another one marked "tabac" in main square.

This village gets its name from San Zoilo, the patron saint of its church, worth a visit, if it is open, for its frescoes of the Ascension and Gothic statue of San Pedro. Very good "aerial view" of Torres del Rio from the forecourt in front of the church (and from where you can also see the path you will take to reach it).

At entry to village turn R into **Calle Mayor**, L into **Calle Real**, R into next street (uphill), next L, next R, next L and you will come out on the road again. Cross it (N111, KM68, view of Torres del Rio below you now, on a hill top across the river Liñares), turn L and then R down FP at side of house and go down to minor road below. Cross over road by bridge, turn R and then turn L down FP to cross bridge over stream *(fountain/lavadero on L)* and go uphill into village of

1km Torres del Río (878/617)

Another small village with very few modern buildings. Twelfth-century octagonal Romanesque church of Santo Sepulcro showing influence of Byzantine and Hispano-Arabic style (ask for key to visit). Fountain near 2nd church.

To continue, fork L at church. Follow road to L then R uphill out of village through orchards, past cemetery (L) to open fields.

This section climbs up and down quite a lot, playing "hide and seek" to avoid the very many hairpins bends in the main road and thus goes in a fairly straight line, though constantly up and down. (Not recommended for cyclists.)

After 1km descend to crossing with another track. KSO (olive groves on R) and pass below the bend in one of the road's many hairpins. Follow track down, then up, fork R to join road at a bend. Continue below road to L on FP, then above it, for 300/400m and you can then either:

a) follow yellow arrows and stay on road;

b) avoid a stretch on the road by turning R and then up along a bank on its RH side, // to road. Pass through and then above a fir plantation.

Both paths meet up again at the **Sanctuario de Nuestra Señora del Poyo** on RH side of road. Shortly further on is an *ermita* (near Bargota). Panoramic views from here, picnic area.

Turn down to road until next bend (N111 KM72), cross to other side and at end of crash barrier, turn R off road up lane and then L after 20m up small path, following its zigzags to the top of the hill. (You can see Sansol behind you, three trees on hill to R.) Go along lane past building (L) and join road again after 200m. Turn L and after 20m turn R along UMUR, taking R fork (it divides almost immediately). From here you can see both Viana and Logroño away in the distance below you.

Continue along path, KSO at next fork and follow path as it zigzags down to valley floor, watching out for the waymarks (*balises*, *flechas* and yellow tape) as you go, in a general diagonal direction towards Viana. At the bottom, cross through an olive grove, go up the slope on the other side, turn L onto a track coming from the R. Continue downhill (track joins from R after approx. 200m). Fork L at bottom, then R after 100m near small white house. 200m later turn L along track coming from the R. (You can see the road over to your L, more or less // here.) When you reach a wood, bear L diagonally uphill (wood on your R). KSO at top past farm building (L) to road; this is **Cornara**, the site of a Roman settlement and inhabited until the fourteenth century. Cross it and turn L into grassy lane. (Here you are aiming for a future bend in the road near the electric pylons / cables at the top of the hill.) Follow path straight up hill (watching out for waymarks) and join road again near (but not going under) cables. Turn L along road. After 100m turn L off road (ie. road bends to R but you continue more or less in a straight line) along grassy track. KSO. Cross another track and KSO till you rejoin road. Continue on road for 1km, continue on FP / / to it for last 500m and enter Viana opposite huge grain silo and by town placename boards.

9km Viana (887/608)
Population 3500. All facilities.

   Attractive small town with cobbled streets and a long association with pilgrims (there were formerly four hospitals). Church of Santa María (almost as grand as a cathedral), fifteenth and sixteenth-century, mixture of styles, with the tomb of Cesar Borgia under the street in front of it. Numerous houses with armorial devices on their facades. The Parque San Pedro (behind remains of church of that name, refugio next to it) on part of the old town walls is a good place for a rest, with excellent views.

   Leave Viana from the **Plaza** in front of the church by the **Calle Navarro Villoslado**. Turn R in front of the ruined church of **San Pedro** (facade interesting), R diagonally then L (**Calle San Felices**) under arch. R again (same street name) to the road. Cross it and take the 2nd turn L (down street behind some seats) and zigzag R to **Calle El Rancho**. At the bottom cross the road and turn R by a large school, along a track which veers L past the school's sports ground. Continue alongside a long brick wall (R) and R again. ie. going around the boundary of a smallholding. Cross stream when you reach it and continue L along lane (100m) to a road. Cross it and KSO under electric cables to farm (R). Turn L at side of dog-kennel (occupied!) with waymark on it and veer R downhill under embankment to lane coming from L. Take *2nd* fork R and KSO (L at next fork) until you get to another road. Cross it, take lane opposite and fork R immediately. After a few hundred metres turn L onto wide UMUR signposted "Virgen de Cievas". (From here Logroño is visible ahead.)

   Ignore next two L turns and veer R below fields until you reach the **Virgen de Cuevas** (once a chapel, now a private house, by a stream, a shaded area with a lot of trees and picnic area). Good view

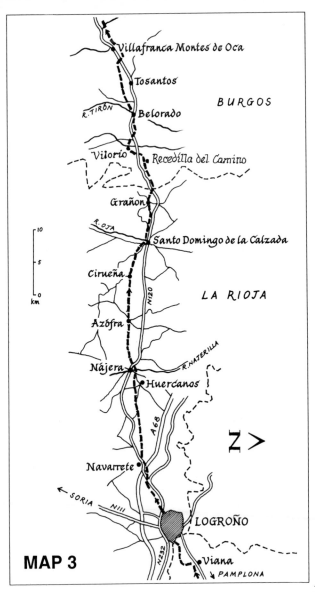

MAP 3

143

back over to Viana.

20m later UMUR forks into 3 - take centre path and then fork R 100m later past farm. After 1km you will see a wood ahead of you near a road; the path leads you to the road which you then cross and continue on a FP under trees on the other side, / / to the road. The path eventually takes you back to the road, near a paper packaging factory; cross bridge over a stream (petrol station on L) and leave the province of Navarra to enter **La Rioja**.

Walk along hard shoulder and then on the FP on RH side of road marked "Logroño norte" and at N111 K337 (post) cross to LH side of road. Turn left off it after 10m onto UMUR.

(This is indicated by the first of the many special "Camino" signs you will see, metal noticeboards depicting a pilgrim with staff and hat in "pinman" format.) Shortly further on (10m) you will also see the first of another type of marker - a concrete stèle, a little larger than a traditional milestone, with a scallop shell embossed on it. The red and white balises of the French GR system, used simultaneously with the yellow arrows, stop at Logroño for the moment.

KSO along this UMUR, slightly uphill for most of the way, across a road, through fields and vines. (The town of Oyon is visible

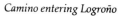

Camino entering Logroño

away to the R on the other side of the road.)

After 2km the UMUR descends downhill into Logroño, past a warehouse (R) and a few small houses to L and R. At the bottom you reach the main road into the town alongside the river **Ebro**, passing the cemetery to your R. Cross over, take path behind flats, // to river, return to road, then cross the stone bridge L over the river into

10km Logroño (897/598)

Population 120,000. Large bustling city with all facilities. RENFE. Buses to Pampelona, Burgos, Madrid. Tourist Office: Calle Miguel Villanueva 10.

Cathedral of Santa María Redonda, with a carving of St. James in the choir stalls. Churches of Santiago, San Bartolomé (interesting portal) and Santa María de Palacio. Logroño is a large town today but it owes its development to the pilgrim route and the old quarter of the town is laid out along the line of the camino.

On the other side of the bridge take the 2nd turn R down the **Calle de la Rua Vieja** (*refugio* on L halfway along), through the old quarter of the town, as its name suggests. At the end, continue along the **Calle de Barriocepa** to the **Fuente de los Peregrinos** in the **Plaza Santiago** (with its modern checkerboard paving depicting sites along the route to Santiago on both the *caminos aragonés* and *francés*) and then to the **church of Santiago** with its massive equestrian statue of Santiago Matamoros, St. James the slayer of Moors, above the south door. (This is best viewed from a distance, down the Calle de Santiago opposite.)

Continue along the **Calle de Barriocepa** to the end, where it bends round to the L, turn R, R again and then L under an arch in the old town walls. On the other side turn L and then immediately R (**Calle de los Depositos**) past a roundabout with fountains (and tap) to your L. (Well waymarked.) Cross a road L and then turn R down **Calle del Marques de Murieta**. Continue down this road for some time, past the barracks of the Guardia Civil. After crossing the railway line the road changes its name to **Avenida de Burgos**.

About 500m after this fork L (**Calle Entrena**) behind a petrol station into an industrial estate. Turn L at end, then R between two factories. Veer L diagonally and cross **Calle Prado Viejo**. KSO on other side up tarred lane which becomes UMUR, leading to dual carriageway after 300m.

Logroño. Church of Santiago el Real with equestrian statue of Santiago Matamoros

Cross (very carefully) and turn R // to road onto track and veer L to fork R along gravel *camino* (ie. not L to factory), lined at intervals with newly planted trees. This is easy to follow and leads, after 1.5km, to some woods and a tarred road just before the Pantano de la Gragera (a reservoir). Continue ahead (L) and then turn R along the wall of the dam. Cross a bridge at the end and turn L under trees to cross FB over stream.

Veer R to pass behind bar and picnic area and then veer L along stony *camino* which leads you around the lake (though not along the water's edge). After passing behind the radio/TV mast turn

146

R at UMUR to cross irrigation channel and 30m later turn L onto tarred lane which becomes UMUR. This veers round to L in a loop (KSO(R) at fork) uphill before returning you to the main road (view of lake and Logroño to rear) at the turn-off to Navarrete after passing *behind* the petrol station and in front of a timber yard. (If raining continue on road as next section may be flooded.)

Take L fork at junction (N120) towards Navarrete (up on hill ahead of you). After 200m cross road and fork R down a UMUR through vines, fields and over the motorway. To the L are the restored ruins of the old Hospital of the Order of San Juan de Acre, founded in 1185 to look after pilgrims. Follow the track down to a farm immediately below another road. Turn L diagonally up some steps to this road, cross it and follow the street into the village of

10km Navarrete (909/586)
Population 1500. Shops, bars, restaurant, bank. Several fountains. Campsite, fonda.

Navarrete has two "Calles Mayor", alta and baja (both under restoration), arcaded and lined with casas blasonadas, houses with heraldic devices on their facades. The town also has several alfarerías, pottery factories and workshops producing goods in the dark red clay seen everywhere in the landscape in this region. Monumental sixteenth-century church with a magnificent seventeenth-century Baroque reredos, gilded from floor to ceiling and wall-to-wall.

To visit Navarrete: turn R up street in front of church and then either: a) follow yellow arrows along 1st street on L (**Calle Nueva**, roofed-in tunnel effect in first part); b) follow yellow arrows along 2nd street on L (**Calle Mayor Alta**). For a) turn R at end to join option b), at the end of which turn L at end of **Calle Mayor** into the **Calle de Santiago** (which becomes the **Calle San Antonio** after some traffic lights). Turn L down the **Calle Arrabal** and KSO when it is joined by a road coming from the L (it now becomes the **Calle San Roque**). Continue to a "stop" sign and then along the main road (ie. straight on). KSO past the cemetery.

This has twelfth-century gates from the former Hospital at the entrance to the village, installed there when the cemetery was established in 1875. Outside it there is a monument to a Belgian woman, Alice de Craemer, who was killed while riding a tandem to Santiago in 1986.

Continue on the main road for 5km, watching carefully for the traffic. Just before the KM16 marker post and a large road bridge ahead there is a turning to the L, waymarked with a pinman pilgrim sign. Turn L along it then R down a lane that follows // to road. Cross a minor road leading from main road to Ventosa and KSO.

[However, to avoid the constant stream of juggernauts, cattle trucks, car transporters, ready-mix concrete lorries, huge vehicles laden with timber, clay, animals, etc, as well as cars and buses doing 100km/h an alternative is available by turning L 1km approx. after passing the cemetery down a road marked "Sotés 3" and "Hornos 3". If you follow this to the village of Sotés and then on to Ventosa you can join the camino at the main road mentioned above, turning L. It is not waymarked but is easy to follow and although it is a couple of km longer is preferable to all the traffic on the busy main road.]

KSO through fields. 200m after hut (L) - handy if raining - track forks R, more steeply up hill, then forks R after 50m, up a grassy lane. Follow this uphill, then downhill, through vines, past a farm at

5km Alto de San Antón (914/581)
Ruins of a convent with pilgrim hospital.

Camino meets the main road at a lay-by on a bend. (This is 2km after leaving the main road at KM16.) Turn L, then R to cross road, go through gap in crash barrier, down steps in the embankment and turn L on to track at the bottom. Follow this for 3-4km, through fields, more or less // to the main road all the time. Panoramic views.

Ignore all turnings to L and after passing a stone hut (L) the track veers round to the R of a round hill (L).

This is the Poyo Roldán, where Roland is reputed to have slain the Syrian giant Ferragut with a huge stone, in the same way that David killed Goliath (from whom the giant is said to have been descended).

When you eventually reach the road at the cement/gravel works turn R and then L after 30m down a UMUR. Veer R past a mountain of sand/gravel and then cross FB over the **Río Yalde** (there is another memorial to Alice de Craemer here too). Turn R after FB. Path veers slightly L. KSO along cart track between vines.

After 1km you reach a huge factory (with a long pilgrim poem painted on its wall, in Castilian with a German translation):

Polvo, barro, sol y lluvia
es Camino de Santiago.
Milláres de peregrinos
y más de millar de años.

Dust, mud, sun and rain
is the road to Santiago.
Thousands of pilgrims
and over a thousand years.

Peregrino, ¿quién te llama?
¿Qué fuerza oculta te atrae?
Ni el Campo de las Estrellas
ni las grandes catedrales.

Pilgrim, who calls you?
What hidden force draws you?
Neither the Field of Stars
nor the great cathedrals.

No es la brava navarra
ni el vino de los riojanos
ni los mariscos gallegos
ni los campos castellanos.

It's not sturdy Navarre
nor the wine from La Rioja
nor Galician seafood
nor the fields of Castille.

Peregrino, ¿quién te llama?
¿Qué fuerza oculta te atrae?
Ni las gentes del camino
ni las costumbres rurales.

Pilgrim, who calls you?
What hidden force draws you?
Neither the people along the way
nor country customs.

No es la história y la cultura
ni el gallo de la Calzada

It's not history and culture
nor the cockerel in Santo
    Domingo de la Calzada

ni el palacio de Gaudí
ni el castillo de Ponferrada.

nor Gaudí's palace
nor the castle in Ponferrada.

Todo lo veo al pasar
y es gozo verlo todo
mas la voz que a mi me llama
la siento mucho más hondo.

I see it all as I pass along
and it is a joy to see,
but the voice that calls me,
I feel more deeply still.

La fuerza que a mi me empuja
La fuerza que a mi me atrae
no se explicarla ni yo.
Sólo el de Arriba lo sabe!

The force that drives me
The force that draws me
I am unable to explain.
Only He Above knows!

E.G.B. [trans. AR]

Cross canal behind it (**Canal Najerilla**) and KSO 400m to minor road. Cross it and KSO along cart track until you come to a housing estate, passing a new sports centre (R) and blocks of flats. KSO into street (bar and shop on R) and continue into the centre of town, the road (**Avenida de Logroño**) veering to the R (and becoming the **Calle San Fernando**) as it nears the **Río Najerilla** in

10km Nájera (924/571)

Population 7000. All facilities.

End of the fourth stage of the camino *in Aimery Picaud's guide. The town takes its name from the Arabic "place between rocks", a name which will become more obvious as you leave the town along a track which wends its way uphill between high cliffs on either side. Monastery of Santa María la Real, containing royal pantheon and interesting choir stalls with pilgrim scenes and cloisters. Church of San Miguel (Antigua), Convento de Santa Elena, Church of Santa Cruz. The present bridge (1886) over the river Najerilla replaces the twelfth-century bridge with seven arches built by San Juan de Ortega.*

On the other side of the river *either* follow the yellow arrows and turn R and then L, following the signs for the monastery *or*, a shorter, more direct way, turn L immediately after the bridge down the **Calle Mayor** (pedestrianised) to the end, into the **Plaza España** and turn R to the church of **Santa María** (set into cliff at rear).

Pass in front of the main entrance (the **Calle Costanilla**) and KSO uphill. Continue on when road becomes a track, trees and woods to either side, up hill and then down (path is in a ravine here). Keep L at fork. KSO past farm (L), cross bridge and KSO ahead. At fork bear R. KSO. When track crosses another KSO along grassy track. When this eventually reaches a minor road [near tree, for RJ] turn L and continue along it for 1.5km to

7km Azófra 559m (931/564)

Village with 2 bars, shop, fountain in main square.

Church of Nuestra Señora de los Angeles with sculptures of St. Martin of Tours and Santiago as a pilgrim, with staff, cape and hat. Just outside the village on the R is the Fuente de los Romeros, near the site of a twelfth-century pilgrim hospital with adjoining cemetery.

KSO down main street and continue to end of village. Turn R along main road for 50m then L along a farm road (UMUR).

Ignore turns to L or R and KSO. After 1km pass a *rollo* (R), a medieval pilgrim cross. KSO. Turn R into UMUR and then L after 20m. Cross a minor road leading to San Millán de Cogilla and KSO, forking L after 10m. Turn L at next junction. KSO.

[The monasteries of San Millán de Cogilla - National Monuments - are definitely worth a visit but are situated 15km off the route to the south. The upper one, Suso, is Visigothic and contains the remains of San Millán, patron saint and protector of Castille. It dates from c.1000. The monumental lower monastery Yuso (it can only be visited on a guided tour) is mainly sixteenth to eighteenth-century. Both are closed on Mondays. There is no accommodation at San Millán but there is a fonda 5km away at Badarán, on the way back to the camino].

The original camino ran in a straight line from Nájera to Santo Domingo de la Calzada but today it is interrupted in three places by changes in land ownership. To avoid a long stretch on the main road an alternative route has now been waymarked, if somewhat sparsely, and is easy to follow. It is slightly longer but has splendid views, taking you through undulating fields to the L of the village of Ciriñuela, passing by the edge of Cirueña.

When you come to another junction, in fact a diagonal crossroads, KSO. Continue for several km. After climbing the route flattens out (village of Ciriñuela plus church and cemetery over to R) and village of **Cirueña** visible ahead. KSO till you come to it, turn R down road and then L after 300m on to a farm road between fields. Ignore any turns to L or R and continue for 3km to

16km Santo Domingo de la Calzada (947/548)

Population 5000. All facilities.

The town takes its name from Santo Domingo (1019-1109). Originally a shepherd, he wanted to enter the monastery of San Millán de Cogilla but was refused admission because he was illiterate. He then built himself a hermitage and chapel in a forest in a notoriously bandit-infested stretch of the camino between Logroño and Burgos and began to look after the needs of pilgrims. He built a hospital (today converted into a Parador) and church in what became the present-day town, a causeway and bridge over the river Oja and devoted the rest of his life to road and bridge building. One of his disciples, San Juan de Ortega, continued his work.

The town contains several places of interest (Convento de San Francisco, Ermita de Nuestra Señora de la Plaza, Cistercian monastery, ramparts and

tower) but the most well known is the Cathedral, where Santo Domingo is buried. However, what is most likely to strike the visitor are its unusual occupants: a cock and a hen (both very much alive) in a cage high up inside the building, reminders of a miracle. A family of three pilgrims stayed in an inn in the town where the innkeeper's daughter is said to have made advances to the son, who refused the offer. In revenge she secretly placed a bag of money in his luggage and the following morning, after they had left, "discovered" that the money had gone missing. The innkeeper pursued the family, the son was brought before the judge and condemned to death. The parents continued their pilgrimage to Santiago, however, but on the return journey spent the night in Santo Domingo de la Calzada once again.

The mother was not convinced, in fact, that her son really was dead and went to the spot where he had been taken to be put to death and found him there alive, though still hanging. Accordingly the parents went to see the judge, to ask for their son to be released. Like his counterpart in the apochryphal account of the death of Judas Iscariot he too was sitting at dinner when the couple arrived and, likewise, refused to believe them. He declared that the boy was no more likely to be alive than were the cock and the hen on his table to get up and fly - which they immediately did, as proof of the son's innocence.

Enter town past farm/factory, continue along farm road when bends to R to join road. Turn L to crossroads (with *rollo*), cross over and take R fork past flats and then KSO down **Calle Mayor** (fountain). Pass cathedral and KSO. Turn L at end of Calle Mayor and then R into **Calle de los Palmarejos** and KSO when it continues as **Avenida de la Rioja**. Cross the bridge over the **Río Oja** (*ermita*, 1917, at entrance to bridge).

After crossing the bridge and causeway walk along the main road for 6km. Turn off it L uphill between KM49 and KM50 and then immediately R uphill into the village of

6km Grañón (953/536)

Shop, bar, pharmacy. Originally a walled town with two monasteries, a castle and a pilgrim hospital. Sixteenth-century Ermita de los Judíos.

Cross road on entering village, go up short flight of steps and walk along main street past church (L). Continue a little further and then turn R (waymarked). At first it may seem as though you are going back on yourself but you then turn L by a modern barn building onto a minor road. Follow road round a bend after 200m (ie. do *not* go straight on) to barn with yellow arrow on it. Cross bridge over river **Relachigo** and take 2nd L along farm road. Fork R after approx. 1km (village of **Recedilla del Camino** visible ahead) and follow track 1.5km to village. Just before you reach it turn R at farm to join road. Pass another *rollo* and fountain (R).

3.5km Recedilla del Camino (956.5/538.5)
Bar. Between Grañon and Recedilla you pass from La Rioja into the province of Burgos. Village with a long tradition of looking after pilgrims (there were several hospitals here), its single main street lined with houses bearing armorial devices. Church of the Virgen de la Calle contains Romanesque font.

Continue along main street at church (fountain) and public garden (fountain). KSO to end of village and join road again (KM55 on leaving village). Continue on main road, cross bridge over river **Relachilo** (carefully: bridge is on a sharp bend).

2km Castildelgado (958.5/536.5)
Petrol station, bar/restaurant El Caserio (has rooms), hostal restaurant El Chocolatería. Church.

KSO along main road. 2km later turn L up minor road to **Viloria de la Rioja** (where the *camino* does a "C" shaped "loop" to take you through the village which was the birthplace of Santo Domingo de la Calzada), before returning you to the main road again. KSO.

5.5km Villamayor del Río (964/531)
Bar/restaurant. Fountain. (Despite its name this is not a "big town on a river" but only a "small village by a stream").

KSO on main road until just after K64. Turn R off road by warehouse, down lane leading, after 1km, to church of **Santa María** in

6km Belorado (970/525)
Small town with all facilities, population 2000.

Churches of Santa María (sixteenth century, contains a Santiago chapel) and San Pedro (seventeenth century), used alternately, summer and winter.

To leave - turn L (church on R), L again, R to arcaded main square. Cross it in a straight line (trees, bandstand) and go down the **Calle José Antonio de Ribera**. Turn L. Then *either* turn L again, then

R to main road *or* KSO behind blocks of flats, joining road at a sawmill. Turn R and KSO.

Cross the river **Tirón**, pass petrol station (L) (after approx. 1km out of Belorado) and after 20m (*before* KM68) there is a turning to the L, down a minor road, signposted "San Miguel de Pedroso 3". Turn L here and then immediately R off it onto a track. Then, turn R again almost immediately and the lane you are on is now / / to main road and remains so, more or less, to Espinosa del Camino.

KSO, watching out carefully for waymarks. Cross a track and KSO along a grassy FP, joining a track from behind L and then another to side L. KSO and after 200m reach village of

3km Tosantos (973/522)
Bar 100m on main road. Cemetery uphill to L. Twelfth century Ermita Virgen de la Peña set into hillside on the R, on other side of main road.

Do not go as far as the main road but fork L uphill up a farm road. Follow this to the village of

2km Villambistia (975/520)
Fork R just before passing church (R). KSO, cross bridge over river, pass fountain (R) and chapel of **San Roque** and KSO (ie. do *not* follow road round to R). Village seems a bit run down. Main road is still away to the R, more or less / / to *camino.*

KSO until you reach the road. Turn L and 20m later turn R into a lane and into village of

1.5km Espinosa del Camino (976.5/518.5)
KSO past fountain (R). Follow road round to R and then turn L behind the last line of houses onto a farm road. KSO, ignoring next 3 turns to R. After you pass the **Abside de San Felices** (ruins of the medieval monastery of San Félix de Oca, R) a UMUR leads round to the L (view of Villafranca Montes de Oca ahead, with its large, prominent church).

Continue till you reach the road. Turn R onto it and follow it to the village of

4.5km Villafranca Montes de Oca (981/514)
Bar/restaurant El Pajero has rooms. Shop, pharmacy, panadería, fountain.

"Town of the Franks", like others along the camino, the village's name refers to the many Frankish settlers and traders who established themselves

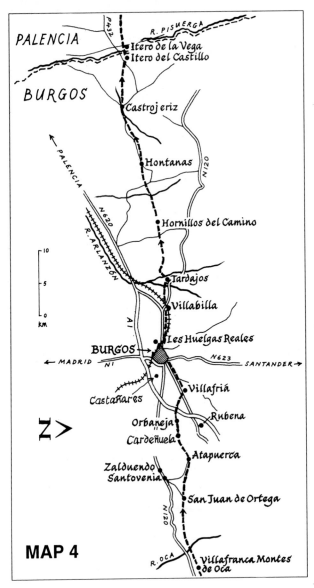

MAP 4

along the pilgrim route in the Middle Ages. Situated at the foot of the Montes de Oca it had its own bishop until 1075 and an important pilgrim hospice as early as 884. This was superseded in 1380 by the 36 bed Hospital de San Antonio Abad, at present under restoration as a refuge. The eighteenth-century parish church of Santiago replaces an earlier building and contains a statue of St. James.

Do not leave here late in the day and allow plenty of time. It is not difficult to find the way to San Juan de Ortega in good weather but it takes at least 3hrs and the route, at 1150m, is wooded and completely unpopulated. In this section the waymarks are the Council of Europe blue and yellow signs with the Milky Way logo.

Go along main street and turn off the the R up the side of the church (L), pass remains of **Hospital San Antonio** (R) and continue uphill beside modern (long) wall. Pass trees and join farm road from L. Turn R along it (level here and good views to rear on a clear day).

Fork R shortly afterwards top join another track coming from R (ie. a crossroads where, in fact, you KSO). KSO up hill and after 2km reach (signposted) the **Fuente de Mojapan** (literally "moisten bread", a common pilgrim resting place in former times in an area too dangerous to cross at night and in which wolves were an expected hazard).

After this the track enters the woods (semi-shaded) and veers to L. KSO, ignoring paths to L and R. Join forest road coming from L and KSO until you reach the memorial to those killed in the Civil War (R), the **Monumento de los Caidos**, (alt. 1163m). Descend steeply after this, cross the river **Peroja** and then climb up again.

(The path is in a dead straight line here, visible from the monument, // to main road and to main road being excavated between the two.)

Path veers L and shortly after this (near road) fork R. After approx. 500m the path emerges into a very wide forest track. Turn R onto it at MP57 (post). [RJ: waymarks and MP57 hidden by trees. Flashes/yellow paint on pile of stones at R. Turn L to small unmarked opening in embankment onto FP. This is approx. 100m after Council of Europe waymarking on R.]

At big crossing (MP61) and trig point type pillar KSO unless you want to visit the Fuente del Carnero, waymarked 200m to L.

(Signposted "fuente" in yellow.) This is at the side of the road, by the Ermita de Valdefuentes, all that remains of a former pilgrim hospital.

Camino in La Rioja

After 1km join road coming from L [RJ fork L]. 1km further on a similar track joins from behind R. A very large wooden cross has waymark on it. KSO.

After a further 2km the church of San Juan de Ortega ("St. John of the Nettles") is visible for a while in the distance through the trees to the L. Turn L at next fork. After 500m track opens out, goes downhill and 500m further on you reach the church of

13km San Juan de Ortega 1250m (994/501)
Small hamlet with the large pilgrim church of San Nicolás de Bari and monastery (recently restored), containing the elaborately decorated tomb of San Juan de Ortega. After his ordination the saint went on a pilgrimage to the Holy Land and on his return set up shelter for pilgrims in the notoriously dangerous and bandit-infested Montes de Oca. One of the most famous architects of his day, San Juan de Ortega constructed the Romanesque church in such a way that at 5 o'clock in the evening on the spring and autumn equinoxes (March 21st and September 22nd) - and only on those days - the rays of the setting sun light up the capital depicting the scene of the Annunciation. Instead of highlighting the angel Gabriel, as happens in most portrayals of this scene, it focuses instead on the Virgin Mary, thus transmitting the idea of fecundity and life. (The saint was also well known for his gift of making childless couples fertile.) Refugio. Fountain.

Continue past the church till you reach the road. Cross it and enter woods. *Very* large wooden cross (some 15-20ft high) and *cledo* shortly afterwards. KSO along forest road. Pass another large cross and another *cledo*. KSO. Road opens out, cross a ravine (path banked

157

up across it). KSO and fork towards R at 3rd large cross, descending towards village of

4km Agés (998/497)
Path joins main street. Follow this past fountain (R) and follow street through village. Continue on road to

2.5km Atapuerca (1000.5/494.5)
2 fountains, bar panadería. *Fortress-like church uphill on R. Archaeological excavations nearby have recently unearthed a spectacular "find" - the fossilised "Atapuerca man".*

Turn L just before bar (R), diagonally off road, and then turn R towards the TV antenna (watch out carefully for the waymarks). The path then divides and the LH option is described here. Fork L and follow track which veers L leading you into the village of

5.5km Cardeñuela (1006/489)
Bar.

Turn R along road, KSO through village and continue on road, ignoring turns to L and R to

2km Orbaneja (1008/487)
KSO. Cross motorway.

After this you have a choice between continuing to Villafría and then along the main road into Burgos (option A) or turning L and taking a slightly longer, no more "scenic" but quieter and a lot safer route to enter the town from the northeast instead, via the suburb of Castañares and the N120 (option B).

A. ROAD OPTION VIA VILLAFRIA
After crossing the motorway KSO on road for 2km till you reach the railway line (Madrid-Irún), / / to it. Follow road round (rubbish tip on L) to cross bridge over the railway. Then *either* follow road till it joins the N1 after 100m *or* turn R at bend in road immediately after bridge and go down lane to church of

4km Villafría (1012/483)
Now a suburb of Burgos. 2 bars near church (whose tower has a complex arrangement of "accommodation" for the storks), shop. Several bars on main road, hostal, *bar with rooms, restaurant. Frequent bus service to*

Burgos Monday to Saturday but none on Sundays.

Continue on N1 into Burgos - 7km of heavy lorries, fast cars, buses - the worst section of the whole *camino*. KSO along the main road towards the city centre. After 4-5km and a large crossing the road becomes the **Calle Vitoria**. When you get to another large junction (traffic divides R for Santander, centre for city and L to Madrid) you can *either* continue along the **Calle Vitoria** into the centre of Burgos *or* take a road // to it on the L, along the river and shaded, the **Avenida General Sanjurio**. This becomes the pedestrianised **Paseo de Espolón** in the city centre. Alternatively, if you have not yet picked up the yellow arrows again you can turn R at the large junction along the **Avenida del General Vigón** and then L along the **Calle de las Calzadas** to follow the waymarked route as described below under **Castañares**.

B. ALTERNATIVE ROUTE VIA CASTAÑARES

After crossing the motorway turn L 50-60m later down UMUR beside military barracks and then R (passing behind it) 30m later, continuing through fields, // to motorway on your L for a while.

This is an alternative to the traditional entry to Burgos along the N1, no more interesting but much quieter and far less dangerous. Watch out carefully for the waymarks, however, as, with nowhere else to put them, they are often on the ground. If you lose them you are heading, in general, towards two large factories on the skyline of chimneys ahead, one of them red and white and probably smoking, with the spire of Burgos cathedral behind them to their L.

[RJ: head for the TV antennae and the motorway all the time.]

Ignore R turn and KSO. Fields give way to waste ground. After approx. 1km cross another track and KSO ahead, keeping straight on after 2nd crossing a few yards later. Track then veers L towards Castañares (factories, water tower, suburb on the N120). Cross bridge over stream, go under HT cables and enter

3km Castañares
Fountain, 2 bar/restaurants on main road.

Turn R at fountain, // to main road, and then R again on track // to road (and beside it). Cross road carefully by bar/restaurant 20m later and go under road bridge (N111 Madrid-Bilbao road) after (also carefully!) crossing slip road (just after road KM107) and continue on hard shoulder.

200m later turn L and then R down track // to road towards a large block of flats, passing to the L of them (factory on your L) down ex-tarred road (the **Calle Mayor de Villayuda**) which becomes a residential street (*shop, bar*). At end KSO on UMUR alongside field (red and white chimney is now to your R), // to N120 all the time.

At last factory go under railway line, go up flight of steps, turn L and then immediately R down more steps behind block of flats (ie. to the L of it, the **Calle Villafranca**).

At the end of the street (*fountain, bar* and sports ground to R) KSO ahead down alley between walls and then L at end, then R down street with municipal sports centre on L. At end of street (**Plaza de Toros** on L, football stadium ahead) turn R, cross road and KSO ahead alongside to R of football ground (ie. a "staggered" turn).

Pass Red Cross HQ, park (L, *fountain*). The two *"caminos"* merge here, ie. the variant with the road route via Villafría.

Cross over and go down street (**Calle Maestro Justo del Río**) beside Guardia Civil barracks (R) and Hotel Puerta de Burgos (L). Cross waste ground ahead diagonally, cross **Avenida General Vigón** and continue ahead down **Calle de las Calzadas** to **Plaza San Juan** at end (Museo Municipal on L near end).

Cross road bridge over a river, go under arch and continue down **Calle San Juan**, cross **Avenida del Cid Campeador**, KSO on **Calle San Juan**, then **Calle de Avellanos** and **Calle Fernán González** to the cathedral.

7km Burgos 856m (1019/1476)

Population 170,000. All facilities. RENFE. Buses to Pamplona, Logroño, Madrid etc. Tourist Office in the Calle de San Carlos.

Capital of Castille and end of the fifth stage in Aymery Picaud's guide. A place to spend at least a whole day. Gothic cathedral with Santiago chapel, many other important buildings, including the Gothic church of San Nicolás and, just outside the town, the monastery of Las Huelgas with its church, very fine Romanesque cloisters, chapel of Santiago and museum and the Hospital del Rey for sick or tired pilgrims.

To leave Burgos *either*: turn L at the end of the **Calle Vitoria** to the **Paseo de Espolón** if you have not already done so and continue along the river on the **Avenida del Generalíssimo**, the **Paseo de la**

The cloisters of San Zoilo at Carrión de los Condes

The Canal de Castilla at Fromista
The Casa de Botines in León

Burgos. Arco de Santa María

Isla, the **Paseo Fuente** and cross the river by the **Puente Malatos** (the last one before the railway bridge).

Alternatively: from the cathedral (with the church of San Nicolas to your R) continue along **Calle Fernán González**, passing seminary (on your R), and go under archway at end. Turn L immediately down flight of steps, cross road and KSO ahead down **Calle del Emperador**, pass church of San Pedro de la Fuente (L, fountain) and turn L at the bottom into **Calle Vilalón**. Continue to end, bringing you to the river **Arlanzón**, and cross it by the **Puente Malatos**.

Turn R on the other side along the main road past the Hospital

161

del Rey (now restored as part of the University's Law Faculty). Weighbridge (*bascula municipal*).

After 3km, at traffic lights opposite the **Mesón Restaurante Bellavista**, the main road veers L. Fork R down a minor road (tree-lined). At the end (0.5km) KSO along a farm track (/ / to railway line to L) past fields, a tree plantation and more fields. KSO ignoring turns to L and R. After 3km reach

6km Villabilla de Burgos 837m (1025/470)
Church (L) on other side of railway line. Cross minor/branch line but *not* the main (Madrid-Irún) line. Fork R, passing to the L of a house in front of a flour factory (R). Follow the road round to the R, cross a bridge over a river and turn L on other side, past 2 bridges on to a farm road through fields. (Main road ahead to L.) KSO for 1km till you reach the road. Turn L along it, cross to other side, and cross bridge over the river **Arlanzón**.

After bridge fork L down a track / / to main road and continue on it until it joins the road at entry to

4km Tardajos 828m (1029/466)
Shops, bars, restaurant, fonda.

Pass *rollo* on L on entry. Fork L opposite bar down **Calle del Mediodía**. Turn R at end and then L on to a minor road. KSO to

1.5km Rabé de las Calzadas (1031.5/463.5)
Fountain.

KSO through village and turn R in a triangular "square". KSO. Fork R at modern chapel (L) by cemetery (L) then fork L 50m further on.

Track joins from R and the path levels out to a vast, seemingly endless plateau.

This is the meseta, *lush and green in spring, a dustbowl in summer. Depending on your preferences you will either find it extremely tedious or, if you like undulating expanses reaching out to infinity in all directions, hauntingly beautiful, especially in the early morning light. Although it is so far removed from the noise of "civilisation" it is, in fact, far from silent, as it now becomes obvious quite how much sound the wind, the insects, the birds and the grass actually make.*

500m further on path descends to a valley (approx. 1.5km to village ahead). Join UMUR coming from R. When you get to the road cross it and enter village of

8.5km Hornillos del Camino (1040/455)
Small village with a large Gothic church, formerly an important pilgrim halt with a hospital and a small Benedictine monastery.

Continue to the end of the village (no shops or bars) and turn R at the public weighbridge. Turn L after 1km and fork R (ie. keeping straight on) 500m further on. Fork R again after 10m, uphill all the time. Turn L at next junction.

At the top of the hill and beginning of the plateau cross a track and KSO.

Apart from electrity pylons in the distance to the L there is no sign of any sort of habitation at all in any direction, giving a feeling of being on the "roof of the world".

KSO at next 2 junctions (1st is a crossroads, 2nd a T junction to L).

Cross a UMUR and KSO. Shortly afterwards track descends to valley. Keep R at fork. Cross another UMUR (ruined houses to L and R) and KSO uphill again. Turn L at next fork (ie. straight on) and then the path levels out again. Nothing in sight for miles and miles around.

Cross a minor road and KSO (2 large clumps of trees away to R in distance). Cross grassy track and KSO. Cross another track and KSO again.

2km past the last minor road a valley suddenly appears on your R. KSO. 500m later another valley appears ahead and just after that another path joins from behind L. Then - all of a sudden - the church and village of **Hontanas** appears below you. Go down the path into the village, following the path to the R and then to the L down the main street. Fountain (L) and church (L)

11km Hontanas 870m (1051/444)
Pilgrim village (its name means "the fountains") dominated by its church.
   Fountain, bar (meals), swimming pool with bar (summer).

Continue past fountain (L), church (L), weighbridge (R) and swimming pool (R). When you get to the road the waymarks direct you to cross it and fork R (ie. to L before you've crossed over) along a track on the other side. However, although this takes you off the road, // to it, there is hardly any shade at all and you may prefer, instead, to stay on the road as it has very little traffic and is tree-lined almost all the way to Castrojeriz.

Otherwise, after crossing the road, turn L 300m further on, at a junction after three large trees. When you reach the ruins of the **Molino del Cubo** take the upper path (ie. keep your height) and KSO, uphill slightly, to the ruin of **San Miguel**. Pass below it. The track then descends to join another from the R. Fork L. 10m later a track joins from behind L - KSO (still / / to road). KSO at next fork. Track then veers L to join road. Follow it for 1km to the ruins of

5km Hospital San Antón (1056/)

Gothic hospital founded by the Antonins, the French order believed to possess powers of healing St. Anthony's Fire (a type of gangrene which appeared in Europe in the tenth century) and which pilgrims who have come along the route from Le Puy will already have encountered in the village of Saint Antoine. Pilgrims came here too in search of a cure and were sent on their way after a blessing with the "Tau" (T-shaped) cross. The remains of the hospital are on both sides of the road, which passes under an archway. Bread for pilgrims was placed in a niche to be seen on the left of the road.

Continue along tree-lined road (ruins of *alcázar* on hill above town visible ahead) to

3km Castrojeriz 800m (1059/436)

Population 1185. Shops, bars, restaurant, bank. Hostal, *campsite.*

Town built by the Romans and an important stoppng place for pilgrims in former times: there were still seven hospitals left at the beginning of the nineteenth century. Collegiate church of Nuestra Señora del Manzano (thirteenth and seventeenth centuries, with statue of St. James), church of San Juan (interesting cloister), church of San Domingo (with small museum).

Turn R at entrance to Castrojeriz to church of **Nuestra Señora del Manzano** (worth a visit) and then turn L through village (very long). To leave, pass church of **San Juan** (R) and go down to road. Veer L to crossroads. Turn L, cross road and after 50m turn L down a UMUR. After 1.5km cross bridge over **Río Odrilla** and shortly afterwards (house visible away to L), at staggered junction, KSO up path that winds its way, veering L, uphill to the top of the hill and the monument you can see on the skyline. You are back on the *meseta*

Colegiata de Nuestra Señora del Manzano

again (1km from bridge). At the top KSO (ie. don't turn L) towards iron crosses (waymarks).

KSO, following these waymarks (crosses with yellow plastic on them) and shortly afterwards, after approx. 500m you look down to a huge valley (bowl-like) below you. Panoramic views. From here the path leads more of less straight ahead to **Itero del Castillo** (though it doesn't actually go into the village).

Descend on track through fields for 1-2km. Cross a farm road and KSO. Fork L slightly downhill when track divides. Cross another farm road and KSO and approx. 1km afterwards join a minor road, going slightly uphill, at the **Fuente del Piojo** (fountain).

Turn R along road for 1km to crossroads. (Itero de la Vega visible ahead.) Turn L along road (ignore farm track back to L). Pass **Ermita San Nicolas** (L), which has now been converted into a *refugio* by the Italian association of the Friends of St. James and then cross bridge over **Río Pisuerga** - the boundary between the provinces of Burgos and Palencia. (The 65km stretch of the *camino* which passes through Palencia is particularly rich in historic monuments.) Fork R on other side of bridge down minor road for 1.5km to village of

10km Itero de la Vega (1069/426)

Shop. Thirteenth-century Ermita de la Piedad (with statue of St. James the Pilgrim) at entrance to village, sixteenth-century church of San Pedro.

KSO through village (**Calle Conde Vallellano, Calle Santa María**), cross end of main square (*fountain, rollo*). Continue straight on and then turn L down **Calle Marqués de Estrella**, following white arrows painted on road. Turn R into **Calle Comandante Ramirez**. Pass five large trees (L) (another *fountain*) and KSO to crossroads.

Cross road and continue along UMUR flanked by water channels on either side. Pass turning (L) to hamlet of Bodegas after 1km and KSO. Cross bridge over **Canal Pisuerga** and continue straight on to top of hill (three humps visible ahead on skyline). View of Boadilla del Camino (3km ahead) at the top.

Cross canal and turn R along bank. Then either follow street round to R to leave village or head for church to enter it. [RJ: fork R at *fountain*.]

8km Boadilla del Camino 782m (1077/418)

Bar/shop. Fifteenth-century rollo.

To leave continue past bar and then turn L alongside football ground (R) and L again past warehouse along UMUR. KSO. Go through a gap in the irrigation channels (raised up) and 200m further on fork R up a bank to join the towpath of the **Canal de Castilla**. KSO along it for 3km. Cross FB over the canal by a lock, veer R down a FP down a bank, go along a tree-lined path for 100m and turn R onto road. Follow it, veering L under railway bridge to crossroads (by Tourist Office). [RJ: follow signs for "Astadillo" to bend in road (to R) and then cross canal at FB.]

6km Fromista 780m (1083/412)

Population 1400. All facilities. RENFE.

End of the sixth stage in Aimery Picaud's guide. Small town with Romanesque church of San Martín, a National Monument, and one of the most well preserved of the whole *camino. It has 315 carved figures of animals, humans (some humorous), flowers, monsters etc. in a line round*

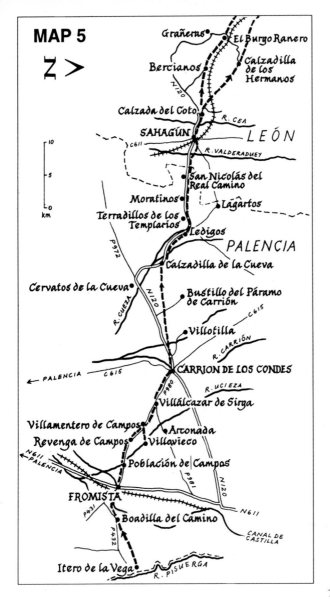

MAP 5

N >

Grañeras
El Burgo Ranero
Calzadilla de los Hermanos
Bercianos
Calzada del Coto
R. CEA
SAHAGÚN
LEÓN
C611
R. VALDERADUEY
San Nicolás del Real Camino
Moratinos
Lagartos
Terradillos de los Templarios
Ledigos
PALENCIA
Calzadilla de la Cueva
Cervatos de la Cueva
Bustillo del Páramo de Carrión
R. CUEZA
N120
P972
Villotilla
C615
R. CARRIÓN
PALENCIA
C615
CARRION DE LOS CONDES
P980
R. UCIEZA
Villálcazar de Sirga
Villamentero de Campos
Arconada
Revenga de Campos
Villavieco
N611
PALENCIA
Población de Campos
P981
N120
FROMISTA
N611
P431
Boadilla del Camino
CANAL DE CASTILLA
P432
Itero de la Vega
R. PISUERGA

10

5

0
km

167

the church under the eaves, all in perfect condition. Church of Santa María del Castillo (also a National Monument), erected on the site of an ancient fortress, has an altarpiece with 29 paintings. Fifteenth-century church of San Pedro, Ermita del Otero.

To leave - KSO along road to Carrión de los Condes (ie. cross road at crossroads by Tourist Office).

The new route now takes you alongside this road on a specially prepared senda de peregrino, *running parallel to it like a cycle track all the way to Carrión de los Condes, passing the entrances to Población de Campos and Villovieco, through Villarmentero de Campos and past the entrance to Villalcázar de Sirga.*

Alternatively, you can continue on the old route, turning R after 4km on the road into

4km Población de Campos 790m (1087/408)

2 bars, shop (unmarked), very small refugio.

Small village with the remains of a former pilgrim hospital, Thirteenth-century Ermita del Socorro. Ermita de San Miguel, seventeenth-century church of the Magdelena, Fuente San Miguel L near cemetery.

Fork R up concrete road (**Paseo del Cementerio**) to visit village, aiming for church. At junction behind church take minor road ahead with raised irrigation channel down LH side. Otherwise, turn L past village, join above road and turn L.

KSO. After 3km pass a fountain on RH side, built in 1989, with a wayside cross, shell and red/white cross motif. KSO to

3km Villavieco 790m (1090/405)

Turn L over bridge over the river **Ucieza** and then immediately R along its bank and KSO. Follow the bank for 5km, as far as the **Ermita de la Virgen del Río** (contains alabaster statue of St. James the pilgrim).

Sometimes it is necessary to cross small irrigation channels running at right angles to the river - some have stepping stones - and then go back onto the path again. The last km is fairly shady.

Turn L along the road when you reach the *ermita* (a large building, similar to a church but now a private house) which is near a bridge. Then pass the **Ermita del Cristo de la Salud** (small - still in use) (L) and after 1km enter

6km Villálcazar de Sirga 809m (1096/)

Bar/shop, 2 mesóns, fountain in public garden.

Also known as "Villasirga". The village is dominated by the thirteenth-century church of Santa María la Blanca, a National Monument, with very fine portals, chapel of Santiago with tombs and statues, including one of St. James, all in a very fine state of preservation and well worth a visit.

Turn R to enter village. Otherwise KSO to main road. Turn R and continue along it, with cornfields to both sides in an undulating landscape.

This road is not usually too busy but there is no shade at all. Bodegas in fields to side of road.

6km Carrión de los Condes 840m (1102/393)

Population 2800. All facilities. Campsite near river. Churches of Santa María del Camino (or de la Victoria), Santiago (splendid portal, church burnt in 1809 War of Independence), Monastery of San Zoilo (National Monument) with sixteenth-century cloisters, Convento de Santa Clara and museum.

To enter town - turn L off road at flour factory. To leave - continue past square and church of **Santa María** and turn R. Pass in front of **church of Santiago** and veer L to cross the river **Carrión** by the main bridge.

Pass in front of the **Monastery of San Zoilo** (L) and come to a large crossroads 300m later. KSO for 300m further, past a petrol station, to another crossroads where the N120 veers L. KSO along a minor road which is signposted to "Villotilla 6". KSO for 4km.

Pass the **Abadía de Benvívere** (R), former abbey but now a private house, just before a sharp bend in the road where a bridge crosses a small river. 300m after the bridge there is a junction with a minor road: cross it and KSO along a farm road (scallop shell waymark) through cornfields. The landscape is flat in all directions.

KSO for 2.5km to plantation of *chopos* (poplars, R) and road. Cross it, KSO for 6km, ignoring turnings to L and R. The church tower and cemetery are visible to the R shortly before you enter the village of

17km Calzadilla de la Cueva (1119/376)

Bar/restaurant (has rooms). Shaded area with seats at end of village (R).

Continue straight on through village to road. Cross the river

Cueza and KSO on the road, passing the remains of the eleventh-century pilgrim hospital, formerly very important, of

2km Santa María de las Tiendas (1121/374)

From here the landscape becomes less flat and slightly undulating. Woods to L and R, away from road. Mountains in distance to R. This is roughly the half-way point on the Spanish section of the camino, three-quarters of the way to Santiago if you started in Le Puy.

Continue on main road to

4km Ledigos 883m (1125/370)

Bar, shop. Church of Santiago with a statue of St. James.

At entrance to village fork L off road and continue on track through fields // to road, emerging to rejoin it after bend at exit, crossing the river **Cueza** again. KSO on road.

4km Terradillos de los Templarios (1129/366)

Shop, fonda. *Eighteenth-century church of San Pedro.*

Continue on the main road, passing turnings to the L to Moratinos and then San Nicolás del Real Camino (fountain).

After this you leave the province of Palencia to enter León. There is a fair amount of traffic on this stretch (but less on Sundays, when there are no heavy goods vehicles) and the stretch from Calzadilla de la Cueza to Sahagún can therefore be rather tedious. Sahagún is now visible ahead.

After this you can either (a) continue along the road for 7km more, directly to Sahagún, turning off the N120 at the flour mill or (b) turn R off the road, shortly after the provincial boundary, onto a track. Turn L along a clear track which now runs // to main road. KSO through fields, ignoring turnings to L and R. Panoramic views. Then, at a large rubbish tip (probably smoking) another track joins from the R. Here you can either turn L and return to the road again at KM235 (and in which case you will simply have done a "rodeo" to get away from the traffic for a while, admire the view and perhaps have a quiet sit down) or KSO downhill, aiming for the river **Valderaduey** at the bottom, opposite the **Ermita Virgen del Puente** on the other side (a former pilgrim hospice). This is the old route. There is no longer a bridge at this point but as the river is extremely shallow here (only a few inches deep) it should normally be possible to cross it.

(If you rejoined the road again after the rubbish tip KSO on road until after you have crossed the road bridge over the **Valderaduey**. Turn R immediately along a track along the river bank for 100m until you reach the *ermita*. Trees and a good place for a rest.)

The path leading from here into Sahagún is still known as the *camino francés de la virgen*. Turn L at the *ermita* and follow the path until you reach the embankment of the Sahagún bypass. Turn L under bridge and KSO on other side, aiming for a very large white grain silo ahead. When you get there, cross the N120 and enter

11km Sahagún 816m (1140/355)
Population 2700. All facilities. RENFE on León-Palencia line, campsite, swimming pool. Tourist Office.

End of the seventh stage in Aimery Picaud's guide. Sahagún takes its name from a contraction of San Fagún or Facondo, a Roman martyr. A monastery was founded here as early as 904 and then, in 1080, the order of Cluny established itself and Sahagún became the foremost Benedictine abbey in Spain. Nothing remains of the five pilgrim hospitals founded in the eleventh century but there are several churches of outstanding architectural merit: San Tirso, San Lorenzo and La Peregrina (all three National Monuments), San Juan de Sahagún, La Trinidad and, 5km to the south, San Pedro de las Dueñas (also a National Monument).

After crossing the main road continue down a small street (**Calle Ronda Estación**). As you approach the railway line (with the station on your L) follow it for a short distance and then cross it at the bridge. KSO down the **Calle José Antonio**, the **Calle del Peso** (fork R after this for the town centre), the **Calle Rua** and the **Calle de las Monjas**. At the end you will come to an open space, with the Convent of the Madres Benedictinas and the museum of religious painting on your R. (Turn R here for the **Arco de San Benito** and the church of **San Tirso**.)

To leave Sahagún continue straight from the **Calle de las Monjas** along the **Calle de Rey Don Antonio** and out of the town across the bridge over the river **Cea**.

This is bordered with poplar trees and legend has it that at a time when both Moors and Christians were battling for control of northern Spain a Christian force camped near Sahagún. Before retiring for the night some of the men stuck their lances in the ground and woke up the following morning to find that they had sprouted roots, branches and leaves.

171

Pass the swimming pool (R) and follow the main road to León to

6km Calzada del Coto (1146/349)
Leave the road here along a turning to the R.

At this point the camino *divides, the two paths running more or less // to each other with the railway line in between them for much of the way, merging when they reach Mansilla de las Mulas.*

A. CALZADA DE LOS PEREGRINOS

This is an old Roman road, the Vía Trajana, but is very isolated and there is little or no water, no accommodation, no shops or bars and virtually no shade from the sun for 30km. It is definitely not recommended in July or August but for fit walkers who like space, silence and unlimited solitude it is perhaps the more attractive of the two routes at other times, provided you carry plenty of food and water and set out very early in the morning. There are not many waymarks on this route but it is easy to follow as there are few turnings to make and, like most of the rest of the camino, *you are always walking in a straight line due west.*

Turn R into the village of **Calzada del Coto** (*shop*) past the **Ermita de San Roque** on your R and follow the street through the village. At the end ignore the track to the L (this leads to Bercianos) and KSO(R). After 2km cross the bridge over the railway line (artificial lake to L on other side) and KSO.

After this you enter a wooded area, going gradually uphill. Small, scrubby trees and a little shade. After 3km (from the railway bridge) and just before you leave the woods pass the **Granja Valdelocajos**, a large farm with modern houses and some very large dogs (probably loose!). 1km further on, on your R, is the newly installed **Fuente de los Peregrinos** and a picnic area. KSO for 3km till you reach

9km Calzadilla de los Hermanos
Enter the village and KSO along the main street, past the *ermita* (L) and continue to the end where a road joins from behind R.

Continue on the road.

This crosses an immense plateau stretching to the horizon on all sides. From time to time you can see the poles along the railway line away to the L and the grain silo at El Burgo Ranero and you may see/hear a train in the

distance but otherwise all you can see around you are the cornfields seemingly reaching away to infinity.

After 3.5km you will come to a junction where the *camino* ceases to be tarred and continues as a UMUR, on the other side of the tarred road that crosses it (L to El Burgo Ranero, R to Villamartín de D. Sancho). KSO for 13.5km, ignoring any turnings you may see to L and R, until you reach the deserted railway station (*apeadero* means "halt, stopping place") at

17km Apeadero Villamarco
Trains do in fact still stop here, though only on request.

Do not cross the railway line at the station (the road on the other side leads to the village of Villamarco, some 2km to the south) but KSO more or less // to it. After 4km you will pass through the valleys of two dried up rivers and from time to time you will see tracks leading off to L and R. KSO. After a further 6km you will enter two more river valleys - the path veers L here: follow it and KSO. 200m after emerging from the 2nd valley there is a junction: KSO and the church tower of Reliegos is suddenly visible ahead. If you want to go there (bar) and finish by the Camino Real Francés KSO (you are about 500m away from it). Otherwise - turn R down a track shortly after the junction. Go downhill along a track in a straight line for 6km until you reach **Mansilla de las Mulas** (and which you will have seen ahead of you in the distance since nearing Reliegos). Enter the town by a canal and turn L along the main road. KSO at junction, enter town and KSO along main street.

B. CAMINO REAL FRANCÉS
This route passes to the south of the other one, though leading directly west. Much of it has now become like a cycle track, prepared for the "invasion" in the 1993 Holy Year. It is tree-lined on one (the sunny) side only and has picnic areas at intervals.

At the point where you turn off the main road from Sahagún towards Calzado del Coto do *not* enter the village but take the L turn along an UMUR lined with recently planted trees.

This is the road to Bercianos and is used by quite a lot of vehicles, even though it is not (yet) tarred, and sends up huge clouds of dust in the dry summer months.

Pass a *laguna* (R) after 1.7km and then, after 2km, the **Ermita de**

MAP 6

Perales (L). KSO. After 1km and after crossing the bridge over the river **Coso** (probably dry) enter the village of

5km Bercianos del Real Camino (1151/344)
Bar, shop. Church of El Salvador.

Follow the main road through the village. In the distance you will see the silos of **El Burgo Ranero**, 7km away.

It was in between these two places that the seventeenth-century Italian

pilgrim Domenico Laffi came across the body of a fellow pilgrim who had been devoured by wolves - this was one of the loneliest stretches of the entire pilgrimage, as it still is today.

Continue directly west along the well-defined track until you reach the village of

7km El Burgo Ranero (1158/337)
Shop, bar/restaurant, fonda, refugio.

Follow the main road through the village past the church (R), cross a road that intersects the village from north to south and past the cemetery (L).

2km further on the L is a group of ten trees (which you will see before you get to them) with a brick fountain set back from the road - a good place for a rest.

KSO. The road carries straight on, and after 6km passes a turning, on the L, to the village of Villamarco (the village itself is 1km off route).

2km further on the route crosses the railway line and continues with this to its left for a while. The route is still well waymarked with yellow arrows. It enters a small valley, crossing first the "river" **Valdearcos** and then, 1km further on, the "river" **Santa María** (usually dried up).

Shortly after this there is another shaded area with trees and the landscape becomes less flat, with bodegas (storage cellars for keeping wine cool) set into the hilly ground at intervals.

2km further on enter

13.5km Reliegos (1171.5/323.5)
Bar. KSO through village and out the other side on a stony track across a plain, where you will see **Mansilla de las Mulas** 6km away in the distance. Continue west until you reach the main road, cross it and the bridge over the canal and enter the town.

6.5km Mansilla de la Mulas 799m (1178/317)
Population 1800. Shops, bars, restaurant, hostal, *campsite.*

Substantial remains of the twelfth-century town walls. Thirteenth-century church of Santa María, Capilla Nuestra Señora de Gracia.

Continue along the main street to the end of the town and cross the bridge over the river **Esla**. Fork L onto the old road and then onto a track which continues // to the main road, apart from a few exceptions, for 5km until you reach the village of

6km Puente Villarente (1184/311)
Shops, bars, restaurant, hostal.
>*Small village with a 20 arch bridge over the river Porma.*

After this the *camino* follows the main road (with a *lot* of traffic) all the way to **León**. At the petrol station to the R on leaving Puente Villarente a path is waymarked to the R but is hard to follow, although, in theory, it goes as far as **Valdafuente** (*bar, farmacía*) before rejoining the road again.

As you approach León fork L as road veers R at **Avenida de Madrid**. Cross the river **Torío** at **Puente Castro** (by the FB). KSO to roundabout with fountains playing amidst very modern sculptures. Cross road and veer R along **Calle Santa Ana** (at the back of church of same name) into the centre of León and the cathedral via the **Calle Barahona**, **Calle Puertamoneda**, past the church of **Santa María del Mercado** (R), and the **Calle de la Rua**.

13km León 822m (1197/298)
Population 135,000. All facilities. Youth Hostel. RENFE. Buses to all major towns. Tourist Office opposite Cathedral.
>*End of the eighth stage in Aimery Picaud's guide and another place worth spending a whole day. The three most important monuments are the thirteenth-century Cathedral in French Gothic style with superb stained-glass windows, the Basilica of San Isidoro containing the Royal Pantheon (with twelfth-century wall and ceiling paintings) and a fine Romanesque church and San Marcos, formerly an important pilgrim hospital (now a Parador). León also contains one of the few Gaudí buildings outside Barcelona - the Casa de las Bottines, once a private house but now a bank.*

To leave León - cross bridge over **Río Bernesga** by the **Hotel San Marcos**. KSO past public garden (Parque Quevedo, R, good place for rest/picnic; note *black* swans in lake) and continue along this road, taking L turning at fork. Cross the railway line by FB and KSO, passing the **Iglesia Capilla de Santiago** (R), and KSO, uphill all the time. Turn R at a bus stop and some traffic lights halfway up hill onto the **Camino de la Cruz**, which veers round to the L (still uphill) between bodegas. Continue ahead and at junction 300m later with another track coming from L KSO(L) on UMUR (not road) by scrap dealers. (This may sound complicated but all you are doing is playing "hide and seek" to avoid the main road.)

KSO ahead, passing factories, forking R uphill (away from main road) at marble factory. At top of hill continue on track coming from L (the *very* tall spire of the modern church of Virgen del Camino is visible ahead) and take next L fork by long wall on R.

At start of residential area (**Calle Tras las Casas**) *fork* (not turn) L onto tarred road ahead (leading towards church spire). Continue down **Calle del Orbigo** and take second L into the **Calle Cervantes** and then turn R onto main road, continuing to church in

6km Virgen del Camino 905m (1203/292)

Small town with shops, bars, restaurant, hostal.

Church of San Froilan (modern) has a very interesting facade which includes thirteen huge bronze statues, one of which is St. James pointing the way to Santiago. Its interior is very plain apart from an extremely ornate baroque reredos, retained from a former church on this site.

Cross the road after (visiting) the church and continue on minor road downhill behind crash barrier (to L) (signposted "Fresno del Camino 3.5km") and leading to cemetery.

100m later the two caminos divide, as from here to Hospital de Orbigo, some 25km, according to which you choose, you have two options, both of which are described here: a) the traditional (road) route and b) a recently waymarked, longer alternative which passes to the south of the N120 on minor roads (see page 178).

A. ROAD OPTION VIA VILLADANGOS DEL PÁRAMO

In the next section you basically follow the road but often take parallel tracks to avoid actually walking along it.

Continue up hill past cemetery (L) and rejoin road in front of a factory. Continue on path above road (L): ahead of you you can see a (complicated) motorway junction.

When you rejoin the road cross the first part (a sliproad) carefully, crossing where you see the yellow arrows painted on the road itself, and walk on the hard shoulder of the main Madrid-Astorga road. KSO, go under *both* bridges and KSO. Continue along the road.

4km Valverde de la Virgen 887m (1207/288)

Bar, fuente.

2km San Miguel del Camino (1209/286)

Shortly after San Miguel fork L off road onto track // to it. Veer R at farm and follow track across open land more or less // to road. When you think you are going to rejoin the road KSO instead down dip to track // to road. KSO.

6km Urbanización de Santiago (1215/280)

Continue on road to

2km Villadangos del Páramo (1217/278)

Shops, bars, fonda, *pharmacy, restaurant.*

> *Originally a Roman town. Church of Santiago has a painting of Santiago Matamoros in its main altarpiece. (The word* páramo *in this and many other place names means "bleak plateau.")*

Cross road at entrance to village (*refugio* in former school on R), fork R and enter village. Turn L at end to return to main road for a short while. Then fork L off it onto a track // to road. Follow this for as far as is practicable and then rejoin road to walk on hard shoulder. Unfortunately there is no alternative in this section as all the land to L and R of the road is criss-crossed with canals, dykes and deep irrigation channels. Continue to

4km San Martín del Camino (1221/274)

Small shop, 2 bars.

KSO and shortly outside village cross road and fork R onto track // to road. At farm veer slightly R to pass it (on your L) then veer L again to follow track // to road. KSO until, after 2km, the track forks away from the road. Turn L, cross bridge over dyke and return to road over crash barrier.

KSO. 1.5km before Hospital de Orbigo, opposite a gravel works, turn R down a lane. Follow path through fields to **Hospital de Orbigo**, veering L at fork into the Calle Orbigo along the river and then turn L to cross the bridge over the river into the town. Continue as described on p180 from "Hospital de Orbigo".

B. COUNTRY ROUTE VIA VILLAR DE MAZARIFE

This is somewhat sparsely waymarked but is easy enough to follow.

Turn L and veer L up side of wall uphill. KSO ahead. Join minor road coming from back R and KSO along it. Ignore next L turn, KSO downhill and go *under* road to enter

3.5km Fresno del Camino

Fountain. KSO ahead uphill (unmarked bar in social club on R) on road marked "Oncina de la Valdoncina, 2.3km". Go downhill, cross minor railway line, bridge over stream (probably dry, small fountain/water supply to L) and enter village of

2.3km Oncina del la Valdoncina

Veer R then L uphill and KSO on stony track (sign to "Chozos de Abajo, 5km"). Continue uphill to open plateau, fork and then veer L. Continue ahead on open plateauland, more or less flat, ignoring turns to L and R. Cross minor road and enter

5km Chozos de Abajo

Bar (meals), camping.

KSO(R) on **Calle Real** (signed "Villar de Mazarife, 4km"). Turn L and then R in village, cross bridge and KSO on UMUR, ignoring turns, to

4km Villar de Mazarife

2 bars (neither does food), shop.

Continue to **Plaza Mediovilla** and continue ahead along **Calle Camino** to road (**Carretera Valcabo**). Cross it and KSO (signposted "Villavente 9.3km") on minor tarred road, past sports ground (L). KSO.

The páramo *is almost completely flat (if, in fact, the earth is!), with cornfields, sunflowers in season, irrigation channels and the occasional tree. The Montes de León are visible away to your R on the horizon (and, later, gradually ahead of you). Few waymarks in this area as there is little else to do but continue straight ahead all the time.*

After 4-5km cross a minor road and continue ahead on what has now become a UMUR, turning L at small junction of similar tracks 100m later. Cross bridge over canal, veer R and KSO, ignoring turns to L or R. After 2km cross bridge over a large canal and then a road and KSO again into

9km Villavante

Bar. Turn R into village at junction with tarred road and then L into **Calle Santa María**. Turn R *after* junction with the **Calle Pradico** and veer L into another street. Turn L again at bar down **Calle Iglesia**.

Pass church (on your R) and KSO, forking L down side of *huge*

179

water tower. Cross bridge over railway line (a notice at start says "Hospital de Orbigo, 3.5km").

Turn L along minor road at end of bridge, continue on UMUR after last house, along side of railway track (ie. it is on your L) at first, then veering R towards **Hospital de Orbigo** (visible ahead).

KSO for 2km, cross minor road, continue ahead (still on UMUR). Approx. 600m later reach minor roaad (fountain on R), passing between factory buildings. Turn R, cross main road (N120) carefully and continue ahead on **Avenida de la Constitución** into

7km Hospital de Orbigo 819m (1228/...)

Small town, population 1320, with shops, fonda, *restaurant, campsite, 2 fountains.*

The longest pilgrim bridge in Spain, crossing the river Orbigo. It is 204m long and has 20 arches. It is known as the bridge of the Paso Honroso in memory of a month long jousting tournament which took place in 1434, breaking 300 lances and leaving one person dead. Its champions continued to Santiago where they left a golden necklace on the processional statue of Santiago Menor (reportedly still there).

Cross Roman bridge and continue ahead, passing **Casa Consistorial** (R, fountain opposite on L), church of **Santa María** (R) and KSO down main street to end o
f town (down the **Calle Camino de Santiago**). At the crossroads with an UMUR at the end you again have two options: either

a) KSO (waymarked) to continue on the road route to **Astorga** or

b) (also waymarked) turn R for an alternative country route as far as **San Justo de la Vega** (the one described here).

KSO along minor road to

2km Villares de Orbigo 919m (1230/265)

Ignore turns to L and R. Enter village, turn L then R, then veer R (past *lavadero*). Veer L and then turn R onto road, cross it (and canal) and KSO. After 200m turn L up junction with green lane. KSO for 1km and join road again. Turn R to village of

2km Santibañez de Valdeiglesias 845m (1232/263)

Enter village down **Camino Villares** and continue ahead down **Calle Real** then turn R up **Calle Carromonte Alto** and KSO, uphill all the time, into open country. At top of hill descend to take L fork, past large sandstone quarry to L. Descend to wide shallow valley (watch out for waymarks on the ground) and then KSO ahead up other side, taking RH fork part way up. KSO then take L at next fork, uphill all the time.

At top of hill join track coming from back L and KSO downhill ahead. Take RH fork (four options to L) and go uphill under trees to open plateau. (HT cables ahead, woods to L ahead.) Descend to next valley (line of trees along stream) and then up again to another open plateau.

At junction of similar tracks when you are level with *second* farm building to R veer L under electric cables (view of Astorga ahead, below), taking RH of two forks leading to the **Crucero de Santo Toribio** (and splendid views of Astorga).

(Toribio, along with Genadio, both from Astorga, Isidore of Seville and Ildefonso of Toledo, was one of the four bishop saints.) This is where this camino *joins the other one coming from Hospital de Orbigo along the road.*

Go downhill ahead and 200m later turn R onto section of old main road which then leads to the new one. Continue along it into

8km San Justo de la Vega (1240/255)
Bars, shop, hostal.
Church with old tower but very modern windows and brick nave.

Continue through village and out along main road until you have crossed the road bridge over the river **Tuerto**. Turn R 100m after bend onto UMUR marked "merendero" (ie. picnic area) then L along a shaded lane / / to the road. Follow this for 2km past field, factory and another field until you cross an old three-arch bridge over a small canal. Turn L onto UMUR and KSO to main road. Turn R along it, cross two level crossings. Turn R along this road, cross two level crossings and follow road uphill into town. Turn R to visit cathedral.

5km Astorga 869m (1245/250)
Population 14,000, all facilities. RENFE. Buses to León, Ponferrada and Villafranca del Bierzo. Tourist Office opposite Cathedral.
A town dating from Roman times, with extensive remains of its original town walls behind the Cathedral. Astorga was (and still is) the junction of two pilgrim routes, the camino francés *(described here) and the* camino mozárabe *or* Vía de la Plata. *This explains the unusually*

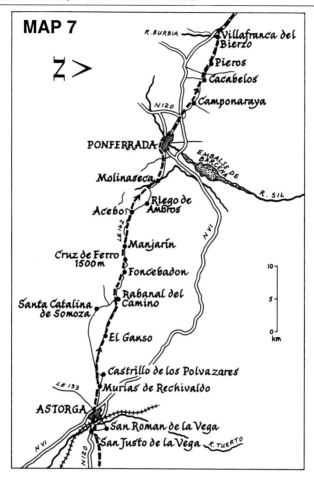

MAP 7

N >

R. BURBIA

Villafranca del Bierzo

Pieros

Cacabelos

Camponaraya

N120

PONFERRADA

EMBALSE DE BARCENA

Molinaseca

R. SIL

Riego de Ambros

Acebo

LE142

Manjarín

N VI

Cruz de Ferro 1500m

Foncebadon

Rabanal del Camino

Santa Catalina de Somoza

El Ganso

10 ┐

5 ┤

0 ┘
km

Castrillo de los Polvazares

LE133

Murias de Rechivaldo

ASTORGA

San Roman de la Vega

San Justo de la Vega   P. TUERTO

N VI

N120

large number of pigrim hospitals formerly in existence (there were twenty-two in the Middle Ages), the last of which, the Hospital de las Cinco Llagas (the Five Wounds), was burned down earlier this century. Gothic Cathedral with interesting choir stalls and museum, Bishop's Palace built by the

Catalan architect Antonio Gaudí, with pilgrim museum. Several other interesting churches, Baroque town hall. It is worth spending half a day here.

Between Astorga and Ponferrada the camino passes through the isolated area of the Maragatería (as far as the Cruz de Ferro) and then into the Bierzo region, which continues until you leave the province of León and enter Galicia. For many people this is one of the most beautiful stretches of the camino, most of it in the Montes de León, but as there are few villages and few bars or shops along the way it is advisable to carry a certain amount of food and water. Since the route is also quite high (the Cruz de Ferro is at 1504m) warm clothing is needed, even in summer.

Much of the camino between Astorga and Molinaseca is in fact on the road but it is very quiet and there is very little traffic.

To leave Astorga - turn L at traffic lights on main road out of Astorga to the west onto minor road signposted "Santa Colomba de Somoza" and "Castrillo de los Polvazares". KSO to **Valdeviejas**, passing a memorial sign (L) to "peregrinos identes" and then an old people's complex (L). Pass the **Ermita Ecco Homo** (L) and then either KSO on road itself or along a track beside it as far as the bridge over the river **Jerga** and then return to the road. Continue to village of

4km Murias de Rechivaldo 882m (1249/246)

Bar, *mesón*. Fork L onto a track between two trees just past the village name sign and pass along to the side of the village to its L. Enter street (**Camino de Santiago**) and continue along to the end, when it becomes a track leading to open country.

[1km further on a short detour is recommended to Castrillo de los Polvazares, a cobbled village typical of the Maragatería which is a National Monument and in a very fine state of preservation. Bars, restaurant. To leave you can either retrace your steps or continue on a FP (not waymarked but leading straight ahead all the time) directly to Santa Catalina de Somoza.]

Follow this track straight on for 2km, until you reach the road. Cross over and KSO ahead (signposted "El Ganso 5") and KSO to village of

5km Santa Catalina de Somoza 977m (1254/241)

Bar. Fork R at entrance to village along lane towards church and

KSO along **Calle Real**. Rejoin road at large green wooden wayside cross and KSO along road to

4km El Ganso 1020m (1258/)

Bar in summer. Small village which formerly had a monastery and pilgrim hospital. Church of Santiago, with chapel of "Cristo de los Peregrinos".

Fork R at entrance to village along lane (village to your L). KSO and then turn L back onto road at church. KSO along road, pass a turning to "Rabanal Viejo" after 3km, at the **Puente Panote**, and continue to

6km Rabanal del Camino 1149m (1264/231)

2 bars (meals available at both, one has rooms), fountain.

End of the ninth stage in Aimery Picaud's guide. Ermita del Santo Cristo at entrance to village, church of San José and parish church of Santa María. Today the population is only twenty-seven, except in summer when migrants return for their holidays, but in former times it was an important pilgrim halt and considerably larger, as the presence of three churches testifies.

Turn R off road after church (L) to enter village. Pass churches of **San José** and **Santa María** and *mesón* and KSO along green lane for 1km to rejoin road again. KSO ahead along it. (Fountain to R of road after 2km at KM25, with icy cold water.) Continue to climb and KSO to village of

5km Foncebadón 1495m (1269/226)

Today this village is almost abandoned but in the twelfth century the hermit Gaucelmo built a church, hospital and hospice for pilgrims, of which the remains still exist.

Fork L off road, enter village and continue to end. KSO, passing ruined church and rejoin road after 1km. Turn L and 300m further on reach the

1.5km Cruz de Ferro 1504m (1270.5/224.5)

A very tall iron cross atop a huge cairn. Traditionally pilgrims brought a stone with them from home to add to the pile. Fantasic views on a clear day, with Monte Teleno over in the distance to the south. Modern Ermita de Santiago, built in the 1982 Holy Year. From here the route is almost all down hill to Ponferrada, some 25km.

[RJ: turn R off road between 21st and 22nd snow pole on road

View of El Acebo

after passing the cross. If you miss it, continue along the road to rejoin the *camino* at the entrance to Foncebadón.]

KSO on road, passing highest point of the entire route (at 1517m) to another almost abandoned village of

3.5km Manjarín 1451m (1274/221)
Fountain on L on leaving village.
Continue on road for 2km, pass turning to military base (visible on hill above road, with radar, etc.) and KSO. Mountain ranges visible ahead of you and to the L.

After 1-2km watch out for a turning off the road to the R, 200m after road KM37 and 100m after an iron cross on R fork R off road and which climbs up between two small hills; this short-cuts some of the road's many hairpins and cuts off quite a long section of the road, which you rejoin on the other side (good view of Ponferrada ahead). [RJ: turn L uphill, near drain, before road veers R.]

400m further on, at sign marked "Ruta peatonal". fork L off road onto FP going downhill below the road (which remains on your R). Continue along it, descending steeply, until below you, abruptly, you reach the slate-roofed village of

7km El Acebo 1156m (1281/214)

Fountain on roadside as you leave the FP and 2 others in village. Bar.

Another village which formerly had a pilgrim hospital, a single long, narrow street whose old houses have overhanging balconies at first floor level and outside staircases. Their slate roofs are a sudden change from the red pantiles encountered up to now. Church has statue of Santiago Peregrino.

KSO through village, past *ermita* and cemetery and a memorial in the form of an iron bicycle sculpture to a German pilgrim killed there whilst cycling to Santiago in 1987. Continue on road. 1km before the next village of **Riego de Ambrós**, visible ahead, watch out for a turning to L off road just before a bend onto a FP below the road. Follow this down to the village.

In the section from Foncebadón to Riego de Ambrós there are a lot of wayside crosses with scallop shells below: memorials to pilgrims who died en route?

2km Riego de Ambrós 920m (1283/212)

2 bars, shop, fountain.

Enter village, follow street straight on (downhill all the time) and then turn R down a grassy lane. Continue downhill through trees, for 1km (in a straight line all the time), then join a farm, track. Join a road a few metres further on and turn L along it. 80m after this turn R off the road to a track. KSO then fork R downhill and zigzag down to clearing in a wood with enormous chestnut trees. KSO downhill.

After a while, although the path remains level, the land falls away into a valley so that you are actually walking quite high up here, in an area perfumed with cistus, a bush that smells like church incense. Track veers R and eventually descends to the road. 100m before this turn L along track coming from R. After this you can either turn L to road (at bridge) or continue for a short while longer up hill to R on path, joining road further down at a large wayside cross. After that continue down the road to large village of

5km Molinaseca 595m (1288/207)

Shops, bars, restaurant. Swimming area in river by bridge.

Enter village passing **Ermita de las Angustias** (R), partly set into the cliffs, and cross the Romanesque **Puente de las Peregrinos** over the river **Meruelo**. Continue along the **Calle Real** (the main street) and when this runs into the main road KSO along it until you reach a tennis court on your R. Turn off road to R and then turn L along a lane // to road. KSO along it as it passes behind the houses on the main road, cross a minor road and KSO slightly uphill along the side of fields. Rejoin road at the top of the hill, just before a crossroads.

At top of hill road goes downhill (good view of Ponferrada ahead, church tower to LH side is the Basilica de la Encina). 100m later you have a choice of two routes into Ponferrada (both waymarked), R or L. The RH route is slightly shorter, much of it on a busy road; the LH route is slightly longer and is not particularly scenic but it does take you onto quieter roads with a great deal less traffic and some parts also have more shade.

LH ROUTE VIA CAMPO

Fork L down minor road and then KSO(L) after 50m down earth track. Fork L again 100m later downhill on earth/grassy track/lane, which climbs uphill again after going over a stream. KSO (uphill) at crossing with similar track (vines to your L). [RJ: KSO at R fork uphill.]

KSO downhill again. Approx. 1.5km after making your LH/RH choice enter village of

3km Campo
Take RH fork down **Calle Real** (lined with old houses on both sides). (Stone sitting area at junction.) [RJ: fork R at 2 earth tracks at top of Calle Real.] (Eighteenth-centry church to L.)

At small plaza at the bottom of the **Calle Real** continue ahead along LH of two roads (no name at start) which is gravelled and, later, tarred. KSO(L) at junction with **Calle de los Mesones** passing through waste ground, sports ground (to R), past rubbish tip, slaughterhouse and large factory. KSO at "stop" sign. [RJ: L fork at junction.] 500m further on road runs into a (more) main road coming from back L. Bar at crossing. [RJ: take LH fork marked "Los Barrios".]

Continue 100m to next junction (shop to the L) and turn R to cross the medieval **Puente Mascarón** over the **Río Boeza** to enter Ponferrada. Turn L on other side up **Calle Camino Bajo de San Andres**, go under railway line and uphill. At the Junction at the top you have a *choice* (both marked):

a) RH along **Calle El Camino Jacobeo**, turn L 50m further on and then R into **Calle Hospital**;

b) KSO(L) along **Calle Buenavista** and then R almost immediately along **Calle Hospital** (fifteenth-century Hospital de la Reina at No.28). Turn L at top then R up **Calle Gil y Carrasco** (up side of castle) (Tourist Office on L) and follow it uphill into the **Plaza Virgen de la Encina**.

RH (ROAD) ROUTE

KSO ahead on road for 1.5km and veer R at fork by furniture warehouse, just before road KM54. Continue downhill, cross bridge over **Río Boeza** and shortly afterwards take path beside road on LH side. Veer slightly L off road behind factory 500m later and KSO along lane between low walls with fields on either side, following HT lines. After 1km fork R uphill, cross bridge over railway line, veer L along cemetery wall and past entrance to road. Turn L and at crossing with small roundabout take **Calle del Pregonero**. KSO along it, along **Calle El Templo** to castle, and then up **Calle Gil y Carrasco** to **Plaza de la Encina**.

8km Ponferrada 543m (1296/199)
Population 50,000. All facilities, RENFE. Tourist Office.

Large industrial town at the junction of the rivers Boeza and Sil, taking its name from the iron bridge over the latter. (Today a metal bridge is nothing surprising but was a luxury when it was built, at the end of the twelfth century, and something only possible in an area rich in iron.) The new part of the town is on the west side of the river Sil, the old part on the east, with the thirteenth-century castle built by the Knights Templar, the sixteenth-century basilica of Nuestra Señora de la Encina (Our Lady of the Evergreen Oak), seventeenth-century town hall and sixteenth-century Torre del Reloj, the only surviving remnant of the former town walls. The tenth-century mozarabic church of Santo Tomás de Ollas is in the suburbs, to the north of the town (and where the camino *originally passed).*

To continue (the exit from Ponferrada is both ugly and rather sparsely waymarked): from the **Plaza de la Encina** next to the Basilica veer L across square and down **Calle El Rañadero** (stepped street), turn L at bottom, cross river and take 2nd R down **Calle Río**

Urdiales which veers L into a big square/parking lot. KSO and at end turn R down wide tree-lined avenue (**Avenida del Sacramento**), which veer L at end, rising uphill to **Plaza Lutero King** (surrounded by big blocks of flats with an *enormous* slag heap behind them).

Turn R (waymark) along **Avenida de la Libertad** (slag heap is now on your L). KSO on road (despite misleading waymark near RH fork leading to a disused factory) and 400m later turn L at junction in front of electricity headquarters into tree-lined road. Ignore 1st L fork, KSO and then turn R at end, then L, L again, KSO and then turn R alongside the church of **Santa María de Compostilla** (*sic*). (Note modern statue to L, opposite entrance, and modern murals, painted in the 1993 Holy Year, in entrance arcade.)

Cross road, continue down **IV Avenida** (note private house on your L with two very tall chimneys, one of which has a stork's nest on top) and through a residential area (with numbered, not named, streets). Turn L then R (into **3a Transversal**) past tennis courts (on L), the **Ermita** (not church) **Nuestra Señora de Compostilla** (modern mural at end) and modern *cruceiro* (St. James the pilgrim is on one side, the Virgin and Child on the other).

KSO towards new housing, KSO under crossing of two sets of HT cables (waste ground to R). (Main road leading to NVI visible above you to the R.)

KSO at junction with **Calle Santa Rosa** and continue with **Calle de Finisterre** which then becomes a lane (church bell tower visible ahead of you). KSO, ignoring turnings (vines to your L), go under the NVI and KSO ahead on road at end passing (to your L) church of

3km Columbrianos (1299/196)
(Church has a large covered porch with seats - a good place for a rest, plus view of the mountains.)

KSO ahead downhill (**Calle El Teso**), cross bridge over railway line, go down steps at bend, cross road and continue ahead down **Calle la Iglesia** (not marked at the beginning). Fountain and seats near end in front of Centre Civico.

Join **Calle Real** (coming from your L), continue along it, veer L at chapel (bar to R) down **Calle San Blas** (again not marked at start) with fields to either side. Cross minor railway line and KSO for 2km, ignoring turns to L or R. Road joins from back L [RJ: L fork - earth road], which becomes **Calle Paraiso** in

3km Fuentesnuevas (1302/193)

Emerge at crossing, continue on **Calle Real** (bar on R, *cruceiro* to L) in village and KSO, passing church (on your R) and then continue through fields for 1.5km until track joins road (from back L) in

2km Camponaraya 490m (1304/199)

A very long, straggling village with shops,.bars, bank.

Turn R onto road [RJ: turn L at house no. 337] and continue through village past church and over **Río Naraya**.

At the end (1km), when the NVI veers R (wine cooperative to your L) KSO(L) uphill on earth road/track through vines.

From here you can see the mountains of the El Bierzo region all round you and the camino leads through orchards and vines for much of the time.

Continue ahead, ignoring turnings, until you cross the road again shortly before the entrance to

4km Cacabelos 483m (1309/186)

Fountain on R 100m before village. Shops, bars, restaurant, fonda, bank. Swimming area in the river. One of the last storks on the camino has its "residence" on the church of the Sanctuario de las Angustias on leaving the town (though others have been reported near the Castillo in Villafranca del Bierzo).

At the entrance to Cacabelos a very large board explains the history of the town with its five former pilgrim hospitals, including San Lázaro, built in 1237 on the site of the present Moncloa restaurant (on your L). On leaving the town note old wine press to RH side of road.

Go downhill into the town, KSO down main street, pass fifteenth-century **Capilla de San Roque** (R) and continue down pedestrianised street. (If you turn L you emerge into a tree-lined square with seats, shade, shops.) Pass to L of church and KSO down **Calle de las Angustias**. Continue ahead, cross bridge over river (swimming area in summer when it is dammed up) and KSO on main road.

Continue for 2km past hamlet of **Pierros** (fountain by bus shelter) and two other unmarked ones. Just past a bridge, 200m after a signpost to "Valtuille" and immediately after a stone house (R) and a *mesón/sidrería* turn R off the road and veer L onto a track through vines, // to road and becoming very narrow. KSO ahead (do not take more obvious L fork) and on down other side of hill,

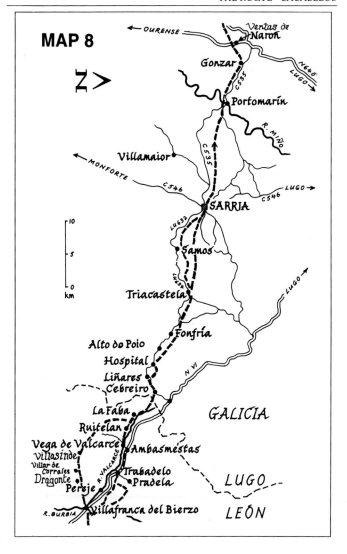

MAP 8

N

← OURENSE

Ventas de Naron

Gonzar

N640 LUGO

C535

Portomarín

R. MIÑO

Villamaior

← MONFORTE

C546

C535

LUGO →

C546

SARRIA

10
5
0
km

LU633

Samos

LUGO →

LU633

Triacastela

Fonfría

Alto do Poio

N VI

Hospital

Liñares

Cebreiro

GALICIA

La Faba

Ruitelan

Vega de Valcarce

Villasinde

Ambasmestas

LUGO

Villar de Corrales

Dragonte

R. VALCARCE

Trabadelo

Pradela

Pereje

LEÓN

R. BURBIA

Villafranca del Bierzo

coming close to road.

Turn R (tractor opening in hedge by roadside 20m away to your L) and then L at the bottom up a clear track going uphill, diagonally R away from the road. Continue on this track until you reach the Romanesque church of **Santiago** (L), by cemetery on the outskirts of **Villafranca del Bierzo**.

This church has a finely carved Puerta del Perdón, through which pilgrims who were too weak, ill or injured to continue to Santiago entered in order to obtain the same indulgences and remission of their sins as they would have done had they been able to complete their pilgrimage. Two refugios near church, one next door to L, on the site of a medieval hospice, the other on the R.

8km Villafranca del Bierzo 511m (1317/178)

Small town with all facilities. Tourist Office in Calle Alameda Alta, near church of San Nicolás.

This is the end of the tenth stage in Aimery Picaud's guide. There are a number of other interesting churches including sixteenth-century Colegiata de Santa María, the seventeenth-century Anunciada and the seventeenth-century convent church of San Francisco with Baroque cloister. The Castillo-Palacio de los Marqueses dates from the fifteenth century and the Calle del Agua contains some fine old eighteenth-century houses, many with armorial devices above the doors.

Between Villafranca and the small Galician village of El Cebreiro at 1300m 27km away there are more mountains and a very stiff climb, whether you opt for one of the two high level routes or the lower one along the old (and some parts of the new) main road. If you intend to spend the night in El Cebreiro make sure you leave Villafranca early in the day.

From the church of Santiago go downhill to the **Castillo** (privately owned) and take 2nd turn R downhill (at side of castle). Cross street, go down a flight of steps and KSO past a small square and the "Correos" along the **Calle del Agua**. Turn sharp L at the bottom (**Plazuela Santa Catalina**), go up steps and cross the bridge over the river **Burbia**.

After this you have three choices (all waymarked): a (very slightly longer) high level route to the R of the main road and a low level one, both of which join up in Trabadelo and a longer, strenuous option which passes to the L of the main road via Dragonte, rejoining the other two in Herrerías.

The Cathedral and Bishop's Palace at Astorga
The castle of the Templarsand the River Sil at Ponferrada

Descending to the village of El Acebo
The route between Villafrance del Bierzo and O Cebreiro

A. ROAD ROUTE

Take this option in bad weather. Continue on the road, flat but busy, though in some parts you use the old sections where it has been straightened out. To do this KSO ahead along the road on the lower (L) of the two waymarked routes. This takes you to the exit of the road tunnel under the mountains at the exit to the town, after which you turn R onto the main road. KSO, leaving it from time to time as indicated by the yellow arrows (eg. through **Pereje** and 1km before Trabadelo, *panadería* at end of village on R) when the *camino* takes the old road in places where the new one has been "straightened out".

Continue until 200m before the **Hostal Valcarce** at road KM48. 200m later take the old road to your L at **Portela** (fountain, bar in summer). Rejoin main road but then, 500m after the end of this hamlet, turn L off main road to **Ambasmestas**, 0.5km (*panadería*) and then KSO to **Vega de Valcarce** (see page 197).

B. HIGH-LEVEL ROUTE VIA PRADELA

This high level route is also waymarked and is much quieter, with superb views on a clear day. It is much more strenuous, climbs very steeply to start with and descends very steeply to Trabadelo (not recommended for people with bad knees) but is worth it unless the weather is bad. The NVI is visible way below you in the valley to the L most of the time.

To take this option fork R after crossing the bridge over the **Burbia** and go uphill between houses. This continues to climb steeply, levelling out from time to time before climbing again, following the shoulder of the hillside. After 1.5km pass a grove of chestnut trees to your L (shady place for a rest). KSO(R) here up narrow lane with rocky embankments on either side and which gradually widens out. Track continues to climb, levelling out with HT pylons to RH side.

Pass under HT cables as track veers R. [View of several similar type *caminos* ahead: yours is the high-level one heading for a small wood on the skyline (next to further HT pylons).]

At fork 200m after passing under cables KSO(R) on *higher* of two choices, ignore next RH turn and KSO(L) ahead. At next fork 200m later KSO(R) uphill, passing to R of (ie. above) wood (fir trees).

After this the route is either level or slightly undulating (mountain views all round). After 1km pass under HT cables. [RJ: KSO(L) at fork by pylon.] Ignore next LH fork downhill to trees and KSO(R). Lesser track joins from back R. [RJ: KSO(R).] Route climbs a little again (TV/radio mast above you to R). [100m later minor road joins from back L: ignore on RJ and KSO(L) ahead.]

Track then goes downhill on edge of woods.

(View of village of Pradela ahead). At "U" shaped fork ahead there is a choice of routes, to L or R, either side of the walled field ahead of you. Both routes are equally attractive and both are waymarked. The RH one is slightly longer and may be muddier if it has rained recently. Views to RH side give you a chance to see valley on other side as you walk. This takes you to the village of Pradela (fountain, but no other facilities). The LH option is slightly shorter, has more shade and may be drier. Views to L over NVI.

a) **RH route**. Take RH fork and KSO. [After 20m track joins from back R: RJ: KSO(R).] KSO. After 1km enter village, passing in front of cemetery, and then church. Turn R in front of church up flight of concrete steps (fountain at top) and then L again onto road. KSO along it until you see the RH fork (waymarked) descending off the road 400m later*** and continue as in *option b*).

b) **LH route**. Follow earth road to (tarmac) road, joining it shortly before entrance to village of **Pradela** (over to your R). Then turn L for 800m, veering R at bend with further choice (!) (also waymarked).

Either: i) continue L ahead on grassy track through woods, slightly uphill. Cross small gulley, turn R and then L at track. The path is not always very clear on the ground but the waymarks on the trees are clear. This is the shortest of these three options and is easy enough to follow as it goes virtually in a straight line all the time, joining the road coming from Pradela (ie. from your R) at the point where you fork R off it downhill.***

Or: ii) KSO on road, forking R down track*** on RH side just before sharp LH bend in road.

***Turn R down a track that forks R off it (coming from Pradela), descending steeply. Pass under HT cables and rejoin road at 2nd pylon. [RJ: turn L uphill at pylon to 2nd: track obvious.] Turn R downhill (ie. short-cutting zigzags in road down to Trabadelo) and 20m later fork R down very steep grassy track (plastic tape waymarks only). Track joins from L and then track joins from back R. [RJ:

KSO(R).]
Rejoin road again. [RJ: take 2nd LH turn off road.] Turn R and follow it down to old main road [RJ: turn L at "stop" sign and "Pradela 4" notice by quarry] at end of village of

10km Trabadelo (1327/168)
Bar, panadería, *fountain. Bar/restaurant and bar/*mesón *100m on other side of main road, just over the river. (Trabadelo is 10km by road from Villafranca, 12-13km by the high level route.)*

Continue along the old road road for a short distance before joining the main road. Turn R along it and KSO. Cross river **Valcarce** (several times) and then turn R onto a section of the old road. Rejoin main road, pass *hostal*/bar (R) at Portela and then fork L onto old road again (fountain on R, 50m later).

At a large road junction signposted "Pedrafita 14" veer L down old road though small villages of **Ambasmestas** (*fountain* by Ermita) and **Ambascasas** (you now have the viaduct high above you to the R) and continue to **Vega de Valcarce** (see page 197).

C. HIGH-LEVEL ROUTE VIA DRAGONTE
This is a considerably longer option but worth it in good weather (providing you have already come a long way and are therefore fit). Strenuous, with several long climbs and descents. Take food with you and some water (though there are fountains in some villages). If starting from Villafranca you may prefer to break your journey and sleep in Herrerías: Bar Adela at end of village does simple meals and pilgrims can sleep on the floor.

This is not just an attractive alternative to the main camino, however, but a route used by pilgrims in the past, particularly those who were ill or with infectious diseases. The former monastery of San Fructuoso in Villar de Corrales (only the church remains today) is said to have looked after pilgrims and have been on the site of a spring with healing properties. Start early in the morning.

Leave Villafranca by the method described for the previous two options, cross a *second* bridge (L, over the **Río Valcarce**) and KSO along the **Calle Salvador** to the NVI at the entrance to the road tunnel (bar at crossroads).

Cross the NVI and KSO ahead (marked "LE622 Corullón") and then fork R steeply uphill 300m later up minor tarred road marked "Dragonte 4.3". KSO, uphill all the time, ignoring turnings till you reach the village of

7km Dragonte 900m

KSO through village and continue on earth road, uphill all the time. After 2km turn R down grassy track just before brow of hill: marker stone with conch shell to indicate turn (1090m).

From here you have a splendid view of the villages in the valley below, including Moral de Valcarce, where you are going next.

After 150m of steep descent, veering L, turn R down another earth road and KSO downhill. 150m later fork L down a smaller track (a short cut, village to L, below) and then L again 100m later. After 20m join asphalt road leading into

4km Moral de Valcarce

Fountain at end of village. Chestnut grove at entrance a good place for a rest.

Continue downhill through village and at end fork L downhill at fountain and *lavadero* and descend *very* steeply down lane with concrete surface (and striations). Descend steeply, zigzagging to valley bottom.

Cross stream (old mill building on L useful for rest/shelter in bad weather) and KSO in valley bottom.

Village of Villar de Corrales and church visible high above you on the skyline. Lane may be flooded for short distance by stream.

KSO (small FP to L of stream) and then veer L, slightly uphill at the time. Track gets steeper, zigzagging. After 1km track joins from L. [RJ: KSO(L).] Emerge by church of **San Fructuoso** in village of

5km Villar de Corrales 1050m

The church originally formed part of a monastery which looked after sick pilgrims, its emplacement visible on wall behind church, all that is left of former large complex. Fountain 50m later on L.

KSO(L) at fork 100m later, KSO(R) at next and turn L at junction at top of hill and ridge. KSO then descend (via grassy road), ignoring turns to L and R. Turn L at big junction, crossing steep forest road (no shade at all). Zigzag down through quarry workings, passing workmen's huts, to road below.

You can now see San Fiz do Seo, where you are going next, on the other side of the road, slightly above it.

Turn R along road and then fork L uphill (fountain on LH side of road) to village of

7km San Fiz do Seo 650m

Turn hard L at church and KSO through village. *(Bar, unmarked, not always open, on road above you to R.)* Continue to end of village and KSO on earth lane. Quarry visible away to L on other side of road.

500m later on fork L downhill. Follow the track (clear, // to valley bottom, halfway up hillside) up and down hill, undulating above stream in valley below, climbing gradually.

2km later take (upper) R track (village of Moldes visible high above you to L on hillside) and continue uphill through chestnut woods. Track joins from back L. [RJ: KSO(L) downhill.] KSO uphill to village of

4km Villasinde

Bar (not always open), fountain.

Here you can choose between a) continuing ahead to Herrerías (4km) or b) going down to Vega de Valcarce (2km, eg. to sleep). To do so turn R along road on entering village. At bend by cemetery fork R off road and then turn L immediately down clear lane at side of road. This leads you (waymarked) downhill into Vega de Valcarce, turning L and L again and then R at the bottom to cross the Puente Viejo. Turn L on main road to rejoin main camino.

To continue to Herrerías: on reaching the road in Villasinde cross over, go up short street, turn L at top and KSO, passing to L of church. Fork L at end, veer R and then KSO(R) at fork uphill. Follow road for 1km and then KSO(R) at fork. (First TV antenna on L uphill.)

Pass fountain on L after 1km and then 500m later turn L downhill off road, very steeply, 150m before a *very* large rock and red and white TV masts (500m after fountain). Continue steeply down old track for 1km, veering R near valley bottom. Turn R by bridge in **Herrerías** and then L along road to rejoin main *camino*.

6km Vega de Valcarce 630m (1333/162)

Shops, bars, farmacía, *bank, fonda.*

[The Castillo de Sarracin is visible above the village to the L. To visit it - for the view, as it is in ruins - ask if you can leave your rucksack in one

197

of the bars and go up on foot, 20 minutes each way. Start on road and then fork R onto a track leading straight up to it].

After Vega de Valcarce the camino starts to climb, gently at first and then steeply, up to El Cebreiro. To begin with it continues to follow the course of the river Valcarce but after that wends its way up through chestnut woods, tiny villages and then into open country where it enters Galicia at 1200m.

Continue on the road to **Ruitelan** (bar/*tabac*) and then, just before road bends round uphill to R, fork L downhill into

3km Herrerías 680m (1336/159)

Shop on road. The last houses in this village were known as Hospital Inglés, where there was also a chapel where pilgrims who died en route were buried.

Veer R over the river (the Dragonte variant rejoins the *camino* here from the L) and then follow road through village (bar/shop on L at other end).

(As the ground is often very wet here many people in the village wear wooden clogs over their shoes in bad weather, each foot raised up off the ground on three "legs".)

At a "T" junction (signposted to the L to "San Julian 2") KSO(R). At the end of the houses there is a L turn marked "Lindoso 2"; ignore this and KSO(R) here to "La Faba".

Keep R along road and after crossing the 2nd bridge go uphill for 1.5km. Then, at *two* milestone-type marker posts (one for walkers, the other for cyclists, La Faba visible ahead to L on clear day) fork L off the road down a FP to the valley floor.

[If the weather is bad or very wet walkers are recommmended to continue on the cyclist's route, a minor road with very little traffic, then a UMUR, going directly to Laguna de Castilla (ie. missing out La Faba) and from there to El Cebreiro - waymarked and easy to follow.]

A clear rocky track then zigzags its way steeply uphill through chestnut woods to the village of

4km La Faba 917m (1340/155)

Bar (simple meals) summer only, church, 3 fountains.

Fork L uphill at fountain and continue through village, ignoring turnings to L and R. KSO uphill at end, up shaded lane. Fork R when lane comes out into the open and then KSO uphill along green lane to village of

2km Laguna de Castilla 1098m (1342/153)

Fountain. KSO through village, ignoring turns to L and R.

Just outside the village you will see the first of the Galician marker stones - it is 153km to Santiago from here. These stones, bearing the conch shell motif, are somewhat like old-fashioned milestones, placed at 500m intervals along the route from now on (although in fact they fizzle out some 15km before Santiago itself). They are useful not merely to tell you how many more kilometres you still have left before you reach your destination, to reassure you that you aren't lost (particularly as from here onwards the camino frequently picks its way through a veritable maze of old lanes and tracks, with constant changes of direction) but also to tell you the names of the places you are in, as many of the villages you will go through after this are far too small to have name boards. Galicia is riddled with green lanes, none of which ever have signposts, so that these marker stones, redundant though they might initially appear, are in fact very useful. In the province of La Coruña they are also used as waymarks and have arrows on them to indicate changes of direction, whether or not they coincide with the usual 0.5km sitings.

Unlike Navarre and Castille-León, where the villages are bigger but very widely spaced apart, those in Galicia are often extremely small but very close to one another and you are not usually far from a building of some sort.

After 1km you will enter Galicia, in the province of **Lugo** (large marker stone to R of camino). Then, after a further 1km, past a wall with a wood above it (R) and a large stone barn (R) you will emerge onto the road at

2km El Cebreiro 1300m (1344/151)

3 hostales (meals and accommodation), fountain (no shop).

National Monument. A tiny village consisting partly of pallozas, round thatched dwellings of Celtic origin, one of which is now a small museum. The village originated with the pilgrim route and the Hostal San Giraldo was originally a hospital, from the eleventh century to 1854, founded by monks from the French abbey of Saint Gérard de'Aurillac. The church of Santa María contains relics and a twelfth-century statue of the Virgin which reputedly inclined its head after a miracle that took place in the sixteenth century.

Magnificent views all round in good weather. At night, if it is clear, the Milky Way (used by pilgrims in centuries gone by to guide them as they walked ever due west) is easily seen as there are no street or other lights anywhere in sight - a rare chance to see all the stars against a completely black sky.

[RJ: take 2nd R facing monument, with Hostal Giraldo to your L.]

Leave on road (LU634) in direction of Samos / Sarria and KSO to hamlet of

3km Liñares (1347/148)

Méson, fountain on L. Fork L off road, enter village, pass church and rejoin road at end. Cross over, turn R immediately at crossroads down minor road. Fork L 100m later up rough track which continues // to road and climbs steeply to rejoin it shortly before KM31.

1km Alto de San Roque 1270m (1348/147)

Chapel of San Roque, panoramic views. Enormous modern statue of St. James "on the move" towards Santiago (with his own stretch of "camino") on LH side of road.

Take path on RH side of road (by K147 marker post) and KSO. Continue uphill and at K145.5 enter

1.5km Hospital da Condesa (1349.5/145.5)

Church. As its name indicates, there was originally a pilgrim hospital in this village.

Fork R into village off road. KSO. *Fountain.* At end of village continue on road for another 400m then fork R to minor road (signposted to "Sabugos"). Turn L up lane 200m further on, up hill (small hut on R of road). Fork L at junction, join track coming from L and KSO. Pass through **Padornelo** (K143, 1275m). Emerge onto minor road at church - KSO and when road bends R continue up track that climbs very steeply to

3km Alto do Poio 1337m (1352.5/142.5)

Small group of houses with bar/shop, méson.

Capilla Santa María. From here to Triacastela (13km) the route is downhill all the way. After that, and in Galicia in general, the camino is often shaded so it is cool and pleasant to walk in, even in the middle of the day, with speckled sunlight. It is, however, often wet and/or misty in this

part, especially in the mornings.

Continue on road for 300m, fork R off road onto clear track // to road continue on it. Just before Fonfría another track joins from back R. [RJ: KSO(R).]

3.5km Fonfría del Camino 1290m (1356/139)

There was a pilgrim refuge here as early as 1535 and which continued to function until the middle of the last century. It offered free "light, salt, water and two blankets" to the able-bodied, "bread, an egg and lard" to the sick. The village takes its name from its "cool fountain".

Continue on old road through village (house marked "CL" has rooms). At end, KSO(L) ahead on track // to road. Return to road briefly at K137.5 and turn R off it to lane.

Cross minor road 100m later and continue on lane on other side. Ignore turns to L and R and emerge ahead (opposite bus stop) at entrance to **Viduedo** (K136.5, Ermita de San Pedro on R). Fork L and L again through village and continue on lane with spectacular views to R but spoilt by huge quarry in the middle distance.

KSO slightly uphill after K136 and continue on track which wends its way round the side of **Monte Calderon** (K135.5),

Church tower, Hospital de Condesa

descending to village of **Filloval** at K133.5. Turn L at telephone pole down lane to L of farm building and 100m later cross road and veer R downhill down lane between banks. KSO(L) at fork 150m later (track joins from back R) [RJ: KSO(R) just before reaching road] and continue to road (underpass under construction). Cross over.

Continue down walled lane 100m later on other side, at entrance to hamlet of **As Pasantes** (K132). Track joins from back L [RJ: KSO(L)]. Continue through village (house with "CL" has rooms). Fork L at *ermita*, fork L at end of village down walled lane (note dovecote in field to L) and KSO downhill to **Ramil** (K130.5). Continue through hamlet on paved lane. At K130.5 a minor road joins from back R [RJ: KSO(R)]. Continue down, passing *refugio* to L at entrance, into

9km Triacastela 665m (1365/130)

Shop, bars, restaurant, fonda, *bank. End of the eleventh stage in Aimery Picaud's guide. Church of Santiago.*

Continue down the main street to the "T" junction at the end.

Here you can choose between two routes to Sarria: a) turn L, via Samos, on the road for the first 3km or

b) turn R, via San Xil, along green lanes, paths and a few minor roads. This is a little shorter but is more strenuous and there are no shops or bars and only one fountain along the way. The two routes join up a few kilometres before Sarria. Which route you chose will probably depend on the weather (the San Xil option can be very muddy if it has been raining) and whether or not you want to visit the monastery at Samos or stay in the village. Both options are waymarked but only the San Xil route has the milestone-type marker stones.

N.B. Watch out carefully for waymarking near Triacastela and elsewhere in this region where there are other long-distance walks marked with yellow and white French-style balises. *Occasionally they overlap with the* camino *for short sections.*

A. ROUTE VIA SAMOS

Turn L in Triacastela (K129.5), pass modern pilgrim statue at edge of road (fountain to L by market hall), cross the bridge over the river **Oríbio** and KSO along road (LU634) in the direction of Samos for 3km to **San Cristobo do Real.**

Turn R off road into village at bend in road by bus shelter (watch out for yellow arrows: not well waymarked here) and go down street, passing to L of church. Veer L, cross bridge over **Oríbio** (*lavadero* on L), take LH of two streets and KSO to end of village.

Take lower of two lanes and pass to R of cemetery and go up lane under trees. (Main road is // above you to your L, on other side of valley.) KSO(R) uphill at fork and KSO(R) again (uphill) at next and KSO on track, undulating, more or less // to river below.

At junction of four tracks (small stone hut to your R) KSO(L) ahead (waterfall below you to your L), descending, ignoring turnings, to cross bridge over the **Oríbio** again.

Continue uphill ahead, veer L uphill at fork and L again at church and cemetery to rejoin minor road in **Renche** (bar).

Turn R off road a few yards further on down a very minor tarred road and then R over bridge over Río **Oaga**. Go over second bridge and continue uphill on road, turn L at hairpin in road along street and fork L at end of village along shady lane (// to river but higher up).

KSO on high-level track, ignoring turnings, until you descend to village of **Tredezín**. Pass in front of church (to your R, porch useful for shade), take 2nd L in front of church and veer L through village. Take R fork at end and R again along walled lane (// to river again).

Continue uphill and onto high-level track again. Turn R at fork, L at "T" junction steeply downhill (not very clearly waymarked). Cross bridge over **Oríbio**, turn R uphill along lane and enter village of **San Martíno**.

Turn L uphill on very minor road, KSO(R) at fork and near top of hill cross minor road and veer R diagonally up small path which becomes walled lane, to emerge on main road to Sarria just past village of San Martíno. (*Bar on road: summer only?*)

Turn R along road (not waymarked), L 100m later into lay-by by tunnel under road. Fork L into short lane, cross minor road (signposted "Freixo 4" on main road) and KSO ahead down lane, downhill between walls to valley bottom. Just *before* bridge over river turn *hard* R into Samos down lane which becomes a street, cross bridge (note wrought-iron railings in shell formation, monastery to your R) and join main road in middle of village by **Casa do Concello** in

Samos. Monastery

11km Samos 532m
Shop, bars, restaurant, hostal.

   Small village dominated by a very large Benedictine monastery (National Monument - guided tours available); this formerly housed some 500 monks but today there are only a handful left.

   To leave, continue along the main road towards Sarria (LU632) for 2km. 300m after the hamlet of **Tequín** with *ermita* dedicated to Santo Domingo de Silos fork R *very* steeply uphill on a minor road marked "Pascais".

   This joins the San Xil route at K116 (Hospital). It is a little longer than continuing on the road but is shady and much quieter, passing through the countryside on old lanes.

At the top of the hill, opposite the first building on the R, turn L down lane which then climbs uphill again.

KSO, forking L (lower option) when lane divides. Field track joins from back L; continue along it to a road (100m) and then turn L 50m later at another road, turning L downhill alongside the twelfth-century church of **Santa Eulalia de Pascais** (church porch a good place for a rest/shelter). 100m later turn R downhill down FP along side of field/wall to join "U" of horseshoe and take RH fork to valley bottom and then continue uphill up shaded lane.

At fork shortly afterwards *do not* veer round to R uphill again (river and minor road below you to L) but take L fork down hill on FP and up and down // to river below. Descend to road, turning R along it for a few metres at a chapel and then fork L down shaded lane // to river but above it.

400m later join track coming from above back R and KSO downhill, veering round to R to cross stream. KSO ahead, forking 2nd L at junction 200m later. Join road coming from back L and then follow it round to R. Cross bridge over river and KSO on road. Fork L at bend after 2nd bridge (200m later) at junction marked "Sivil" and KSO on this road. (River in valley bottom to L.)

Turn L in village and continue uphill on road and then downhill again. Follow road uphill (it then becomes a UMUR). Join another road at a "U" bend and KSO(L) downhill. KSO(R) at next fork and KSO through village and uphill again at end.

Go under road bridge and enter village of **Hospital**, fork L and pass K116. This is where you join the route from San Xil; continue to Sarria as described below.

B. ROUTE VIA SAN XIL

Turn R in **Triacastela**, cross main road and go along minor road marked "San Xil". Follow it round uphill. At 2nd fork KSO(R) along gravelled road (signposted to "Balsa") with a decorative stone section/panel down its centre. Continue to climb, fork L at junction down earth lane to **Balsa** (K128). Track joins from back R at entrance. [RJ: KSO(R).]

KSO through hamlet, veer L at end, cross bridge and then turn R uphill past farm and *ermita* (K127.5). After nearly 1km turn R onto minor road. *Fountain*, with stone sitting area, 20m further on on LH side. Continue uphill on road, pass K126.5 and veer L at junction with "stop" sign to San Xil (a small hamlet with only a few houses).

At junction near top of hill KSO ahead then fork R onto higher road. Road levels out a little after this (village below you to L) though still continuing to climb, fountain on R, shortly before K125.5. Good views to L and ahead. Continue on road for 1km to

5km Alto de Riocabo (1370.5/124.5) 896m

Here you again have a choice, the routes (both waymarked) joining up again 2.3km later in the village of Montán. The RH option passes along the other side of the valley and has the marker stones; it is slightly longer but probably quieter and would be more suitable for mountain bikes.

Either a) KSO on road (notice to "fuente") and 100m later fork R off road down lane. 100m later fork L uphill up stone steps onto FP and follow this downhill. 400m later track joins from back R; KSO downhill (wider track). 200m later turn hard R, steeply downhill. 300m later (*fountain on L*) reach road by church at entrance to **Montán**. [RJ: turn L off road up side of church.]

Continue on road and 100m later turn R again, onto lane into village itself. KSO through it (very long and straggling), KSO(R) (ie. fork R) in middle and L at end downhill between buildings onto lane, rejoining other route at K122 (see below).

Or b) turn R at K124.5 and KSO down grassy track. KSO at crossing 40m (which becomes a lane). Pass K124 (**A Focara**), gently downhill all the time before veering sharp L uphill again. Pass K123.5. High level path with good views.

KSO at junction shortly before K123 (**O Real**) and then veer L downhill at fork a few metres afterwards. KSO downhill down walled lane, ignoring turns to L and R. Pass K122.5 (**Montán**). KSO(R) at fork above village (to your L), KSO downhill, veering L into another village and turn R into another walled lane between fields. Pass K122. KSO ignoring 2 RH turns. Track joins earth road coming from back R [RJ: fork R]. KSO(R) at fork 100m further on and when track becomes a minor road fork R at junction past white house (on your L).

After K121.5 (**Fonteainda**, opposite house) road becomes a walled lane leading down to road. Turn R and a few metres later on at K121 (**Zoo Mondareiga**) turn *hard* L off road downhill on wooded lane. Turn R along UMUR in valley bottom, which then veers round to L, past K120.5 and uphill again, passing to L of telephone tower (ie. on your R). Continue to road (K120), ignoring turns and turn L (not waymarked). KSO(R) at fork 100m later (this *is* waymarked).

KSO on road, ignoring turns, pass K119.5 (**Furela**) and fork L off road through village. At end, after (dirty!) pink church fork R and R again uphill and R a 3rd time, along lane between drystone walls, joining road at K119. Turn L along it and fork R 200m later onto more minor road. Sarria visible ahead. Road becomes UMUR. Pass K118.5 (**Pintín**) and go downhill, veering L at fork [RJ: R fork] to village.

Veer R in village to end and KSO(R) onto road shortly before K118, at bend in the road coming from your L. Continue on road. Fork R down walled lane at K117.5 (**Calvor**). Cross over and down path veering L (church to your L), // to road through trees. Pass K117 downhill to road junction. Turn L along road *down*hill. KSO on road, ignoring turnings. [Refuge in old school on LH side of road, opposite turning to "Louseiro".]

Fork R at fork in road after K116.5 (**Aguiba**). Continue through **Hospital** (K116), so named, like many other such villages, because of its former pilgrim hospital. KSO at junction with bigger road and veer L along it. KSO on road, pass K115 (**San Mamede**, just a few houses) and downhill to Sarria, passing K114.5 (**San Pedro**), K114 (**Carballal**), **Vigo de Sarria** (K113) until you reach the main Sarria-Samos road at "stop" sign in the town itself.

18km Sarria 420m (1383/112)

All facilities. The old part of the town is up on the hill and includes a church dedicated to the Galician martyr Santa Marina, the Romanesque church of El Salvador, the Convento de la Magdalena, the remains of the medieval castillo at the top of the hill and several old houses with armorial devices over the doors.

The section from Sarria to Portomarín is one of the most quiet and peaceful of the camino but before you leave Sarria make sure you have enough food (and water) as apart from one bar off the path at Mercado da Sera there are no shops, no other bars and nowhere at all to get anything to eat or drink until you reach Portomarín. The route passes through many villages but they are all extremely small, with no facilities of any kind.

Cross over and follow the road as it veers round to R, passing K112. Cross bridge over the river **Oríbio**, cross main (Monforte-

Sarria) road and go up a steep street with steps (the **Escalinata Maior**), veer L and continue uphill almost straight ahead, up the **Rúa Maior**, passing the church of **San Xoan** on your R (note modern frescoes outside). Pass police station (L), chapel of **Santa Misión** (at top, L) and turn R past the old Prison Penetencial (R) along the **Avenida de la Feria**. Pass market (L) and descend slightly towards the **Mosteiro de Magdalena** (monastery). Turn L downhill beside the cemetery, turn R at bottom by electricity substation and then turn L to cross the medieval **Ponte Aspera** (K110.5).

KSO down a lane to the Madrid-La Coruña railway line. The path continues alongside the track before bending L and then R to become a green lane. Cross railway line (carefully!) at K109.5 (**Sancti Michaelis**) and continue // to the railway line. Cross stream by FB and continue uphill through oak woods, forking L again uphill at fork.

Path zigzags uphill and crosses large field at top. Turn R along track by 1st farm building at end of wall. Continue to road, turn L and then veer R 100m later (K108, Vilei). Follow road through village and continue on road. Good views to L. Fork R ahead at fork by small bus shelter and KSO to church (road bends R just before it) in

5km Barbedelo 580m (1388/107)
Romanesque church of Santiago, a National Monument and worth a visit for its frescoes.

Turn R uphill up road by church (refuge in old school on R by playing field; spectator stand a good place for rest/keeping dry if raining). Veer L at K107 and at the top turn L off the road into a lane at K106.5 (**Rente**). KSO ahead, veer R through village to road coming from back R ("Casa Turismo Rural del Peregrino" - rooms - on L at bend) and continue on road, ignoring turns to L and R. KSO, cross another road and veer R 20m behind buildings on road (ie. *do not* turn L to farm) and continue down tree-lined lane.

At K105 [RJ: fork R] pass modern fountain (with water coming out of "Pelegrin"'s mouth and stone sitting area). Lane joins from back R [RJ: KSO(R)].

Pass K104.5 (**Marzán O Real**) and continue along lane. 150m later turn R (this may be hard to find), slightly downhill alongside wall (Fenosa - electricity company - tower behind it). Continue along walled lane through woods.

Cross road and KSO on minor road. Pass K103.5 at **Leimán**. KSO, veering L at triple fork and continue on road to village of **Peruscallo** (*fountain*).

Here you encounter one of the many hórreos *typical of this region - long narrow rectangular stone or brick storehouses raised up on stilts and used for potatoes, corncobs etc. They have a cross on top of the roof at one end and a decorative knob at the other and vary enormously in size; some are only 2-3m long but others may be as long as 15-20m.*

Veer L shortly after K102.5 and continue down walled lane, often flooded, but with raised path along LH side and then stepping stones in centre. Fork L at fork alongside field, pass K102 (**Cortiñas**) and KSO, ignoring turns, to village itself. Join very minor road coming from back R [RJ: KSO(R)]. KSO(L) ahead at fork.

Fork R at next fork (K101.5, **Lavandeira Casal**) along walled lane. Turn R on main road 150m later then immediately L down another walled lane, continue on road at bend coming from your L [RJ: KSO(L)], passing to R of houses.

KSO(R) downhill down walled lane, pass K101 and veer L at bottom and then uphill again. (This section is often flooded in bad weather.) Continue ahead, ignoring turns, pass K100.5 (**Brea**) and continue to minor road. Turn R and then follow road, veering L through village and continue on downhill to village of **Morgade** (K99.5, *fountain*).

Continue ahead (deserted *ermita* on RH is useful for a rest if raining). KSO(L) at fork (downhill) and KSO(R) at next fork (another section often flooded). Continue uphill to

8.5km Ferreiros (1396.6/98.5)

To enter village (*fountain, refuge*) turn L, otherwise pass above to R of it. At end of village KSO downhill down minor road (tower of cemetery chapel visible 50m below you at K98, **Mirallos**, Romanesque church of Santa María).

Continue through **Pena** (K97.5) and veer R and then L in village (*fountain*) and join road coming from back R. [RJ: fork R into village.] KSO on road ignoring turnings.

Continue through **Couto-Rozas** (*fountain*) and turn R off road up walled lane at K96.5 and take L (lower) option at fork 200m later. Pass K96 (**Pena dos Corvos**) and K95.5 (**Moimentos**), cross similar track and continue downhill, veering R to road. Cross river and continue downhill, turn R along another road and 100m later turn L down lane at K95 (**Cotarelo Mercadoiro**) and large cement wayside cross.

KSO down lane ignoring turnings, through village of **Moutras** (K94.5), continue uphill and join road coming from R [RJ: fork R downhill] and KSO(L) on road.

KSO on road at K94. (After this it is downhill all the way to Portomarín, 4km.) Turn L and then R 500m later (K93.5) when road bends round to R and go down lane (view of reservoir and Portomarín ahead) to road at K93 (**Parrocha**). Fork L through village to end, join road coming from back R [RJ: KSO(R) at fork] and continue ahead on road for 100m.

Turn R down walled lane at K92.5. Join another lane coming from back R [RJ: fork R uphill up rocky lane] and continue downhill, pass K92 (**Vilacha**) and KSO to road. Cross over, go down short lane and KSO(R) ahead, veering R through village to join road coming from R [RJ: fork R]. Turn L at K91.5 then R and KSO(R) ahead leaving village and KSO to road, ignoring turns to L and R.

Turn R at junction (K91) then 2nd L ahead and L again 50m later, steeply downhill *(bar on R)*. At "T" junction below turn L slightly, follow road round and then R at K90. In front of you you will see the river Miño and the Embalse de Belezar (reservoir). Cross bridge over the river, turn L to continue or go up steep flight of steps ahead and enter

8.5km Portomarín 550m (1405/90)
Shops, bars, restaurant, hostal, *Youth Hostel. One of the bakeries in the town is famous for its* Torta de Santiago, *a large plate-sized almond tart (extremely filling) decorated with the cross that is a combination of a sword and a shepherd's crook.*

The original town was flooded when the river Miño was dammed to build the reservoir in the early 1960s and the new town built up on the hill above it. Before this took place, however, the fortified Romanesque church of San Nicolás was taken to pieces stone by stone (the numbers can still be seen today) and rebuilt on its present town centre site. The portal is by Master Mateo (who built the Portico de la Gloria in the Cathedral in Santiago). The other church in Portomarín, San Pedro, is also Romanesque.

There are 7km of roadwalking in this next stretch (and 14km steadily

uphill all the time as far as Sierra de Ligonde) but there is not usually too much traffic.

To leave Portomarín: go down the main street away from the church (the dam and river are to your L), pass in front of petrol station and turn L either over the new road bridge (signed "Club Nautico") or the old FB. Turn R on other side up minor road and fork L 100m later uphill at K89 up shady lane.

After 1.5km, near top of hill, cross minor road leading to **San Mamed(e) Belad(e)** and continue on path // to old main road, C535, behind bus shelter. Pass to R of factory and cross road (K87) to continue on wide track on RH side of road. Continue on road (and *do not* fork R 100m later towards woods).

Cross over to LH side 1.5km later, opposite the Bima (cattle-food) factory and continue on track // to road at K85.5 (**Toxibo**). At junction with main road turn L 150m later, continue ahead up lane passing behind houses and // to road but not immediately adjoining. Take L fork at fork [RJ: fork L].

At junction with another lane/UMUR coming from L turn R shortly after K84 to return to road and track alongside it (LH side), continuing to

8km Gonzar (1415/82)
Small village with Romanesque church of Santa María and refuge in old school by road.

Turn L 20m after refuge and bus shelter along lane and then turn R to continue on UMUR, // to road but away from it. Continue, ignoring turns, to road coming from R at entrance to **Castromaior** (K81) and turn L along it. Veer L and then R along road through village (uphill) and KSO uphill at end to main road at K80. Turn L along path // to road [RJ: fork R off main road at minor road signed "Castromaior"] and continue (still uphill!) L on road, crossing to continue on RH side after 300m.

KSO and then cross back to LH side shortly after K79 and fork L along UMUR. Pass K78.5 (**Hospital de la Cruz**, site of former pilgrim hospice), cross similar type of track and continue down lane to village itself (bar in summer).

Fork L at end past *refugio* (in old school) to main road and cross it (carefully). Go uphill and then turn L at K78 on old road and KSO through village of

4.5km Ventas de Narón (1417.5/77.5)

Pass to R of chapel (K77) and wooden wayside cross and continue (still uphill) on road until you pass K76.5, **Sierra de Ligonde** at 756m (panoramic views on a clear day), after which the road descends. KSO, ignoring turnings. Road joins from back L [RJ: KSO(L) uphill] and continue downhill. Pass K75 (**Previsa**) and K74.5 (**Lameiro**: note chapel to R of road and then, 200m later on L by enormous tree - good place for a rest - an interesting wayside cross with a skull on its base).

Enter village of **Ligonde** (K73.5, site of a pilgrim hospice in former times) and continue to end, passing stone cross on top of wall (R), veering R and then L down to cross bridge over river. Continue ahead uphill *(bar R in summer)* to

Galician marker stone

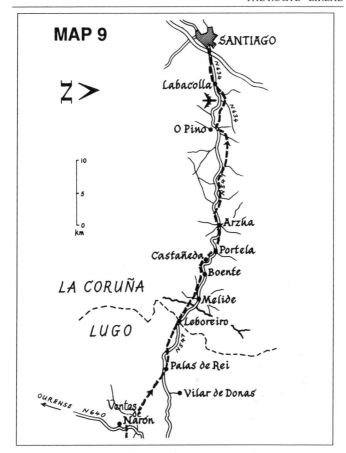

MAP 9

N >

10

5

0
km

SANTIAGO

Labacolla

O Pino

Arzúa

Portela

Castañeda

Boente

Melide

Leboreiro

Palas de Rei

Vilar de Donas

LA CORUÑA

LUGO

OURENSE   N640

Vantas de Narón

4.5km Eirexe (Airexe) (1422/73)
Refugio *in old school on RH side of road.*

The village takes its name from the Galician word for "church" (and this one has a Romanesque portal with sculpture of Daniel and animals on south wall).

KSO(L) at fork in village. Pass *lavadero* and fountain (on L) and continue to a crossroads at **As Cruces** (K72). KSO ahead down road

213

marked "Palas de Rey 10". Pass through hamlet of Portos, **Vilar de Donas** (K71).

[From here a detour of 3km (each way) is recommended, along a lane to R, to Vilar de Donas with its Romanesque church of El Salvador, a National Monument, with fourteenth-century wall paintings and effigies of the Knights of the Order of Santiago who took it over in 1184. Turn R shortly after last hórreo in village (signposted).]

Pass through hamlet of **Lestedo** (K70.5), veer R uphill at *lavadero*, pass church and wayside cross (K70). Continue uphill straight on through hamlet of **Valos** (**Balos**) (K69.5), ignoring turns to L and R. Continue on road, passing K69 (**Remollón Mamurria**).

KSO ahead, ignoring turns to L and R and KSO(L) ahead behind house along track // to main road. Pass K68 (**Ave Mostre/Lamelas**), cross lane and KSO, passing K67.5 (**Alto do Rosario**), till you join main (N547) road at junction with a minor road coming from your L (at road KM32).

Continue on FP to L of road for 250m then turn L down paved lane between buildings at K67 (**O Rosario**, a cluster of houses) by bus shelter. Continue downhill, passing to R of sports centre and KSO ahead at K66.5. Veer R on road past shop (on your L), veer 2nd R and go down steps past church (K65.5). Turn R into the street and then cross main street in town of

7km Palas do Rei 565m (1429/66)
Small town with all facilities but no very interesting features.

End of the twelfth stage in Aimery Picaud's guide and the start of the thirteenth, the last, to Santiago.

To leave: go down more steps (**Traversia de la Iglesia**), down street to R of Correos / Ayuntamiento and turn R down N547 at road KM34 *(fountain)*. Turn L immediately afterwards down paved lane and then R. Turn L and continue along main road.

Pass K64 (**Carballal**) and KSO to top of hill. When road bends R downhill at road KM36 turn L down track at K63.5. Continue downhill, pass K63 **A Laguna** and continue on lane to minor road coming from back L [RJ: fork L uphill]. 20m later KSO(L) down another lane. KSO(L) at K62.5 (**San Xulian do Camino**) and continue downhill to road. Turn L along it, continue through village and pass to R of *hórreo* and church and KSO.

Pass K62 (**Pallota**) and continue on road to "T" junction and then

Galician wayside cross

continue down lane ahead. At road at bottom turn L, cross bridge over river, turn R up lane (paved to begin with) and then L uphill (K61) up lane. Continue through woods. KSO when minor road joins from L and again shortly afterwards when road joins from back R [RJ: fork R]. Pass K60 in hamlet of

6km Casanova (1435/60)
Refuge in old school on R.

Fork L uphill, then L down lane (K59.9). KSO(R) at next fork

215

(after K59) and continue downhill, pass K58.5 (**Porto de Bois**) and KSO to cross bridge over stream. UMUR joins from back R (K58 **Campanilla**) [RJ: fork R] and then from back L 50m later [RJ: KSO(L)].

Join main road coming from back L [RJ: fork L onto track] just before K57.5 (**Coto**) and continue. Enter the province of **La Coruña** at next (minor) road junction.

Here the milestones, normally on your R, are not only at 500m intervals but are also used, with appropriate arrows on them, to indicate changes of direction.

[RJ: they will therefore be on your L - facing away from you.] Continue for a short distance to the main road (N547), signposted "Santiago 60, Melide 6". Turn L at junction [RJ: turn R down minor road signposted "Pedruzo"] *(bar/shop on L, hostal/restaurant to R)* and then turn L off main road after 100m along a track (Melide now visible ahead) leading to village of

3.5km Leboreiro (1438.5/56.5)
Fountain. Simple Romanesque church of Santa María (the building opposite was the former pilgrim hospital), rollo.

Continue through village on paved street, cross reconstructed copy of old bridge over the river **Seco** and continue ahead along lane // to main road (over to your R), ignoring turns. Pass K56 (**Disicabo**) and fork R behind factory (K55.5, **Magdalena**). KSO and then turn L at K55 along tree-lined track // to main road for 2km.

This track winds about quite a bit as it follows the outline of a projected new business park, Parque Empresarial de Melide. Originally the camino was on the main road so this is a safer (though no prettier) alternative.

100m after K53.5 turn L at road KM48 and veer R behind the Blan-Gar factory along the edge of eucalyptus woods. Continue ahead on road at junction and then fork R 200m later (downhill). Turn L (K52.5) at bottom, then R over bridge over the river **Furelos** in the village of **Furelos** itself. Turn L at end on paved road, pass church *(simple bar on L)* and turn L again through village. At end turn R onto UMUR (K52), planted with young trees.

KSO ignoring turns, continue on paved lane, fork R at end (K51 **Melide**) and 20m later enter main street (**Avenida de Lugo**) [by cycle/motor shop for RJ].

5.5km Melide 454m (1444/51)

All facilities. Pleasant small town with public garden in centre, several
pulperías *(stalls or restaurants serving squid). Churches of San Pedro,
Sancti Spiritu (former monastery church, with pilgrim hospital opposite)
and, up on the hill as you leave the town, the Romanesque church of Santa
María.*

Continue along main street past public garden (L) and turn R at
large ornate *fountain* at junction and then turn L along the **Rúa San
Pedro** and its continuation the **Rúa Principal**. (Another *fountain* in
small square to R.) Pass church of **Santa María** (L) and cemetery (L),
both at the top of the hill, and KSO downhill along lane to road at
the bottom. Cross it and enter hamlet of **Santa María** *(shop, bar)*. [RJ:
cross road and go up lane veering R.]

Turn R 200m further on down paved road, past a chapel and
another cemetery, passing the first of the many eucalyptus trees you
will encounter from now on.

*From here too, until the outskirts of Santiago, the route leads in and out
of the woods most of the time so that although the temperature may be quite
high in summer walking is still very pleasant as much of the route is shaded.*

Continue on gravelled lane // to main road (150m or more to
your R), ignoring turns to R. Pass K49.5 (**Carballal**).

KSO(R) at junction shortly after electricity substation (K49) on
your L and enter eucalyptus woods. Continue downhill, KSO(L) at
fork (K48.5), cross river at bottom by FB and KSO uphill again. This
section is more strenuous than you might expect.

Turn L at junction and continue uphill, veering R [track from
back L, RJ]. KSO(L) then turn L then T again to emerge on main road
by bus shelter at road KM52 (K47.5 **Raído**). Continue on FP on LH
side of road for 100m then turn L (by phone box) down UMUR
which veers R to continue through woods.

KSO on forest road, pass **Parabispo** (K46.8), ignore all turns and
continue in more or less a straight line, // to main road away to your
R. Go downhill, veer L out of woods to fields. Cross stream (K46,
boundary of Concello de Arzúa) and KSO on UMUR with young
trees on either side. Ignore all turns, pass **Peroxa** (K45.5), KSO(L) at
junction at entry to

6km Boente (1450/45)

Bar on road. Fountain at crossing, rollo, church of Santiago.

Turn R in village and veer L *(fountain)* to rejoin road at wayside cross and *fountain*. Turn R at church and then L straight away and KSO down UMUR to road (K44.5), cross it and continue downhill towards the river **Boente**. Go *under* main road and after crossing river lane veers L to climb steeply uphill to road at road bridge at top of hill (K43.5, road KM56).

KSO(L) along road, pass K43 (**Castañedra**) and KSO. After 300m turn L to minor road signposted to "Rio Pomar Doroña" *(bar/shop* 200m ahead to RH side of old main road) then KSO(R) 50m later at junction. Pass K42.5 (**Pedrido**). Continue downhill to Río (K42), veer L to cross bridge over stream and continue uphill again.

KSO at next crossing (// to main road) and continue uphill again (steep). Cross minor road and continue uphill (yet) again. Enter eucalyptus woods, veer diagonally R to top of hill and then L downhill. 10m after K40.5 the *camino* crosses a bridge over a new road in a very steep cutting. KSO ahead on path through woods on other side. Cross minor road and KSO downhill, crossing the bridge over the river **Iso** at the bottom in the village of

5km Ribadiso de Baixo (1455/40)
The first house on the R by the river, a pilgrim hospice in medieval times, has now been restored as a refuge.

Continue uphill, turn diagonally L at junction 300m later, continue to main road above (K39), ignoring confusing marker stone to L below road.

Watch out carefully here as there are yellow and white waymarks for another walk that passes through this area.

[RJ: turn L down road signposted to "Rendal".] Join (new) main road after bend and continue on road to

2.5km Arzúa 389m (1457.5/37.5)
Small town with all facilities. Churches of Santa María (parish church) and La Magdalena (former Augustinian convent with a pilgrim hospital).

Continue into town and then fork L (behind the **Casa Teodora**) into the **Rúa Cima do Lugar**, // to main road and KSO. Pass church of **Santa María** (R), go down **Rúa do Carmen**, cross another street and KSO. Fork L (K36.5) just before a factory, down a paved lane and KSO.

Pass K36 (**As Barrosas**), cross track and KSO. Pass **Ermita de San**

Lázaro (L), now in private hands. Turn L at junction at top of hill (main road is now 150m to your R) along UMUR which then veers round to R, downhill to valley bottom. Veer L, track joins from back L [RJ: KSO(L) ahead].

Cross stream and then climb steeply uphill again. Turn L at top along minor road coming from R (this is the **Rúa de Preguntoño**), pass small restored building with "Lugar de Preguntoño" in tiles above the door and KSO(R) at fork: ie. *ignore* the "wrong direction" crossed yellow and whites *balises* in front of you belonging to a local waymarked walk. (No yellow arrow here.) Cross minor road 20m later and continue uphill opposite. Go under main road and turn L and then R on other side, steeply uphill. Continue on fairly level lane ahead which then climbs slightly uphill again between fields, veering L after 200m or so.

(This is not as complicated as it may sound as you are merely "playing hide and seek" with the main road, now on your LH side. The marker stones in this area have no distances on them for a while as the route has been altered to take the camino *off the road and it is therefore slightly longer than before.)*

Cross minor road and continue ahead. (The track you are on becomes a road after the crossing. Arzúa visible behind you.) Fork L along lane 200m later in hamlet and L again 50m further on along track through woods and then downhill.

Turn R downhill at fork and KSO, ignoring turns, till you reach a minor (tarred) road. Turn L up it, steeply uphill (K33 to your L). At slightly staggered junction at top of hill (K32.5) KSO ahead, still uphill.

Track joins from back R at K32 (**Tabernavella**) [RJ: fork R]. KSO ahead past next L turn, enter woods again and go slightly downhill again at junction (K31.5).

KSO ahead at K31 (**Calzada**), cross minor road and KSO ahead all the time, ignoring all turnings. (Road away to your L, // to *camino*.) At junction with minor road (UMUR) coming from back L by houses shortly after K29.5 KSO(L) to L of farm buildings [RJ: KSO(R) uphill on track up lane] and rejoin UMUR a few metres later. Turn 2nd R at K29.2 (**Calle**).

20m later go down muddy paved lane between houses *under* a *hórreo*. At bend in road at bottom KSO then turn L 20m later at junction. Turn R 50m later down lane under vines. Cross stream by stone boulder FB (unstable), cross road and turn 1st R on other side between buildings then L on minor road. 20m later fork R up walled lane (at junction with another minor road coming from back L) and after 100m cross minor road and KSO uphill on gravelled road.

[If the green lane is flooded in bad weather do not fork R but KSO ahead, turning R at minor road crossing and then immediately L uphill.]

KSO, cross another minor road, continue ahead on road marked "Suso" and turn L 60m later (at K28) up smaller tarred road passing cluster of houses at **Boavista** (K27.8). (The main road is parallel for much of this section so, once again, it is not as complicated as it may seem.) At next minor road *do not KSO* but turn L and then immediately R under trees (ie. a "staggered" junction). Join minor road (leading to white house on your R - K27), cross road and KSO slightly uphill to woods again. KSO.

Pass K26.3 **Salceda**, cross a minor road, continue ahead for 50m, fork L at fork, pass K26 and veer L to rejoin main road by road placename sign for

12km Salceda (1469.5/25.5)

Bar/shop. Turn R along main road for 200m [RJ: turn L down lane after last house on L after bar] then fork R up lane (another bar ahead on main road).

Pass memorial (R) to Guillermo Watt, a pilgrim, aged 69, who died there on 25 August 1993, one day short of Santiago, a bronze sculpture of a pair of shoes set in a niche in a curved drystone wall.

Cross minor road, pass K25 and rejoin main road.

100m later cross over and fork L along forest track // to road. Pass K24.5 (**Xen**), cross road, KSO downhill down UMUR, pass K24 (**Ras**), rejoining main road again in hamlet itself.

Cross over main road and continue on lane on other side. KSO(L) at junction. Pass K23.5 (**Brea**) and memorial stone to Mariano Sánchez-Coursa Carro, a pilgrim on foot who died here on 24 September 1993. KSO, turn L at minor road and then R down wide lane. KSO to a farm (K23, **Rabiña**), fork L (farm on R). Turn L at junction and rejoin main road. [RJ: turn L down minor road marked "Rabiña / Arnal".] Turn R along road. Continue along this for 1km and at **Empalme** at top of hill turn R to minor road (bar/café, shop, restaurant). Turn L 100m later by bus shelter along side of woods

(K21.5) Emerge on main road at K21, continue on track alongside it (RH side) for a few metres and then go under the road if you want to visit the chapel of

5km Santa Irene (1474.5/20.5)

Bar. Return by tunnel and continue on RH side of main road, pass K20.5 (**Santa Irene**) and refuge at side of road by junction with minor road to Leborán. Fork R downhill onto gravel track into woods, cross road (carefully) after 300m and turn L down a track and veer R after wood yard (K19.5) to woods. KSO.

At minor road (join it at bend - bar 100m to R on main road) KSO (**Rua** K19). Ignore turns and KSO to main road again after K18.5. Cross it and KSO on other side up lane to eucalyptus woods. Ignore turns to L and R and KSO through woods till you come out at the side of a very large hangar/warehouse (on the R). Turn R in front of it along tarmac road and past college sports ground. Pass K17.5 (**Pedrouzo**) at the end.

3.5km Arca (1478/17)

Shop, pharmacy and 3 bars, refuge on main road.

To enter the village turn L after stadium. To continue on the *camino* turn R and then L (after *bar* on L) into woods again.

Turn L at the end onto a minor road (K16.9 **San Antón**). Turn L and KSO(R) and after 100m fork L to return to woods again at K16.5. Fork R (KSO) at fork after 300m, pass K16, turn L at end of woods and immediately R along track between fields, // to road. Turn L 300m later, then R after 100m on minor road. Pass K15 and at bottom of hill turn R in village of

2km Amenal (1480/15)

Bar/tabac. Small supermarket 200m further on (L) main road.

Fork L, cross river, cross main road (carefully) and continue up steep lane between buildings. Cross road and continue on other side (K14, **Cimadevila**) up lane into woods. Track joins from back R. [RJ: fork L]. 300m later cross track and fork L diagonally uphill and KSO, ignoring turns, uphill for 1km.

At "T" junction at top (Santiago airport is behind the trees ahead of you) turn R (K12.5) down forest lane for 300m to main road (K12). Turn L down clear FP between road (on R) and airport perimeter fence (on L). Pass behind airport observation platform and 200m later rejoin main road. Cross over (pergolas on either side for a short distance) and 100m later turn R down minor road at bus shelter and stone sitting area to small hamlet of **San Paio**. Turn L at church, follow road round up *very* steep hill and fork R at top onto track leading into woods (// to road to begin with).

At crossing with similar tracks turn L to Lavacolla and KSO for 1km, following lane which then joins a minor road coming from back L [RJ: fork L at house no. 28] and KSO into village of

5km Lavacolla (1485/10)

Hostal, bars, shop. The only fountain is 100m up lane off main road (to L, signposted "Fonte de Labacolla") opposite Bar San Miguel (after chapel), down some steps to L of lane.

Small village where, traditionally, pilgrims washed in the river and generally made themselves presentable before entering Santiago.

The original *camino* went past the **Capilla San Roque**, on RH side of what is now the main road (good picnic spot, shady). If you want to do this continue on the road for 3.5km to road KM717 and then, after passing **Fundación Sotelo Blanco: Museo de Antropoloxia** (on RH side of main road), cross road, go along gravel path towards huge "Monte de Gozo" sign by school and turn R along the **Rúa San Marcos**. (Quicker, but there is a *lot* of traffic.)

Otherwise, turn L to main road below parish church in **Labacolla** (temporarily *away from* Santiago), go along it for 100m and then cross it *(shop)* and turn R along minor road signposted to "Vilamaior". This takes you along quiet roads more or less // to the main road.

Follow road round to R and KSO to village of **Vilamaior** (2km: there are no longer any marker posts). Turn L in village and then R. KSO. When you get to a junction (after 2km) with a *campsite* to your L turn L past TV station (Televisión de Galicia) and then R after another TV station (TVE).

Turn R at junction and then L immediately afterwards down **Rúa de San Marcos**. KSO until you reach the **Capilla San Marcos** and the

4km Monte del Gozo (Monxoi) 368m (1489/6)

A very large modern sculpture marks the place from where pilgrims could see the Cathedral of Santiago for the first time after their long journey and

which was thus known as the "Mount Joy". It was formerly a quiet green hill but after the Pope's visit to Santiago in 1989 it was levelled to make room for the vast crowds there for an open-air mass and just below it the area is now covered with a large complex of accommodation (for 3000 people), amphitheatre, car parks and restaurants, resembling a cross between a military barracks and a holiday camp. Pilgrims with a credencial *can stay here (free of charge?) for one night only. Useful if you arrive here late in the day so that you can complete the final stage in a leisurely way the following morning.*

The chapel of San Marcos is surrounded by trees and is a good place for a picnic or final rest.

Continue on past chapel, downhill. When you get to the bottom, just before the main road and just past a house (L) with two stone *rollos* in its garden and a lot of very large concrete animals (dinosaurs etc.) go down a flight of steps to L and cross bridge over motorway. (Like the entry to many cities, the outskirts of Santiago are not very inviting.)

4km San Lázaro (1493/2)

Suburb of Santiago. After crossing the motorway KSO along the **Rúa do Valiño** (ie. the road you are already on) passing the church of **San Lázaro** *(bars etc.).* Fork L off the main road down the **Rúa do Valiño**, continuing as **Barrio das Fontiñas** when you see a very large modern housing complex to the L below the road. When you reach a big junction with traffic lights (the Avenida de Lugo L goes to the new town) continue uphill along the **Calle Fuente de los Concheiros**.

After passing a small square (L) with the cross of the Homo Sancto the road becomes the **Rúa San Pedro**. Follow this down to the **Porto do Camiño**, the traditional pilgrim entry point, then go up the **Rúa des Casas Reias**, cross the **Plaza de Parga**, the **Plaza de Animas**, turn L into the **Plaza Cervantes** and then R down the **Calle Azabachería** to the Cathedral. Go to the front, in the huge **Plaza de Obradoiro** and enter the Cathedral by the Portico de la Gloria.

2km Santiago de Compostela 264m (1495/0)

Population 80,000. All facilities. RENFE. Accommodation in all price ranges. 2 campsites: one on the main road to La Coruña, the other at As Cancelas (on outskirts). Tourist Office: 43 Rúa do Vilar (near Cathedral).

The most important of the many places of interest in Santiago (all in the old town) is the Cathedral, part Romanesque, part Baroque, with its magnificent Portico de la Gloria and facade giving onto the Plaza del Obradoiro. The Cathedral also houses what is probably the world's biggest censer (incense burner), the famous "Botafumeiro". It is made of silver and weighs nearly 80kg, requiring a team of eight men and a system of pulleys to set it in motion after mass, swinging, at ceiling level from one end of the transept to the other. Guidebooks (in English) are available from the bookshops in the Rúa do Villar (near the Cathedral) or in the new town (eg. Follas Novas, Calle Montero Ríos 37). Try to spend two or three days in Santiago, as there is much to see and do.

If you have time two pilgrim destinations outside the city are worth visiting. Padrón is the place where the boat bringing St. James to Galicia in AD44 is believed to have arrived and also contains the museum of Rosalía de Castro, the nineteenth century Galician poet; it can be reached easily by bus (some 20km) from Santiago bus station. Finisterre, the end of the known world in former times and the end of the route for many pilgrims in centuries gone by, can be reached by bus (95km) from Santiago bus station every day except Sunday. If you prefer, however, you can continue there on foot, a 3 day journey described in Appendix C.

Santiago de Compostela

The thirteenth century former monastery church
of San Salvador at Vilar de Donas

En route from O Cebreiro to Triacastela
Santiage de Compostela from the park of Santa Susanna

Appendixes

Appendix A
GR651: VARIANT ALONG THE VALLÉE DU CÉLÉ

This is not the historic route but a pleasant 54km variant along the river Célé until this runs into the Lot in Bouziès and where it joins the GR36. From here you can continue (west) for 21km along the common course of the GR36 and GR46 to rejoin the main GR65 in Les Bories-Basses. The routes are waymarked throughout with the usual red and white *balises*.

Béduer		Shop, campsite, *gîte d'étape*.
4km	**Boussac**	
2km	**Corn**	
7km	**Espagnac**	Bar, *gîte d'étape*
4km	**Brengues**	SCR, campsite, CH
4km	**Saint-Sulpice**	Bar, shop, campsite, CH
7km	**Marcilhac-sur-Célé**	SCR, *gîte d'étape*, campsite, CH
9km	**Sauliac-sur-Célee**	SCR, campsite
3.5km	**Château de Cuzals**	
2.5km	**Espinières**	*Gîte d'étape*
4km	**Cabrerets**	SCR, *gîte d'étape*, campsite, CH, hotels
5.5km	**Conduché**	
1.5km	**Bouziès**	Hotel-restaurant.
4km	**Saint-Cirq-Lapopie**	SCR, *gîte d'étape*, campsite, hotels
10km	**Concots**	SCR, hotel
7km	**Les Bories-Basses**	

Appendix B
CAMINO ARAGONÉS

The *camino aragonés* was the one taken by those who had crossed the Pyrenees by the Somport pass after following the Arles route via Montpellier, Toulouse and Auch and joins the *camino francés* in Puenta la Reina (Navarra: this route also passes through another Puenta la Reina in the province of Huesca). There are several variant routes in different sections of this *camino* but only one, waymarked throughout with the familiar yellow arrows, is described here.

It is some 165km from the Somport pass to Punta la Reina along the *camino aragonés* and should take a fairly fit walker six to seven days. It is not a very strenuous route after Jaca and much of the walking is either on the level or downhill, following the valley of the river Aragón as far as Sangüesa. Much of the area is only sparsely inhabited and it is advisable to carry enough water and a certain amount of food. The *Codex Calixtinus* divided the *camino aragonés* into three stages, the first beginning in Borce on the French side of the Pyrenees. The second went from Jaca to Monreal and the third from there to Puenta la Reina (Navarra).

Jaca can be easily reached by bus from Zaragoza, Candanchú by bus from Jaca. For up-to-date information regarding accommodation on this route it is advisable to consult the Confraternity of St. James' guide to the Arles route.

	Somport		Aldunate
		0.5km	
6km	Canfranc estación	5km	Izco
4.5km	Canfranc pueblo	2km	Idocín
7km	Villanúa	5km	Salinas
6km	Castiello de Jaca	2km	Monreal
6km	Jaca	3km	Yárnoz
4.5km	Santa Cilia	1.5km	Otano
17km	Puenta la Reina	2km	Esperun
17.5km	Mianos	1.5km	Guerendiáin
4km	Artieda	3km	Tiebas
23km	Undués de Lerda	1km	Campanas
11km	Sangüesa	2km	Biurrun
4km	Liédena	3.5km	Úcar
6.5km	Lumbier	2km	Enériz
4.5km	Nardués	2km	Eunate
226		5km	Puenta la Reina

Appendix C
SANTIAGO TO FINISTERRE

Finisterre (*Fisterra* in Gallego) was the end of the known world until Columbus altered things and was the final destination of many of the pilgrims who made the journey to Santiago in centuries gone by. There are various explanations as to how this continuation came about (one such is that it was based on a pre-Christian route to the pagan temple of Ara Solis in Finisterre, erected to honour the sun) but it is known that a pilgrim infrastructure existed, with "hospitals" in Cée, Corcubión and elsewhere. It is still possible to walk there avoiding main roads but although numbers have increased quite a lot in the last few years relatively few people still do so at present and only a very small percentage of those who make the pilgrimage to Santiago continue on to "land's end". This has no doubt been in part because of lack of information and route-finding difficulties but now that the entire route has been re-waymarked those who feel that their journey would be incomplete without continuing to Finisterre will find it much easier to do so.

The route described here leads 75km due west from Santiago, in roughly a straight line, along footpaths, quiet roads and country lanes, and is now fully waymarked. However, as there is no single definitive route and as there are frequently (waymarked) variants to choose from, which meet up again later on, what follows is not a description of all the many possibilities but a guide to one route which should be easy to follow and pleasant to walk. Allow three days to walk to Finisterre, with possible overnight stops in Negreira and Cée, though this will mean a *very* long second day. **Accommodation** is readily available in Negreira, Cée, Corcubión and Finisterre itself but there is a long gap (approximately 50km) between Negreira and Cée where there is nothing. The actual walking isn't hard but there are a lot of climbs and descents. The route is waymarked with the familiar yellow arrows of the main *camino* and they now lead you from the first one, by the Carballeira de San Lourenzo in Santiago, all the way to the town of Finisterre. [The continuation north from Finisterre to Muxía via Lires (10km + 12km) is described (in Spanish) in a supplement (No. 47) to the February 1996 issue of *Peregrino* magazine, along with an earlier version of the route described here.]

Watch out carefully for the *new* waymarks, however, as in the past the route to Finisterre was waymarked in *both* directions (ie. there and back as well). If you know where you are this shouldn't cause any problems but if you get lost retrace your steps to the previous waymark as once you have picked up the first one by the Carballeira de San Lourenzo in Santiago, they do, in fact, lead you all the way to the town of Finisterre. Many villages are also so small that they are not marked with their names at either entrance or exit, so unless you ask (and meet someone you can ask) you may not always know exactly where you are. Moreover, even the more detailed maps available do not indicate all the minor tarred roads or give the names of all the villages on them. The spellings of **placenames** may vary, too. On signposts they will be in Gallego (Galician), on some maps in Castilian, but as definitive spellings for the latter have not yet been settled these too may appear in more than one version.

Some **maps** are available in Santiago bookshops, such as the 1:250,000 map of Galicia (published by the Xunta de Galicia) and the relevant sheets (*hojas*) of the IGN's 1:25,000 series of the Mapa Topográfico Nacional de España: 94-IV (Santiago), 94-III (Negreira), 94-I (A Baña), 93-II (Mazaricos), 93-I (Brens), 92-II (Corcubión) and 92-IV (Fisterra). For the Finisterre-Muxía section you will need 67-IV (Touriñan) and 67-II (Muxía) (*hojas* 93-1. 93-2 and 92-2). These should also be available from Stanfords or the Map Shop in Upton-upon-Severn.

Asking the way. If/when you need to do this you will need to know in advance the name of the *next* village you want to pass through, asking your way from one to the next as medieval pilgrims did. However, as many people may assume you want to get to Finisterre as quickly as possible they may direct you to the main road. You will then have to explain that you want to go through the mountains/along the old tracks and assess the reliability of the information given you, according to whether the person has actually been that way themselves or just heard about it. It will be obvious from this that your Spanish needs to be reasonably good, all the more so since although you ask your question in Castilian the reply may well be given in Gallego.

Food. You will pass some shops and bars along the way but it is better to take at least some reserve supplies with you.

You will have to be more alert to route-finding than you probably had to be on the *camino francés* but continuing to the coast on foot it is definitely worth the effort. Finisterre is the real end of the journey, both in the physical sense and the religious and historical one. You will pass a number of interesting small churches, *pazos* (large Galician country houses) and old bridges along the way, apart from the now familiar *hórreos*, and the scenery is often beautiful. It is very peaceful and as there are still relatively few walkers the route is quite different from the often *autopista*-like *camino* before Santiago in July and August. It does rain a lot in this part of Spain but you will have the opportunity to see something of the real Galicia, away from the big towns. You can return to Santiago by bus, either direct or with a change in Vimianzo and/or Bajo, every day including Sunday. [Space permitting, it is also possible to take one or two bikes.]

THE ROUTE

To leave Santiago: from the **Plaza del Obradoiro** and with your back to the Cathedral pass in front of the **Hostal de los Reyes Católicos** (on your R) and go down the steps and along the **Calle de las Huertas**, veering R at end into the **Campo de las Huertas**. Continue ahead down the **Rúa da Poza de Bar** (unnamed at the start) which then becomes the **Rúa de San Lourenzo**.

At the **Carballeira de San Lourenzo** (a small park with seats and a lot of old oak trees) there is the first yellow arrow; you can KSO ahead to visit the church of **San Lourenzo de Trastouto** (normal visiting hours Tuesdays and Thursdays 11am-1pm and 4.30-6.30pm, otherwise open at mass times) and then return or turn R immediately (ie. if coming from the Cathedral) down the **Roblada de San Lourenzo**. Shortly afterwards veer L down a cement road (the **Corredoira dos Muíños**) leading you downhill to cross bridge in the hamlet of **Ponte Sarela**; the first house by the bridge has a sign: "Parroquia de San Fructuoso, Lugar de Puente Sarela". (The old buildings by the bridge were tanneries and the mills used to power them.)

Turn L on the other side along a lane and then fork L after crossing a small FB over a stream. (Watch out carefully for the waymarks here.) Go uphill, veering R until you reach a minor road.

MAP 10

Turn L along it then 300m later turn R up a tarred hill which becomes a walled lane. This veers L and may be somewhat overgrown after leaving trees (waymarks on the ground). Turn L at fork, veer L towards eucalyptus woods and then R down to houses. Turn R into the **Rúa de Vidan**, past the *lavadero*, to the main road to Noia (C-543)

3km Vidan

Bar. Turn R and continue (carefully) on main road. At present no alternative is available so continue along it through **Barcia**, **Lamas** and **Pedra da Legua**. Just before you reach Roxas *(shops etc.)* it is possible to avoid a section of main road by forking L and then rejoining it after a bend. (There are quite a few *mesones* between here and Puente Maceira.)

3.5km later, just before the entrance to Villastrexe, after a bus garage on the L and before a petrol station on the R, turn R up a minor road, slightly uphill. Take the 2nd L, veer R, pass between houses and then take the 2nd L turn, then R, onto a local road. Continue to hamlet of

2.5km Ventosa

Turn R by bus shelter. Veer R, cross road, KSO and continue down old lane, passing under electricity cables. Return to road and then turn L. *Shop* (rather grandly called "Centro comercial"). Continue to

2km Augapesada

Turn L at junction at bottom of hill in village and pass bar after 150m. Turn R 50m after bar onto road signposted "Trasmonte 3, 5 P. Maceira". KSO, uphill all the time, through eucalyptus woods *(fountain* on R 100m before top), pass two TV masts and then descend, via **Carballo**, to

3km Trasmonte

Bar/shop. Church of Santa María with Baroque tower, cruceiro *with statue of Santiago.*

KSO at crossroads and continue on road to

2km Puente Maceira

Picturesque village in two parts with stone bridge over the river Tambre and wide waterfall. Note houses with armorial devices.

Cross bridge (**Capilla San Blas** at end) and then turn L on other side. Turn R uphill at end of village and then fork L downhill when road goes up to R and 100m later turn L again down road that becomes a lane and runs // to river **Tambre**.

Go under the road bridge (the nineteenth-century **Puente**

Maceira Nueva) over the river *(bar on other side)* and continue on lane until you reach the road at KM18 (on AC-140, 1km from Puente Maceira). Continue on road for 500m then fork L uphill on road marked "Logroso" (river to your L, woods). Continue uphill to village (note Pazo de Chancela at entrance) of

2km Chancela
After top of hill take 2nd L, turn down concrete lane, then turn R onto FP, go down steps to road, turn L and continue on main road into the town of

2km Negreira
Small town with all facilities.

Go uphill, veering R, into town and then turn L into the **Carreira de San Mouro** *(Hostal Mezquito, rooms, on corner)* down main street. Continue along it to the bottom, passing under arches linking the **Pazo do Cotón** and the **Capilla de San Amaro** *(fountain* in public garden to R) and KSO on road, crossing bridge over **Río Barcala** at end of town. At junction turn R uphill, signposted "Outes, Marco del Cornado".

[A waymark to the left *here takes you on a* desvío *via the parish church of San Xulián. Go up minor road marked "Puente Don Alonso 23" and 150m later turn R (marked "Negreira Iglesia") and then R 50m later (cruceiro on L) to pass in front of church and cemetery. Turn L up steps, go through gates and turn R along street (ignore* old *arrows) which then becomes a lane. At sharp bend 200m later turn L onto middle of three FPs uphill through trees and KSO(L) at fork. This brings you out on the road again, where you turn L uphill to Zas.]*

Continue uphill to the village of

2km Zas (Xas)
Turn R here at junction opposite *shop/bar*, pass chapel, veer L and at end of village KSO(R) between *hórreo* and white house down a walled lane. Fork L 100m later to similar lane, R 100m after that, R at following junction and L 100m later, watching out carefully for waymarks as there is nothing but eucalyptus trees all round and no distinguishing features.

Turn L at "T" junction near school 2km later, R onto a road *(bar* to L) in hamlet of **Camiño Real** and continue on road. 700m later turn R onto more minor road and 100m later turn L between the trees in a straight line // to the "main" road. This is an old track which fell into disuse but gradually becomes clearer as you proceed and joins another (clear) track coming from back L after 200m.

Fork L at junction and turn L at crossing of similar tracks. KSO(R) on wider track coming from L, merging into walled lane coming from R. KSO, cross minor road, KSO ahead, veer L and then R into the middle of the village of

4.5km Rabote

At end veer L down walled lane, KSO(R) at fork, slightly downhill all the time to valley bottom and then turn R uphill. KSO(L) at fork and continue ahead through an old oak forest, ignoring all turns and continuing on tarred lane after 1km to *cruceiro* in centre of village of

1.5km A Pena (Peña)

Bar (on road at entrance to village, simple meals; to reach it turn hard *L and then hard R as soon as you reach the tarmac section).*

Turn L at *cruceiro*, L again and then R onto road. At end of village (it becomes **Porto Camiño** 700m later) turn R after last house then immediately take the RH of 3 forks (ie. the 2nd from R of 4 choices). Fork L, veer R to cross stream and veer R uphill on other side. Cross field at top. KSO, veering L, turn L at junction and rejoin road 100m later. Turn R and continue to village of

3km Vilaserio

Immediately before the first house at the approach to the village and just before a road junction turn L off the road down a walled lane to road at bottom. Turn R at fork, R immediately and L *(bar)* onto road. KSO, passing turns to Pesadoira and Cornado.

At junction of roads CP-5603 and 5604 (KM14) KSO ahead down UMUR. After 1km turn R onto a minor road, KSO at junction when tarmac stops, veering L and 300m later at group of seven isolated trees fork L downhill. KSO at next two crossings, cross bridge over river and enter

7km Maroñas

A very long, straggling village. Bar, shop (ask for it) and bar/restaurant.

Fork L in village, follow street round and veer R. Turn L at "T" junction into village of **Santa Marina** (1km), veer R at *cruceiro* and reach main road. Turn L, pass *bar/restaurant* **Casa Victoriano** and another bar and turn R up a minor road 300m further on, signposted "Buenjesús. Guiema". KSO for 3km to scarcely separated villages of **Bon Xesús** (there was a chapel and pilgrim hospital here in former times) and

3km Gueima
Turn R at junction at end of village. 100m later at last building (barn) turn L uphill, steeply, on UMUR. KSO, ignoring turns, to top of hill (this is the **Monte Aro**, good views over the reservoirs on a clear day). Veer R downhill and join gravelled lane, turning R into village of

2km Lago
Turn L and L again. At road turn L and then turn R by bus shelter and KSO down a minor road for 3km, ignoring turns to

3km San Cristóbal de Corzen
Pass church and cemetery and turn L at junction. KSO to next village and turn R at junction onto larger road. Cross bridge over river **Xallas** and enter

1km Puente Olveiroa
KSO on main road (which veers L) for 2km and then, after passing a turning to R to "Santiago Olveiros", turn L off main road onto a minor and go through the village of

3km Olveiroa
(Not to be confused with another village nearby, Olveira.) Here there are a lot of hórreos. *Church over to L with statue of St. James, Bar Mueriñas 50m uphill to R on main road.*

Turn L at end of village onto main road again.

After 100m there is a waymarked turning to the L, which leads along the side of a lake (up to Logosa) but is so overgrown at present as to be impossible to use.

Instead, continue uphill (*very steep*) on the road.

(It is eventually intended to re-waymark the route through the village of Logosa and go from there to Hospital, thus avoiding present stretch on road, so watch out carefully for new waymarks.)

At the top (2km) there is a wayside crucifix on the RH side (the Cruz de Olveiroa, placed there in 1917) and you will see two large,

234

Stone formations near Logosa

ugly belching carbide factories ahead of you on the skyline: the first one is just outside the village of Hospital. Continue up on the road and then turn off to the R into village itself.

4km Hospital

Bar Casteliño on road near factory. A village likely, given its name, to have had a pilgrim hospital here in centuries gone by, although no evidence remains.

Turn R again uphill, veer L by house then R onto old road. At a roundabout (the factory is now near you on the L) turn L onto the main Dumbria-Cée road and then fork R, opposite the factory entrance, onto a track. 500m later fork L and KSO.

This is the old camino real, *9km of old drove road leading you through the mountains to Cée, more or less in a straight line.*

At a minor road KSO ahead, forking L 100m later. KSO for 2-3km more and at a clear "T" junction turn R. 300m later turn L down track coming from R to

4km Santuario de Nosa Señora das Neves

Chapel, currently being restored, which was formerly known as the Fonte Santa because of the fountain, at the foot of a cruceiro, *which had healing*

235

properties. A mass and festival is held there annually on December 8th.

Go downhill and then up the other side, continuing ahead all the time on a clear track, recently waymarked, which is easy to follow and with good views in clear weather. Shortly before you reach Cée you will reach the **Ermita de San Pedro Mártir** on the R, with its own *fonte santa* and site of a local pilgrimage. Good place for a rest. Continue on mountain track until you reach the C550 and KSO into

6km Cée

Coastal town with all facilities. Hospedaje Crego (in Avenida Finisterra), Hostal Cruceiro (on hill near entrance to town) and Hostal Galicia (on road to Corcubión) all have rooms.

Continue through the town on the road along the waterfront to

1km Corcubión

All facilities. Café/restaurant Sirena has rooms.

Follow the main road (signposted "Fisterra") uphill out of town for 3km (it zigzags a lot but there appear to be no short-cuts) until you reach a large play / picnic area and tennis court at the top, where the road turns sharp R. KSO straight ahead here, down a minor road (waymarked) and then turn R immediately down a green lane (not waymarked straight away). Veer L along wall and past *fuente*. This cuts out quite a long section of road before you return to it again at a red bus shelter.

Fork L 200m further on (on road) down a FP into the woods (watch out for waymarks on trees), pine at first and then eucalyptus. When you reach a junction at the bottom (field and stone wall to L, sea ahead of you) turn R (the path you were on turns sharp L here). This too is not waymarked immediately but there are yellow flashes on the ground later on. Follow this path slightly uphill until you rejoin the road. (This has now been considerably widened so it is now possible to short-cut many of its former hairpins.)

5km Sardiñeiro

Shops, bars, campsite and nice beach at entrance to village.

Here yellow arrows lead you off the main road onto quieter streets near sea: turn L alongside football pitch (**Rúa da Playa**) and continue along **Rúa de Marina** between main road and sea. Turn L onto main road at end of village and KSO along it, entering woods again, until you reach the hamlet of

View towards Finisterre

4km Anchoa

Turn L down minor road opposite *autoservicio (shop)* and *café* and then turn R. When you reach a small "roundabout" head for the beach and continue along it to the buildings at the end.

Bar/restaurant in the somewhat grandly named Calle San Roque: presumably this was once a much bigger place, referring, as it does, to the saint associated with pilgrims. The beach here is strewn with literally thousands of shells, scallop and others, recalling the legend of the equestrian bridegroom.

Go up track to L of bar (waymarked) and KSO(L) along road at top by tall wayside crucifix into

2km Finisterre

Small fishing port with all facilities and several hostales.

From the village of Finisterre itself it is a further 2km along the road to the lighthouse *(el faro)*, where plans are underway to turn it into a *parador* (hotel). Continue uphill past the parish church of **Santa María das Areas** (St. Mary of the Sands).

Romanesque in part with a statue of St. James, Gothic cruceiro, chapel which was formerly a pilgrim hospital and its own Porta Santa in jubilee years. (Visits 10.30am-1.30pm, 4-7.30pm.)

This is the real "land's end" and is clearly signposted.

(Fountain on RH side of road at sharp LH bend.) A rocky outcrop known as the Piedras Santas, a possible focus of pre-Christian worhip, is apparently to be found on the north shore of the peninsula. As the weather is often misty until about midday in this part of Spain you may have better views from here in the late afternoon and evening.

Appendix D
OUTLINE GUIDE TO THE CAMINO MOZÁRABE
OR VIA DE LA PLATA

As explained in the introduction, there was not just one *Camino de Santiago* but several, one of which was the *camino mozárabe* or *Vía de la Plata*, so named, it is now thought, *not* because it followed the old Roman silver road from Huelva in the south to Astorga but as a corruption of the Arabic *Bal'latta*, used to describe wide paved or public roads. This was the route taken by pilgrims from southern Spain and led north, in more or less a straight line, via Seville, Zafra, Mérida, Cáceres, Salamanca and Zamora until it joined the *camino francés* in Astorga. It is well waymarked throughout with yellow arrows and is easy to follow but as yet not many people take it, presumably because, as a walk, it is less well known than the northern route. There is now a concise guide to it (in Spanish) with sketch maps, produced by the "Amigos" in Seville, but apart from a certain amount of route-finding information given in the Confraternity of St. James' accommodation guide to the *camino mozárabe* nothing is available in English.

However, since the the *Vía de la Plata is* easy to follow (it is not a "map-and-compass" walk) a skeleton outline is given here to enable (and encourage) interested people to undertake it. This contains a list of the places, large and small, through which this *camino* passes, and should be used in conjunction with Michelin maps 446 (Southern Spain), 444 (Central Spain) and 441 (Galicia/Asturias-León).

The route is very varied, both in climate, scenery, history and architecture (you are very much aware of being in Roman Spain), and differs from the northern road in a number of practical ways. It is much warmer (July and August are definitely *not* recommended) and the best time is either April-May or in the autumn. In the south there is very little water (and very few fountains, though fortunately these increase in number and reliability the farther north you go) so you will usually have to carry everything you need for the entire day. In Andalucía and some parts of Extremadura there are a lot of very large properties (farms known as *cortijos*) and very few tracks or roads other than the main road so that in some places this unavoidably coincides with the *camino*. Later, though, you may spend complete days in the countryside on old tracks, never meeting a single person or passing a single village from morning to evening. You are also unlikely to meet many other walkers and for this reason some people may prefer to go with a companion. The walking is not difficult as such but as there are often long gaps between accommodation you will need to be fit and able to cover long distances (ie. upwards of 30km) on a daily basis, carrying all your food and water.

Not only is the route well waymarked from the outskirts of Seville but the tracks/lanes themselves are very clear and obvious, with none of the *sendas* or very small footpaths sometimes encountered on the *camino francés*. However, unlike the northern route, the existence of the *Vía de la Plata* as a walker's pilgrim route is less well known amongst the people who live along its path, so that if you have trouble, for example, finding your way *out* of a place you will need (as well as good Spanish) to know the name of some prominent building/street/other feature near its exit so that you can ask for that instead. It is therefore a good idea to go for a *paseo* in the evening to check where you will leave from the following morning; in small places this is not usually too difficult, since the *Vía de la Plata* heads north all the time, but in bigger towns it can be more complicated, especially if there have been roadworks.

How long does it take? The distance between Seville and Astorga is 738km so the amount of time you need will depend on your pace, stamina and the number of rest days you want to take. A month is probably a minimum, plus another 9 or 10 days if you want to continue on from Astorga to Santiago.

Language. A better than basic knowledge of Spanish is even more essential on the *Vía de la Plata* than on the *camino francés* and regional accents may be particularly difficult to follow. In Andalucía, for instance, and in parts of Extremadura, all the intervocalic and terminal "s's" disappear from words so that, as an example, *dos meses* ("two months") will sound like "doh may".

Accommodation. There are only three refuges along the Vía de la Plata (and only for the use of those with a *credencial* or "pilgrim passport") and in some places (eg. between Cáceres and Salamanca) there are very long stretches without any accommodation within reasonable walking distance. However, places of any size, particularly if they are on a main road, usually have some kind of facilities, if only *camas* in bars for *camioneros* (lorry drivers) and which are often surprisingly good value.

Getting there. a) By air direct to Seville from London (Iberia has scheduled flights). b) By train. There is now a high-speed train (the TAV or AVE) from Madrid to Seville via Córdoba. c) By coach, either direct to Seville from London or Paris via Madrid, from where long-distance buses are also available to Mérida, Cáceres, Salamanca and Zamora.

THE ROUTE

Figures after placenames refer, respectively, to the distance from Seville and the number of kilometres remaining to Astorga, and, where known, a place's height (in metres) and its population. Thus, for example, Camas 5/733 is 5km from Seville and 733 from Astorga.

0km	**Seville** 0/738 (12m, 650,000)
5km	**Camas** 5/733 (13m)
5km	**Santiponce** 10/728 (16m)
13km	**Guillena** 23/715 (22m)
3km	**Venta la Casa de Pradera** 26/712
17km	**Castilbanco de los Arroyos** 43/695 (329m)
29km	**Almadén de la Plata** 72/666 (449m)
16km	**El Real de la Jara** 88/650 (460m)
12.5km	**Ermita de San Isidoro** 100.5/637.5
4km	**La Nava** 104.5/633.5
4km	**Cruz del Puerto** 108.5/629.5 (753m)
1.5m	**Monasterio** 110/628 (752m)
22km	**Fuente de Cantos** 132/606 (583m)
6.5km	**Calzadilla de los Barrios** 138.5/599.5 (556m)
14.5km	**La Puebla de Sancho Pérez** 153/585 (522m)
4km	**Zafra** 157/581 (509, 12,900)
5km	**Los Santos de Maimona** 162/576 (528m, 8100)
15km	**Villafranca de los Barros** 177/561
19km	**Almendralejo** (337m, 23,600)
16km	**Torremegía** 212/526 (302m)

16km	**Mérida** 228/510 (218m, 51,600)
6km	**Embalse de Prosperpine** 234/504
7.5km	**El Carrascalejo** 241.5/496.5 (308m)
2.5km	**Aljucén** 244/494 (270m)
15km	**Cruz del Niño Muerto** 259/479
6km	**Alcuéscar** 265/473 (489)
9km	**Casas de Don Antonio** 274/464 (413m)
7km	**Aldea del Caño** 281/457 (396m)
12km	**Valdesalor** 293/445 (380m)
12km	**Cáceres** 305/433 (464m, 69,193)
11km	**Casar de Cáceres** 316/422 (369m)
22km	**Hostal Miraltejo** 338/400 (250m)
15km	**Cañaveral** 353/385 (362m, 2100)
6km	**Puerto de los Castaños** 359/379 (500m)
24km	**Galisteo** 383/355 (308m)
6km	**Aldeahuela del Jerte** 389/349
5km	**Carcaboso** 394/344 (271m)
13km	**Venta Quemada** 407/331
6.5km	**Cáparra** 413.5/324.5 (400m)
18.5km	**Aldeanueva del Camino** 432/306 (529m)
10km	**Baños de Montemayor** 442/296 (708m)
13km	**Calzada de Béjar** 455/283 (796m)
7.5km	**Valverde de Valdelacasa** 463.5/274.5
3.5km	**Valdelacasa** 467/271 (964m)
8km	**Fuenterroble de Salvatierra** 475/263 (955m)
10.5km	**Navarredonda de Salvatierra** 485.5/252.5 (982m)
5km	**Pico de la Dueña** 490.5/247.5 (1140m)
6.5km	**Calzadilla de Mendigos** 497/241 (950m)
8km	**San Pedro de Rozados** 505/233 (980m)
4.5km	**Morille** 509.5/228.5
20.5km	**Salamanca** 530/208 (808m, 167,000)
6km	**Aldeaseca de la Armuña** 536/202 (820m)
5km	**Castellanos de Villiquiera** 541/197 (830m)
4.5km	**Calzada de Valdunciel** 545.5/192.5 (807m)
5km	**Apeadero de Huelmos** 550.5/192.5
14.5km	**El Cubo de Tierra del Vino** 565/173 (846m)
13.5km	**Villanueva de Campeán** 578.5/159.5 (765m)
19.5km	**Zamora** 598/140 (658m, 57,734)

6.5km	**Roales de Pan** 604.5/133.5 (700m)
12.5km	**Montamarta** 617/121 (690m)
11km	**Fontanilles de Castro** 628/110 (725m)
4km	**Riego del Camino** 632/106 (705m)
6.5km	**Granja de Moreruela** 638.5/99.5 (708m)
9km	**Santovenia** 6477.5/90.5 (715m)
5.5km	**Villaveza del Agua** 653/865 (700m)
2.5km	**Barcial del Barco** 610/80 (717m)
5km	**Castropepe** 660.5/77.5 (720m)
7.5km	**Benavente** 668/70 (747m, 12,500)
8.5km	**Villabrázaro** 677/61 (710m)
8.5km	**Maire de Castroponce** 685.5/52.2 (748m)
3km	**Puente de la Vizana** 688.5/49.5
3km	**Alija del Infantado** 691.5/46.5 (740m)
21.5km	**La Bañeza** 713/25 (777m, 8501)
3km	**Santiago de la Valduerna** 716/22 (775m)
3km	**Palacios de la Valduerna** 719/19
14km	**Cuevas** 733/5 (840m)
5km	**Astorga** 738/0 (899m, 14,000)

Asociación de Amigos del Camino de Santiago "Vía de la Plata", Calle Paraiso 27, 41940 Tomares (Sevilla), Spain. Tel: 95.415.44.85.

Appendix E
REFUGIOS IN SPAIN

The following is a list of the main *refugios* along the *camino francés* in Spain and which are available only to those with a *credencial* or "pilgrim passport". As the availability of such accommodation varies considerably from one year to another only the more permanent ones have been included here. Prospective pilgrims are advised to obtain the Confraternity of St. James' annually updated guide for more detailed information.

Refugios vary greatly in the facilities they offer and in their opening/closing hours and some are extremely spartan. You will need a sleeping bag as blankets are not often provided and a sleeping mat in the simpler accommodation or for when the beds/mattresses are already occupied. Not many have the sort of cooking facilities you would find in a Youth Hostel in Britain or a *gîte d'étape* in France. Note that you cannot reserve places, which are allotted on a first-come-first-served basis, that many *refugios* do not take groups and several do not accept cyclists either, if there are too many walking pilgrims, and that these facilities may be *extremely* crowded in July / August as no one with a *credencial* is normally turned away.

Please note too, as indicated in the Introduction, that they are *not* provided as cheap substitutes for hotels but as alternatives to sleeping rough. If there is no charge as such you should expect to leave a donation. Many are staffed by volunteer wardens during the summer months.

Roncesvalles	Hospital de Órbigo (2)
Zubiri	Astorga
Larrasoaña	Rabanal del Camino (2)
Trinidad de Arre	Molinaseca
Pamplona	Ponferrada
Cizur Menor	Villafranca del Bierzo (2)
Puenta la Reina	Vega del Valcarce
Estella	Cebreiro
Los Arcos	Hospital de la Condesa
Viana	Triacastela
Logroño	Samos
Nájera	Calvor
Azófra	Sarria
Santo Domingo de la Calzada	Barbadelo
Grañon	Ferreiros
Belorado	Portomarín
San Juan de Ortega	Gonzar
Burgos	Ventas de Narón
Tardajos	Eirexe
Hornillos	Palas do Rei
Hontanas	Casanova
Castrojeriz	Melide
Fromista	Ribadiso
Carrión de los Condes	Santa Irene
El Burgo Ranero	Arca
Mansilla de la Mulas	Monte del Gozo
Villadangos del Páramo	

Appendix F
SUGGESTIONS FOR FURTHER READING

Donald Atwood and C.R. John, *Penguin Dictionary of Saints*. 3rd ed., Harmondsworth: Penguin, 1995.

Pierre Barret and Jean-Noël Gurgand, *Priez pour nous à Compostelle*. Paris: Hachette, 1978.

> An account of the authors' journey from Vézelay to Santiago on foot, interspersed with parallel accounts of pilgrims from previous centuries. Contains a very extensive bibliography.

Jean Bourdarias and Michel Wasielewski, *Guide Européen des Chemins de Compostelle*. Paris: Fayard, 1997.

> Guide to all the European routes to Santiago (from Holland, Denmark, Poland, Hungary, Brenner, Croatia, Italy and Portugal), not the currently more well-known routes through France and Spain. Contains maps, distances, over 800 photographs, history and descriptions of places, lives of saints and relevant Biblical extracts.

Laurie Dennett, *A hug for the apostle. On foot from Chartres to Santiago de Compostela*. Toronto: Macmillan of Canada, 1987.

> An account of the author's walk, undertaken to raise money for the Multiple Sclerosis Society. Some of the book covers the pilgrimage in France though much of it is devoted to the route in Spain, including much interesting historical material.

Michael Jacobs, *The Road to Santiago de Compostela* (Architectural Guides for Travellers series). London: Viking, 1990.

> A guide to the churches, monasteries, hostels and hospitals along the pilgrim route, analysing their architectural styles. Contains photos, maps and detailed plans.

Domenico Laffi, *A Journey to the West*. Trans. James Hall, Leiden: Primavera Pers/Santiago: Xunta de Galicia, 1997.

> A translation of and commentary on the diary of a seventeenth-century pilgrim from Bologna to Santiago. Includes maps and 84 original black and white illustrations.

Edward Mullins, *The Pilgrimage to Santiago*. London: Secker & Warburg, 1974.

An account of the art, architecture, history and geography of the pilgrim route from Paris to Santiago.

Rob Neillands, *The Road to Compostela*. Ashbourne: Moorland Publishing, 1985.

An account of the author's journey from Le Puy to Santiago by bicycle.

Annie Shaver-Crandell and Paula Gerson, *The Pilgrim's Guide to Santiago de Compostela: a Gazeteer*. London/Langhorne: Harvey Miller, 1995.

730 entries and 575 illustrations describing all the relics of saints, important monuments, towns and buildings encountered by the twelfth-century pilgrim along the four routes through France and then in Spain. Includes a new translation of the Latin text of the *Codex Calixtinus* plus discussion of the pilgrimage phenomenon in the Middle Ages as well as the tradition of travel literature.

Bert Slader, *Pilgrim Footsteps*. Newcastle, County Down: Quest Books (NI), 1994.

Walter Starkie, *The Road to Santiago. Pilgrim of St. James*. London: John Murray, 1957.

An account of a pilgrimage to Santiago, part travel, part history, part autobiography.

Brian and Marcus Tate, *The Pilgrim Route to Santiago*. Oxford: Phaidon, 1987.

Explains the pilgrim phenomenon and the history of the shrine as well as discussing the different routes. Contains 137 photographic illustrations by Pablo Keller, 50 of them in colour.

Jeanne Viellard, *Guide du Pèlerin de Saint Jacques de Compostelle*. Paris: Klincksieck, 4th ed., 1989.

A French translation, on facing pages, of what is probably the first known guidebook: Aimery Picaud's twelfth century description of the pilgrim routes to Santiago.

Peregrino magazine, 6 issues a year, articles (general, historical, practical accounts of journeys) on the pilgrimage.

The Pilgrim's Guide: a 12th century Guide for the Pilgrim to St. James of

Compostela. Translated from the Latin by James Hogarth, Confraternity of St. James, 1992.

Song of Roland. Trans. G. Burgess, Penguin Classics, 1990.

En Chemin vers Saint Jacques: guide spirituel du pèlerin.

Conques (Communauté des Prémontrés) / Estaing (Hospitalité Saint Jacques), 1993. Pocket-size (A6) booklet intended as a spiritual aid, containing themes for personal meditation, prayers and hymns and notes on the many saints whose churches, chapels and sanctuaries line the route.

USEFUL ADDRESSES

Confraternity of St. James
First Floor
1 Talbot Yard
Borough High Street
London SE1 1YP

Los Amigos del Camino de Santiago
Apartado de Correos 20
Estella
Navarra, Spain

Peregrino, Boletin del Camino de Santiago
Apartado 60
26250 Santo Domingo de la Calzada
La Rioja, Spain

Appendix G
GLOSSARY

France

balise	waymark
barry	suburb (Occitan: cf. Sp. *barrio*)
bastide	walled hilltop town (SW France)
borie	farm (Occitan)
buron	shepherd's bothy
calade	paved road or path (Occitan)
carriera	street (Occitan)
caselle	small round hut of dry stone construction
chasse guardée	private ground / hunting
causse	limestone plateau in SW France with scrubby vegetation
château d'eau	water tower
cledo	flexible gate made of wire and palings
col	mountain pass
commanderie	commandery (ie. of military order)
couderc	enclosed field / village green (Gascon)
draille	drove road
écluse	lock (on canal)
gave	mountain stream / river in the Pyrenees
gaviote	stone hut, similar to *caselle*
halle	(covered) market place
hameau	hamlet
jacquet	pilgrim going to Santiago
lavoir	outdoor washing-place, (public) wash-house
lieu-dit	locality
luy	river (Gascon)
mairie	town hall, town council
mas	house / farm in south of France (Occitan)
mirador	watchtower, mirador
montjoie	cairn
montredon	rounded hill (Occitan)

palombière	hide in forest used by pigeon-hunters
passage canadien	cattle grid
passerelle	footbridge
pech	hill, mountain (Occitan)
pélèrin	pilgrim
pigeonnier	dovecote
puy	hill, mountain
réserve de chasse	hunting preserve
romieu	pilgrim (esp. one who has been to Rome)
sauvetat/sauveté/	
sauveterre	town or area serving as safe haven
tampon	(rubber) stamp
temple	Protestant church

Spain

albergue	inn; also used to refer to a *refugio*
alcázar	fortress, castle
aldea	hamlet
alto	hill, height
arroyo	stream, small river
ayuntamiento	town hall
barrio	suburb
bascula	weighbridge
bodega	wine cellar; also used to describe a store place for wine located in hillsides and other places in the open countryside
cafetería	a café that also serves snacks (not a self-service restaurant for hot meals)
calzada	(paved) road, causeway
camino	track, path
cancela	outer door/gate; wrought-iron/lattice gate
capilla	chapel
carretera	(main) road, highway
Casa Consistorial	town hall in small places
Casa do Concello	town hall (in Galicia)

cierren la puerta /el portillo	"close the gate"
cigüena	stork
coto de caza	hunting/game preserve
coto de pesca	fishing preserve
crucero	wayside cross
desvío	detour, diversion (eg. on roads)
embalse	dam, reservoir
ermita	hermitage, small chapel
finca	smallholding
fonda	guesthouse, inn
frontón	pelota court
fuente	fountain, spring
gallego	Galician
hórreo	(raised) granary
hospedaje	*fonda* (in Galicia)
hospedería	inn, hostelry
hostal	hotel (less expensive than a hotel)
igrexia	church (Galician)
ixti ataka mesedez	"close the gate" (Basque)
jacobeo	(adj.) of St. James
lavadero	outdoor washing-place, (public) wash-house
merendero	picnic area, refreshment stall
meseta	plateau, tableland
mesón	restaurant (often simple, with period decor)
mosteiro	monastery (Gallego)
palloza	round thatched dwelling of Celtic origin
palmero	pilgrim who has been to Jerusalem
panadería	bakery
pantano	marsh, swamp (natural); reservoir, dam (artificial)
páramo	plain, bleak plateau (often used in placenames)
paseo	stroll, walk; avenue

peregrino	pilgrim
plaza de toros	bull ring
posada	inn (simpler than a *fonda*)
pueblo	village, small town
puente	bridge
puerta	door, gateway (esp. fig., often found in placenames)
puerto	mountain pass; port
rollo	stone wayside cross, often at junctions; raised up and may be highly decorated
rodeo	roundabout or indirect route
romería	pilgrimage to a local shrine
romero	pilgrim (originally one who had been to Rome)
rúa	street (Galician)
sellar	to (rubber) stamp
sello	stamp, seal
senda	(small) path, track
señal	waymark, signal
sirga	*camino*
tapas	light snack taken with drinks in a bar
ultramarinos	grocer's shop
vega	fertile plain, lowland area, valley (often found in placenames)

Appendix H
INDEX OF PRINCIPAL PLACENAMES

Aire-sur-l'Adour 104
Alto do Poio 200
Arca 221
Aroue 112
Arthez-de-Béarn 109
Arzacq-Arraziguet 106
Arzúa 218
Astorga 181
Atapuerca 158
Aubrac 58
Aumont-Aubrac 55
Auvillar 90
Azófra 150

Bach 79
Barbadelo 208
Béduer 74
Belorado 153
Bercianos del Real Camino 174
Burgos 160

Cacabelos 190
Cahors 81
Cajarc 76
Calzadilla de la Cueva 169
Camponaraya 190
Carrión de los Condes 169
Castet-Arrouy 92
Castrojeriz 164
Cée 236
Cirauqui 135
Cizur Menor 132
Condom 97
Conques 67
Corcubión 236

Decazeville 70
Dufort-Lacapalette 87

Eauze 100
El Acebo 186
El Burgo Ranero 175
El Cebreiro 199
El Ganso 184
Espalion 62
Espeyrac 65
Espinal 125
Estaing 64
Estella 1136
Estrets (Les) 53

Faycelles 74
Ferreiros 209
Figeac 73
Finisterre 237
Flamarens 91
Fromista 166

Golinhac 65
Gonzar 211
Grañon 152
Gréalou 75

Herrerías 198
Hiriburia 113
Hontanas 163
Hornillos del Camino 163
Hospital de Órbigo 180

Itero de la Vega 166

La Cassagnolle 74
La Romieu 96
Larrasoaña 128
Larressingle 98
Lascabanes 84
Lauzerte 86
Lavacolla 222
Le Puy-en-Velay 43
Lectoure 93
Ledigos 170
León 176

Limogne-en-Quercy 78
Logroño 145
Los Arcos 139

Manciet 101
Mansilla de la Mulas 175
Marsolan 94
Mas-de-Vers 80
Maslacq 109
Melide 217
Moissac 88
Molinaseca 186
Monistrol-d'Allier 48
Montbonnet 46
Montcuq 85
Montgros 56
Montréal-du-Gers 99
Murias de Rechivaldo 183

Nájera 150
Nasbinals 57
Navarrenx 111
Navarrete 147
Negreira 232
Nogaro 102

Ostabat-Asme 114

Palas do Rei 214
Pamplona 131
Pimbo 106
Pomps 108
Ponferrada 188
Portomarín 210
Puenta la Reina 134

Rabanal del Camino 184
Roncesvalles 123

Sahagún 171
Saint-Alban-sur-Limagnole 52
Saint-Antoine 90
Saint-Avit-Frandat 93

Saint-Chély-d'Aubrac 59
Saint-Côme-d'Olt 60
Saint-Félix 72
Saint-Pierre-de-Bessuéjouls 62
Saint-Privat-d'Allier 47
Saint-Jean-le-Vieux 116
Saint-Jean-Pied-de-Port 117
Samos 204
San Juan de Ortega 157
San Justo de la Vega 181
Sansol 140
Santiago de Compostela 223
Santo Domingo de la Calzada 157
Sarria 207
Saugues 49
Senègres 66
Séviac 99

Tardajos 162
Torres del Río 140
Trabadelo 195
Triacastela 202
Trinidad de Arre 129

Valcarlos 119
Vega de Valcarce 197
Viana 142
Villadangos del Páramo 178
Villafranca del Bierzo 192
Villafranca Montes de Oca 154
Villafría 158
Villálcazar de Sirga 169
Villava 129
Virgen del Camino 177
Viscarret 126

Zabaldica 128
Zubiri 127

—◆—

Printed and bound by The Cromwell Press,